'He's one of our own'

The story of Chris Wilder's Blades revolution

Danny Hall

'He's one of our own'
The story of Chris Wilder's Blades revolution

Danny Hall

Vertical Editions
www.verticaleditions.com

Front/back cover illustrations by badlydrawnicons. Front/back cover original main images by Sportimages. Front matter illustration by Luke Prest/www.lukeprest.com. Back cover images by Tyrone Hoyland, Edward Lambert, Danny Oxley, Abbey Kirwin and Steve Hoole

First published in the United Kingdom in 2018 by Vertical Editions, Unit 4a, Snaygill Industrial Estate, Skipton, North Yorkshire BD23 2QR

www.verticaleditions.com

ISBN 978-1-908847-10-2

A CIP catalogue record for this book is available from the British Library

Cover design by HBA, York

Printed and bound by Jellyfish Print Solutions, Swanmore, Hants

Contents

Acknowledgements

It always feels like a bit of a cliché when an award-winner stands on stage and says 'I couldn't have done it on my own' but in the case of writing this book, which began with the first word in February 2018, it is true. But, at the risk of missing someone out and inevitably upsetting them, it would be impossible to list them all. Rest assured, though; my sincere gratitude goes out to every single friend, stranger or contributor who took the time to pen something for the book, provide a picture or an interview or just show even a modicum of interest.

I must give thanks to Karl Waddicor – the publisher at Vertical Editions, for his support, guidance and above all patience with me as I tried to take over every aspect of this book in an attempt to make it perfect – and Kevin Cookson, Sheffield United's media man and all-round good guy for his help in a variety of ways. It was also an honour to use a couple of pictures by the late United club photographer, Martyn Harrison, who is sadly missed by all at Bramall Lane. Simon Bellis, who had the unenviable job of stepping into Baldy's inimitable shoes, is an unbelievable snapper, too, and my thanks also go to him for providing photos of the Wilder years for the book.

My fiance, Natalie, has been a constant source of support and patience – no doubt hoping that this book will pay for the dream wedding she insists she isn't planning in her head – and so, from the both of us, thank you for buying the book. I hope it lives up to expectations. And if your mate asks to borrow it, direct them to their nearest bookstore.

I'm also indebted to the two people in my life, one actually a teacher, who told me I'd never amount to anything in life. Your words have helped drive me on to prove you wrong every day since. Thanks to my bosses at *The Star* for allowing me to write this book in my spare time, and doing so has given me an outlet to keep my mind occupied. Many men, including some close to me, are still affected by mental health issues and I would urge anyone who is struggling to find the courage to talk to someone; to a loved one, to a stranger. Even, if all else fails, to me.

Above all, I guess, none of this would have been possible without the work of Chris Wilder, his staff and players at United. Together they have made United united again and the chant from the Bramall Lane Kop after every game sums it up so well, that I nicked it for the title of the book.

He's one of our own.

Danny Hall, author

Foreword

By Keith Edwards, Sheffield United 1975-78 and 1981-86

My first thought after being asked to contribute the foreword to this book was: what on earth would the author feel I had to offer to the story of Chris Wilder's time at Sheffield United? Our paths hardly crossed when we played at the club at the same time because our careers were at very different stages and I was shortly to leave after my second spell. And although I remained aware of his progress on the pitch and then into management, we have spent little time in each other's company. But our conversations have made it very easy for me to understand why he has captured the hearts of so many Blades supporters in two years as manager. He almost uniquely offers virtually all the desirable characteristics Sheffield United supporters would demand of someone in charge of their team; you will be aware of those qualities, of course, and when they come from a lifelong fan and ex-player it adds up to a beguiling package.

As a player I had my moments with managers and there were a number of reasons for that. We often disagreed about one thing or another and occasionally it resulted in words being exchanged, sometimes pretty forcibly on my part. As a result I have pondered a great deal since on just who was right or wrong. With the benefit of age I began to appreciate that the manager's position was much more difficult than I had imagined in my own little world of just being paid to play football. Those thoughts naturally extend to wondering just who I would enjoy playing for if I was turning out today. For me it comes down to mutual respect, humour and honesty. I had that with Billy Bremner and sense that would be the case with Chris Wilder, too. Real football men, the pair of them. I would love to have played under Chris as well.

There is no doubt that the manager's role is far more encompassing and complicated than it was 25 years ago when Chris was a young player. He will have absorbed and taken advantage of everything he thinks is helpful to him in modern football. But I believe that first and foremost he will have retained and built upon a solid base of the principles of the game and a man management style that players and fans can relate to. It's a good trick if you have what it takes to carry it off and the United fanbase embrace it totally. His bond with the supporters outstrips that of any I have known at the Lane and when they sing about Chris being "one of their own", there surely can't be any doubt about that.

They trust him; not just because he is one of them, but because his DNA matches theirs. Shared triumph and pain is very powerful and none would doubt that he still walks in the fans' shoes in terms of supporting their team. Ex-Blades very often retain a great affection for the club and are generally welcomed back with open arms by supporters and staff. I'm pleased to say that Chris has taken that to a new level by going out of his way to meet us, asking for our views and making us feel both involved and valued. But make no mistake, he can be tough; he won't allow sentiment to cloud his judgement or curb his censure if he feels it justified. Believe me, I have witnessed the death stare – even if, thank God, it wasn't aimed at me!

Our paths cross quite regularly now within the media circle after matches and I often admire the honest and refreshing way in which he critiques the games and his team. In fact, it's really nice to be able to chat to a manager in a friendly way after being ignored by quite a few in recent years! Who would have predicted this scenario back in 1986 when I probably hardly noticed the new 19-year-old as I prepared to move on? Now, 32 years later, I'm incredibly impressed with what he is achieving at our club, and humbled by the genuine respect he offers. This book can't fail to impress either.

Keith Edwards

Introduction

Modern-day football is a very different animal to the game that many of us fell in love with, as little boys and girls kicking a ball around and dreaming of pulling on the shirt for our childhood clubs. The game is richer, certainly, and arguably more popular than it ever has been. But a better spectacle as a result? I'm not so sure.

Just after I had completed this book, I bought another; the excellent *Provided you don't kiss me* by sports writer Duncan Hamilton, documenting his 20 years working alongside the great Brian Clough at Nottingham Forest. An absorbing account of the life of a local newspaper journalist, one line stuck out in the prologue ... 'the beautiful game can seem ugly and dull when viewed through tired and jaded eyes'.

After coinciding my time covering United with their relegation to League One, and working with Danny Wilson, Chris Morgan, David Weir, Morgan again, Nigel Clough and Nigel Adkins, 2016/17 was my first season covering United every week, home and away, alongside my colleague James Shield, for the city's daily paper, *The Star.* And although my eyes may not yet qualify as tired and jaded, the beautiful game seemed anything but ugly and dull as Chris Wilder's history-makers took on League One and, week by week, tore it apart.

Hamilton also quotes B. S. Johnson, a novelist, poet and part-time sports journalist, from his novel *The Unfortunates* ... "Always at the start of every match, often the only moment of excitement [is] that this might be the ONE match ... where the extraordinary happens, something that makes it stand out, the match one remembers and talks about for years afterwards, the rest of one's life."

This was not just a match, but a season that will be remembered and talked about for years. The rest of one's life. Put in context, it is even more remarkable. Wilder took over a club still reeling from its lowest finish since the 1980s and facing up to its sixth season in the third tier of English football. Some within the club felt it was rotten, decaying. Others warned Wilder not to come anywhere near it. Instead, he didn't just awaken the sleeping giant; he poked it right between the eyes and rode it all the way to the league title, with club records shattered left, right and centre.

The extraordinary moment of the season, though, came away at Northampton in April 2016 when promotion was sealed. Billy Sharp was hoisted from the field with his red and white scarf proudly above his head, grown men leaped around at nothing in particular while some cried, and others stood motionless; just taking it all in. One of the matchballs from the game sits proudly in my home as a memento but the memories, for everyone there that day, will last even longer. Less than 12 months after one of the club's darkest days, United were united again. And two boyhood Blades, Wilder and Sharp, had led the the healing process.

Football doesn't do fairytales, they say? Don't believe a word of it. With the help of the players, staff and fans who saw it happen first-hand, I hope this book does Wilder's Blades revolution some justice.

If the manager has his way, this will only be the beginning.

Danny Hall, author

Prologue

Sunday, September 24, 2017. Hillsborough Stadium, Sheffield, 1.31pm. Sheffield Wednesday 1, Sheffield United 2, live on *Sky Sports Football*. Commentators: Daniel Mann and Danny Higginbotham.

Daniel Mann, *61:49***:** Well, Jake Wright is going to depart, Mark Duffy replacing him. He has been a fairly regular presence in the starting line-up lately, Mark Duffy … his pre-season was disrupted in very pleasant fashion by the arrival of a new baby. So he certainly won't be complaining about that, but he had started the last four games …

Owls goalkeeper Keiren Westwood claims the ball routinely from Duffy's cross, off the head of Tom Lees, catching teammate Adam Reach in the process.

Mann, *64:38***:** Here's van Aken, Lee Bannan … Lee again … he's got the skill, tremendous work by Kieran Lee … ooh, and it will reach JOAO … devastating finish! Well, just christen him supersub!

64:58. Lucas Joao levels for Wednesday. Hillsborough is shaking under the bouncing of 30,000 jubilant Owls fans.

Danny Higginbotham, *65:17***:** [Wednesday] have worked the width really well and have done it all second half, and have got their just rewards for it. No-one's stopping that … pure pace and power. Give great credit to Reach, lovely first touch and it's into the back of the net … it's an emphatic finish and Wednesday will be absolutely delighted with the turnaround.

Mann, *66:02***:** Well, a man whose Sheffield Wednesday career certainly appeared to be on the wane has just written his own place in the club's legend there, with a goal that could well turn the derby tide in their favour. Well, I have to say, underneath my feet it is moving.

66:37. Duffy latches onto Basham's header and plays a one-two with Leon Clarke.

Mann: Ooh and Duffy has got there for Sheffield United, inside and outside he goes ... THAT'S A STUNNING GOAL, how on earth did he manage that? Extraordinary stuff! Well that's how to answer back, and then some!

66:45. Duffy puts United back in the lead. Wednesday were level for 38 seconds of play.

Higginbotham: What a response from Sheffield United. You talk about team goals and then talk about individual quality ... this from Duffy is absolutely brilliant. He's just been introduced to the game and turns van Aken one way and then the other ... he has no right to score there. Absolutely no right. Westwood maybe a little bit disappointed that he got beaten at the near post but take nothing away from Duffy ... this is absolutely brilliant, [turns] once then twice and just the pure power, and what a response from Sheffield United.

Mann: And what a reaction from Chris Wilder as well. Well just when I was talking about Lucas Joao maybe turning the derby tide in Wednesday's favour, Mark Duffy has an extraordinary answer.

United go on to win the game – the first Steel City derby since 2012 – 4-2.

1

The making of the man

Every time a former top-flight footballer walks into a plum job for their first managerial role, Chris Wilder can't help but let out a wry smile. Steven Gerrard at Rangers. Frank Lampard at Derby County. In recent times, with up-and-coming managers in the lower leagues frequently overlooked in favour of 'big names', there are countless others.

Wilder smiles because he knows he did it the hard way. After first taking a team – the Bradway, a pub side made up of many of his mates – in the Meadowhall Sunday League, Wilder then served an apprenticeship at Alfreton, then in the ninth tier of the English football pyramid, before taking over at Halifax Town, until they went out of business. After leading Oxford United out of the Conference and back into the Football League, he took over at relegation-threatened Northampton Town, kept them up and then, amongst a backdrop of financial crisis the following season, led them to the League Two title.

Perhaps even more remarkably, in the 15 years as a manager bookended by Alfreton and United, he was never sacked – something of an anomaly in modern football, where the thirst for success is omnipresent but any patience in the pursuit of it is increasingly rare.

"I really appreciate the grounding I've had," Wilder said. "I've got my hands dirty and had to put up with things that the Premier League boys who go into big jobs haven't. I'm not critical of that approach, by any means, but I have done it the tough way and I'm pleased to have had those experiences as they have helped me along the way."

Under the guidance of Wilder, by this point a professional with his boyhood club Sheffield United, and his pal Ian Whitehorne, Bradway graduated from the Imperial League to sweep all before them at the higher level of the now-defunct Meadowhall Sunday League, winning an unprecedented treble along the way. After his playing career – which saw him twice win promotion with his boyhood Blades under Dave Bassett, play in the top flight and later represent clubs including Rotherham United and Bradford City – was ended by a back injury, Wilder accepted an invitation from Alfreton chairman Wayne Bradley to become the club's new boss.

His time at North Street proved short, but sweet; in his seven months in charge, the Reds won four trophies with a team that included Ryan France, who later played in the Premier League for Hull City but delayed his inevitable move into the Football League to complete his degree at Nottingham Trent University and play for Alfreton. "I think in a world where we are bombarded with the importance of tactics and sports science, for me the most important side of managing a football team is managing its players," France said. "The ability to know what to say to one player, which often can be completely different to the next.

"Chris did this better than any I've seen at any level. I knew the minute I played under him he was destined to do good things. He brought out the best in me, the best in my teammates. Yes he has an eye for a player, but he knew how to get the best out of us, always. On and off the pitch, he wanted a group of players that would be together, which is massively important at any level of football. Chris brought that absolute togetherness in us and if you weren't in, you weren't welcome. He was, and is, a pal, a leader and someone you'd follow through thick and thin."

France remembers receiving a letter, on the day he made his professional debut for Hull against Kidderminster, from Wilder, wishing him luck. A former teammate said the manager was equally capable of giving out a rocket or a cuddle, depending what was needed – "He could make me feel ten feet tall or two feet tall" – and those man-management skills were severely tested after taking over at Halifax Town, when he turned up on his first day to find no training ground, fixtures, players or even footballs.

Forced to train in the local park – apart from occasions when a dog show got there first, or the local council needed to paint the lines for an important Sunday League game – Wilder somehow led Halifax to the 2006 Conference play-off final, and the Shaymen were ten minutes away from a place in the Football League before losing in extra-time to Hereford at Leicester's Walkers Stadium. Wilder likened his time at Halifax to "trying to win Formula One in a Ford Escort" and although they avoided relegation in 2007/08 despite a ten-point penalty for entering administration, the club couldn't escape its financial problems and folded weeks later, under debts of around £2m.

"I wouldn't change my time there for the world," Wilder said. "There were so many times when all we could do was laugh at whatever was being thrown at us, which is why I look back now and see keeping Halifax in the division for so long as a major achievement. It was a frustrating time, of course, but at a club like that, where your fingerprints are on everything that happens, it's a real education."

Wilder was forced to break the news of Halifax's liquidation to his players in the pub and for the first time since 1999, when his contract from his second spell at United expired, he was unemployed. In the end it lasted for a matter of days as Alan Knill, who knew Wilder from their days together at Southampton, offered him a route back into football as his assistant at Bury. Six months later, the lure of management proved too great and Wilder was back as a No.1 at Oxford, a proud former first division club now languishing in the Conference. After being denied a play-off place in his first season by another points deduction, the result of an administrative error from before he took over, a 3-1 play-off final victory over York City saw Oxford back in the Football League – and sent Wilder sliding down the Wembley touchline in celebration.

Despite leading them to promotion at a key time in their history, one Oxford fan blog described supporters' opinion of Wilder as "bipolar" and the manager later admitted he stayed a year too long at the Kassam. Although Oxford were well in the hunt for promotion, Wilder's contract was in its final year and chairman Ian Lenagan was reluctant to extend it. So Wilder left for Northampton, then six points from safety in the same division.

He kept them up, beating Oxford on the final day for good measure, and led them to the League Two title the following season amidst a backdrop of financial difficulty. A £10m loan from the council to finish a stand at Sixfields had disappeared, HMRC tried to wind-up the club over a £166,000 tax bill and they were days from extinction when Wilder issued a passionate plea, which subsequently went viral, pleading with then-Cobblers chairman David Cardoza to 'do a deal' with Kelvin Thomas, who Wilder had worked with at Oxford.

With time running out, Cardoza did indeed do a deal with Thomas and the Cobblers breathed a collective sigh of relief. Wilder, his coaches and office staff went unpaid for periods of the season before Thomas' takeover, and the players had their wages paid by the Professional Footballers' Association. But Wilder kept them going. Northampton were the first team in the English Football League that season to be promoted, finishing with 99 points and the league title. One Cobblers fan, Adam Johnson, had previously been unable to leave his own house due to an anxiety disorder, but didn't miss a game of that season. Wilder's stock had never been higher. The only personal disappointment was how events were playing out 82 miles north, at his beloved Bramall Lane.

Once a Blade, always a Blade
By Andy Pack, former Sheffield United media manager

It would be an exaggeration to say that I have known Chris Wilder, man and boy, despite first meeting him around 30 years ago. But he was a young man then, excited about being at United for the first time and hoping to make his way where he really wanted to be. Strangely, I already knew his parents who ran a sports shop in Arbourthorne, only a good defensive clearance from the comprehensive school at which I was teaching PE. The shop was ideally placed for me to negotiate good prices for the purchase of kit and equipment whilst chatting about Chris' development with a very proud mum and dad – but I haven't been able to work out whether Joan's insistence that the school's business kept the shop open is a genuine observation, or a tongue-in-cheek hint that I didn't buy enough!

My own career at Bramall Lane obviously hadn't yet started although I was contributing to the programme with match reports for the reserves, some of which Chris featured in. Consequently, my first memory of meeting him wasn't at a match but at the Millhouses pub in Sheffield where a local football club I was running held a function. It was a big surprise when Chris and Mark Todd arrived – courtesy of Chris Lee, a talented amateur footballer himself and one of my players who happened to be a good pal of the pair. They were young professionals just doing a favour for their friend, probably without the club even knowing, but it meant a lot to everyone there. They had a drink, chatted for an appropriate period of time and went on their way ... I'm sure to go straight home to bed and cocoa! Our impression was that they were down-to-earth, polite, chatty and on their best behaviour. But most importantly, happy enough to give up a bit of time to help out and make our night a bit more special.

Meanwhile, the rivalry for the right-back spot, largely with Andy Barnsley – another Sheffield lad – played out during Billy McEwan's reign, which began brightly enough but ended a year later in relegation after Dave Bassett had taken over too late to avoid the drop. Bassett shook up the squad, recruited heavily but retained faith in Chris who was selected for well over half the games as the team won promotion. Barnsley, Cliff Powell and Brian Smith also contested the position when all, including Chris, suffered injury spells.

The signing of Colin Hill at right-back for the new season proved a big challenge for Chris whose tidy, ball-playing, more flamboyant style often missed out to Hill's defensive capabilities. But he remained reliable and happily was in the side for the final three fixtures which saw the squad achieve back-to-back promotions and reach the top flight. Needless to say the emotions of the likes of Wilder, Dane Whitehouse, Carl Bradshaw and Mitch Ward carried an extra level of pride having achieved it for their city of birth. It was to stand them in good stead in years to come as more recruits from London swelled their ranks and gave birth to the friendly but fierce Sheffield/London rivalry in training, which fuelled an invaluable team spirit.

Given Chris' subsequent and self-acknowledged high regard for Bassett, it is very easy to surmise that these experiences, along with elements of Bassett's management style, played an integral part in the formation of Wilder's own future philosophy and values. Make your own mind up but for me it seems very much so when you hear the current manager talk about, for example, not making the game too complicated and winning individual battles. That he didn't totally nail down his position regularly whilst competing with a succession of rivals under Bassett, yet still holds him in such regard, is revealing. Here is a man who understands the nuances of the game and who is strong enough to put personal vanity aside, and seek guidance from someone who used him comparatively sparingly. No hard luck story here; more a clever appreciation of the game overall and of how 'Harry' kept a squad of players happy at the same time.

The arrival of John Pemberton (and later Kevin Gage) again blocked Chris' way although he enjoyed a decent run in the side in the top flight in 1990-91. Whether in the team or not he remained a committed competitor and unwavering supporter of the side, and I often spotted him watching away games he wasn't involved in up and down the country. His presumed disappointments didn't make him bitter or disaffected. It was always his club and he remained loyal to it, just as he was towards his Sheffield mates with whom he spent time with on the terraces even when he was a professional player. When he did eventually bite the bullet and move on in search of more regular football, his pain was evident. There is nothing fake or contrived when he talks about being a fan, knowing how they feel and being one of them. I can vouch for that and so can other fans who have seen him sitting with them – even when he was later playing for other clubs.

I was media manager at the Lane by the time he rejoined United from Bradford City in March 1998, signed by caretaker boss, Steve Thompson. Steve remembers: "Chris was a young player when I played at the Lane and I always thought he had the ability to go far. He has had a decent career in the game ... but I can't help feeling that he should have played consistently at a higher level. People forget that he did play in the top flight with United.

"And his love for this club was brought home to me once again when, in the aftermath of the Coventry win in the FA Cup quarter-final, I went onto the pitch and felt a supporter clapping me on the back. When I turned round it was Chris!"

And that was a week *before* he re-signed. I remember him saying that the fans would see a more mature Chris Wilder. "Maybe I was a bit reckless in those early days but you learn good habits," he added. "I have always loved to go forward and bomb on, but I think my defending has improved a lot – whatever I can or cannot do the fans know I will give them a 100 percent wholehearted display." That promise was maintained in every single game he played for the Blades until he left again a year later. In a sense he had no choice but to keep that promise because his background and love for Sheffield United demanded that he wore the shirt with genuine pride and determination. Giving his all for the club and its fans was non-negotiable.

What was noticeable was that – despite now being older, more experienced and definitely comfortable with his teammates – he retained every semblance of being a regular Sheffield lad; friendly, down-to-earth and with a sense of fun and humour. And he still mixed predominantly with his long standing local pals. It led to him eventually going back to his roots ... Bradway FC in the Meadowhall Sunday League, along with Ian Whitehorne. Grounded or what? Personally I've always admired ex-pros who still play the game for the sheer love of it rather than for money or glory, and running such a team falls into a similar category.

Inevitably there was considerable success. I guess the experience was invaluable and working with blokes (mates, just as inevitably) who definitely played seriously, but for nothing but enjoyment, would be right up his street. Years later, when he was in charge at Oxford and things weren't going too well politically, I chatted in his office before a Blades fixture, not enjoying him being relatively subdued and kind of fretful about how the situation could be improved. But his stock was still high enough for Northampton to lure him and we all know his achievements there. What I didn't bargain for was seeing such a riveting, impassioned interview after a game in the earlier days, before they won the division.

This wasn't the young, breezy footballer I had previously known but an inspiring, convincing football man spelling out some sensible home truths about off-field matters. Where have we heard that before? Things changed – they went up, as did my regard for Chris Wilder the manager, one who has the knack of seeing things clearly and is able to put across his thoughts in a coherent, genuine and compelling way that doesn't alienate himself. It suggests trustworthiness and concern for the right things and the right way for everyone's benefit, not just his own. It commands respect and the fact that he has never been sacked is only partly down to that – chairmen have realised that whatever faults he has, he is as close to the real thing they are going to get as far as good governance is concerned.

Upon being appointed at the Lane, Chris was quick to respond positively to my offer of bringing in Keith Edwards and Gage to give him their slant on what/who they had been seeing leading up to his arrival. Some managers would be too aloof to take advantage of that and not see the value in canvassing opinion, however informed it was, before making their own decisions. Several other ex-United players like Len Badger and Ted Hemsley are regularly invited to contribute and this inclusivity is both well received and typical of the feel he has for United.

Invites for end-of-season drinks to ex-players, associates, media correspondents and the like are handed out with what feels a real sense of loyalty, gratitude for support, and camaraderie, and you don't always get that from high profile personalities. He still operates in a Sheffield sort of way; genuine, warm, down-to-earth, honest and brooking no nonsense. Chris Wilder is a high profile personality with a low profile way about him. And I mean that in the best possible way.

2

The boos of Bramall Lane

As the champagne soaked into Chris Wilder's suit and the curtain closed on Northampton Town's remarkable League Two-title winning season, the campaign ended memorably for his boyhood club Sheffield United, too, albeit in vastly different circumstances. Under Nigel Adkins, a three-time promotion winner with Scunthorpe and Southampton, they had limped to an 11th-placed finish in League One and despite having what was considered by far the biggest playing budget in English football's third tier, actually ended the campaign closer to the relegation trapdoor than champions Wigan.

Indeed, without Billy Sharp's 21 goals, many Blades fans are convinced they would have been relegated. All was not well at the Lane. But Adkins remained positive until the end. As the season ended in a 2-0 defeat at Bramall Lane to Scunthorpe United which almost perfectly summed up his reign, Adkins insisted that he would lead his players on a post-game lap of honour afterwards.

Of the 21,445 crowd there that day – impressive for the third tier, remarkable given United's struggles over the season – probably a few hundred bothered to stay behind, as anger gave way to the even more damaging feeling of apathy. One fan hadn't quite made the transition yet, though, and was filmed berating Adkins from the Kop with shouts of 'Look around you … this is what we think of you' and 'You're an embarrassment … to the club and to the city'. The video subsequently went viral on *Twitter*, a damning indictment of how far the club had fallen.

Life in League One was far from kind to United. In the first season after relegation from the Championship they appointed

Danny Wilson, the former Sheffield Wednesday player and manager who faced protests in the Bramall Lane car park on the very day he was unveiled. His brand of football, and a team packed with talent including future England international Harry Maguire, saw United score 92 goals and win 90 points, but they never recovered when striker Ched Evans was jailed after being wrongly convicted of rape and they fell just short of automatic promotion.

To rub salt in the wounds, Wednesday pipped United to promotion and they then lost 8-7 on penalties in the play-off final at Wembley, when goalkeeper Steve Simonsen blazed United's 11th spot-kick high over the Huddersfield bar. Wilson was then sacked the following season with United six points off automatic promotion, before they lost again in the play-offs to Yeovil Town, and his successor David Weir suffered the same fate after winning just one of his 13 matches in charge of United, leaving them 22nd in League One.

A remarkable upturn in results under Nigel Clough saw United finish just outside the play-offs that season and, faced with a fixture pile-up on their run to the FA Cup semi-finals, Clough took his side to Marbella. The focus was solely on beers, though, rather than balls and a superb display, and an eventual 5-3 defeat to Premier League side Hull at Wembley, followed.

United did make the top-six the following campaign, only to lose 7-6 on aggregate in the semi-finals to Swindon after an epic 5-5 draw at the County Ground. Clough's men made do with two full-backs, Craig Alcock and Jay McEveley, at centre-half after Neill Collins was stubbornly jettisoned and others were overlooked. Clough, whose legendary father called him 'our No.9' at Forest, wore that on his United training gear rather than his initials and seemingly inherited several family traits from Brian, both good and bad.

Clough Jnr. also led United to the semi-finals of the League Cup in his second season, but was sacked anyway and the Blades, feeling the financial squeeze in the grip of League One more and more as the seasons went by, were on the hunt for a manager once again. After receiving over 50 applications, Phil

Parkinson, Mark Warburton and Karl Robinson were all seriously considered before United pulled off what Jim Phipps, then-club chairman, insisted was a "statement of intent"; they hired Adkins.

With three promotions from League One on his managerial CV, and another into the Premier League with Southampton, Adkins was the overwhelming fans' favourite for the Blades job amongst supporters and his appointment was the most popular United had made since falling out of the Premier League in 2007. A man of unwavering positivity, Adkins – who once recited Dale Wimbrow's poem 'The Man in the Glass' in a press conference after being asked how he deals with stress – certainly lifted the mood around United's newly-refurbished Shirecliffe training base, given a makeover largely with funds raised from the FA Cup semi-final run under Clough.

But Collins, handed a lifeline by Adkins after being shunned completely by Clough, remembers having concerns about United's pre-season preparations. After a spell at Champneys, the plush spa resort in Hertfordshire where Adkins berated one member of his squad for drinking a coffee, United took on Ilkeston, Cheltenham Town and Exeter City with a trip to Macclesfield Town sandwiched between friendlies against Premier League sides Newcastle United and Stoke City.

"Pre-season went relatively well, results wise, but that doesn't mean anything really," Collins said. "What concerned me was that I felt the games we played weren't anything like we were going to experience in League One. What happened on the first day of the season at Gillingham was almost exactly what I expected to happen ... the pitch was dry, they pressed the life out of us and we tried to play pre-season type football." United lost 4-0 at the Priestfield, and one fan remembers that contracting severe sunstroke on the uncovered away end was the highlight of the day.

Four straight wins lifted optimism levels a little, but comprehensive defeats at Bramall Lane to clubs like Bury, Colchester United and Shrewsbury followed and Adkins brought in Dean Hammond, his former captain at Southampton, on loan in October. Despite struggling to adjust to the pace of League One football, Adkins persevered with Hammond in midfield while Paul Coutts, one of the best passers of the ball in United's squad, was shunted onto the right wing. "Nigel was adamant that Dean was his main central midfielder, which is his call, but he wouldn't give me a run out there," Coutts said. "There was a game when he was suspended and we had a few injuries, and he played David Edgar as his playmaker in midfield and I was still on the right. I remember thinking 'ah come on, give me a chance'. Collo was stepping into midfield and had no passes on, so I went inside and got the ball off him.

"For the first time, Nigel had a go at me for that and then took me off just before the hour mark. Then afterwards he made a comment to the media about me not keeping the shape, so I went to see him the next day, explained why I'd done it and said I disagreed with his comments. He apologised to me, said he'd watched it back and was wrong, but had already made the comments to the press by then. I thought 'you've killed me now … everyone thinks I deliberately messed your shape up'. I disagreed with some of the stuff he did but playing me out of position was one time I thought he didn't have a clue, to be honest.

"He was a nice enough guy but there was so much frustration around, and we were getting criticism from the terraces. That's fair enough and it happens, but we didn't have a chance to show our best game and to be played out of position, asked to do a job for the team, and then be criticised for it seemed a bit harsh. There was frustration from the players too; everyone was hating it. It wasn't a good place to be. Once the crowd turned then it became a difficult place to play, and I don't think he quite 'got' the fans and what they demanded from the team."

Adkins, working with a bloated squad left over from the days of Clough's transfer excess, would often have queues of players outside his office wanting to know why they weren't playing, while he wandered around the training ground to avoid conflict. "He didn't want to upset anyone," Coutts remembers, "but ended up annoying everyone, rather than being upfront and honest about certain decisions. It was quite unusual … especially in football, when the manager doesn't normally care about upsetting anyone's feelings."

Months of constant positivity in the wake of disappointing results began to grate on fans, and members of the press alike, and one memorable incident before a game against Oldham saw Adkins ask BBC Radio Sheffield's Jonathan Buchan, mid-interview, which was the biggest room in his house. Taken aback, Buchan offered 'The living room?' before a period of uncomfortable silence eventually ended with the answer: 'The room for improvement'. Players were often baffled by his methods too and after one particularly ignominious away defeat, Adkins elected to shine his shoes without a word about the game before eventually saying he'd see them on Monday morning.

While his record clearly showed that Adkins was not a bad manager, and he remained to the end an affable man, what is now clear is that he was not at all in touch with the ethos of United, as a club and fanbase. Modern managers talk a lot about their 'philosophies' but successful ones work alongside the culture of the club they are employed by, not in spite of it. Serious concerns were raised by senior players during the Adkins season, about the standards of players; Jose Baxter, the talented former Everton youngster, was fined but welcomed back into the first-team fold after committing an assault, described as "out of order" by a teammate who witnessed it, in a Dublin bar on United's Christmas break.

"That probably should have been it, 'you're done'," the player remembers. "The standards weren't great." By that point, Baxter had already been suspended by United for failing a drugs test, and was banned by the FA when he claimed his drink had been spiked with ecstasy. In February 2016, he was suspended again – this time for 12 months – when traces of cocaine were found in his system and was released when his United contract expired.

The result which perhaps typified the Adkins era came in early March, at home to Burton Albion. Days after United lost 2-0 away at Rochdale, Burton – who were a non-league side when United last tasted the riches of the Premier League – were excellent value for a 1-0 win which extended their lead at the top of the table and sent Adkins' men down to 11th. "We absolutely dominated the game," remembers Mark Duffy, who played 85 minutes for Clough's Burton that day. "When I've been to Bramall Lane before, it was a case of 'we're going to be in for a tough game today, maybe we can nick one on the break and even then we'll be under the cosh', but it was easy. I think some United players came off the pitch buzzing that it was only 1-0, and this was against Burton Albion – who, with no disrespect, were a Conference club six years earlier. I remember thinking 'wow, how far has this club fallen?'

"We created chance after chance and they had one shot on target the whole game. I came off the pitch thinking 'this is a joke, what's happened to this place?' I remember looking at the teamsheet and really fancied myself, thinking 'these won't get the ball off me'. I was playing with a lot of confidence at the time, but I couldn't see who was going to kick me or outrun me, and couldn't see what they were good at. That was the feeling in our dressing room; 'these aren't really good at anything. They were slow at the back and dropped deep, allowing the other side time on the ball. We were happy to play them. It was sad because the fans were still turning up in their thousands, as they always have, and supporting the team, but how long can you do that for when the team plays like that? The standards had dropped so far from what I knew of coming to Bramall Lane. Basically, it was just crap."

Duffy's assessment is a withering one, but one not many Blades fans will disagree with. During the promotion season at Northampton, Wilder organised Town's staff Christmas party and borrowed a close pal's executive box at Bramall Lane for United's game against Coventry City. United won 1-0 in a game probably best remembered for skipper Jay McEveley's horrific challenge on Ruben Lameiras that somehow warranted only a yellow card, and Alan Knill – by this point Wilder's No.2 at Sixfields – remembers the game as "boring" with fans in front of the box talking to each other while the game was going on. The box owner recalls calling Wilder to see how the game was, remarking on how noisy the place sounded. The Cobblers party had left the game at half-time and decamped to the Railway pub across the road.

Like Wilder, Adkins had also started his management career in his local Sunday League but that was where the similarities began, and ended. And on the final weekend of the season, as one celebrated an against-all-odds title win with his squad just months after they faced going out of business, the other presided over the 16th and most costly defeat of United's worst season since the early 1980s. But the atmosphere inside Bramall Lane, as goals from Tom Hopper and Paddy Madden secured a routine 2-0 win for Scunthorpe, was tepid rather than toxic. Blades correspondent James Shield wrote in his report for *The Star:* "Complete indifference was the order of the day. That, given this is a stadium where opponents once feared to tread, represented possibly the most damning indictment of United's performances en route to their lowest league finish in three decades."

Arguably the biggest cheer of the day greeted the news that Hammond, at fault for Hopper's opening goal, would not reappear for the second half and sporadic chants, from his own fans, of 'you're getting sacked in the morning' suggested that Adkins' Bramall Lane future may have been fading fast. But the manager did little to strengthen his position with what some fans saw as thinly-veiled criticisms of the club's support, in what turned out to be his final press conference after the game. "I've come [to Bramall Lane] as a visiting manager and you know what the atmosphere is going to be like here," he said. "Always has been ... probably always will be. That's just the nature of it."

Adkins would never find out if that would always be the case as, four days later and just 11 months into his three-year contract, he was sacked. "Nigel is a gentleman and, as proved by his record, a very good manager," the club statement read, "but the overriding aim is promotion from League One and the club feels that this is the correct time to make a change." Jointly made by United's co-owners – Kevin McCabe, a boyhood Blade who orders special diaries without the word Wednesday, and Saudi royal HRH Prince Abdullah bin Mosaad bin Abdulaziz Al

Saud, who bought 50 percent of United's football operations in September 2013 – the decision left United searching for their fifth manager since relegation from the Championship in 2011. Staring down the barrel of a sixth season in the wilderness of League One, they had to get this appointment right.

The next move happened almost by chance. Given Wilder's success at Northampton, overtures from clubs higher up the food chain predictably followed and Charlton, facing up to relegation from the Championship, made an approach to make Wilder their seventh manager in just over two years in a bid to quell growing supporter unrest. Bolton Wanderers were also keen and amongst what he described as "an interesting few days" after Northampton's title celebrations finally came to an end, Wilder returned to Sheffield to present the trophy at a local Sunday League cup final. He was in the bar of Bramall Lane's Copthorne Hotel when McCabe, convening a board meeting to discuss Adkins' future, walked in.

"I thought, 'I need to talk to that lad'," McCabe later admitted. "It's funny how things happen in life. He'd been on the list before when we were looking for a new manager and if there was any reticence, it was the whole situation of a local lad coming back to his local club. It's pretty unusual."

Nevertheless, McCabe took the plunge. Wilder, accepting that the timing was right to leave Northampton after leading them into League One, had met with Charlton's owner Roland Duchatelet in Belgium and as speculation linking him with United grew, he confided privately with close friends that it was perhaps a case of right club, wrong time. With several teams, some with managers still in post, interested in their services, Wilder and Knill spent almost as much time in London as Sheffield as they weighed up their next move and were impressed by Duchatelet and Katrien Meire, the Addicks' former chief executive. Knill had even contacted Duffy, released by Birmingham City, in an attempt to persuade him to join them at Charlton but, well past the eleventh hour, McCabe made his move and approached Wilder to be the next United manager. He'd never actively coveted the job but now, Wilder had a decision to make.

Despite his previous insistences to the contrary, he couldn't say no to this club – to *his club*. There was work to be done but, after years plying their trades in the lower divisions with smaller sides, Wilder and Knill felt like this was their big chance. The Wilder era had officially begun and for the third time in his career, he was back at Bramall Lane.

The Wilder side of life
By John Garrett, Blades engagement officer and club historian

I think that we had really come to a grinding halt a couple of years ago. Sheffield United FC had always taken pride in being a family club in every sense of the word – close, from the terraces to the dressing room, offices and boardroom. Connected. The club has always been at its most potent when it is not trying to be something that it isn't. Change is seldom a bad thing as long as it is evolution and not revolution. You cannot stand still – but, we are Sheffield United FC and not Manchester United FC. And that is important.

In essence, all football clubs are basically the same. All have loyal fans, a football ground with (mostly) four sides, a pitch and floodlights. Some are bigger and more successful than others, but all share the same hopes, fears and ambitions, albeit at varying levels of expectancy. The fact that we had stalled, after long spells out of the top two flights of the game, was evident to all.

The previous manager was a good man who had an excellent track record with his previous clubs, of that there is no doubt. A thoroughly honourable and honest professional who wanted only the very best for the club that had employed his services to get them out of the division. But it just didn't happen and that is a tragedy for both employer and employee. No manager ever wants anything but the best, do they? The departure of another manager meant, inevitably, the task of someone being found who could kick-start the entire club, from top to bottom. One to instil self-belief in those players not departing, raise the battered morale of the paying supporters and bring together a backbone of admin staff who had ridden every punch thrown at them for a number of years. A tough task to say the least.

The front-facing staff are often the ones overlooked when results on the pitch don't go the right way, but those that are front-facing and known are the ones who work seven days a week, and 24 hours a day. You are never off-duty. That can be fantastic and also painful at the same time. It would be fair to say that the tank was very empty after the dreams of another season ended in mid-table reality, and the flames of ambition were very much quenched. An answer to the club's issues was not an option, but a necessity.

Football is a strange animal. A season ticket holder is almost a stakeholder in a business of complete uncertainty. Sheffield United has an incredible number of fans that will give their money in advance of every new campaign in the hope that it will bring something to cheer about, as opposed to cry over, but even the resolve of the hardiest soul at the Lane was being tested.

Chris Wilder is a Blade. Born and bred in Sheffield, despite a short spell in the smoke, he is a son of the city and a proud one at that. A standout player as a youngster for school and Sheffield Boys, he had been a ball boy at Beautiful Downtown Bramall Lane, throwing it back quickly to heroes like Keith Edwards and Colin Morris when the pace of play dictated and slowly to the opposition when the pressure was on, as every good ball boy back in the day would have done. But long before that he had taken his place on the terraces, as every fan does, and cheered the Blades through bad times and good.

He served his time and throughout his career in the game, when not playing or managing, he could be found with the same mates that he always associated with, getting behind his club. A fan, first and foremost. United wanted him as a youngster, but his dad was warned away by a friend in the game, that the United youth set up was not the place for him to be at that point. A connection with Southampton took him down to Hampshire – a long way to serve an apprenticeship, but one that has proved valuable after over three decades in the game.

The fickle finger of football fate is a strange thing. Ian Porterfield and the Blades parted company and the man who had won the club two promotions was replaced by former youth team coach, Billy McEwan. He had a brief to find young, hungry players on free transfers who could give it a go and seize an opportunity. He had an eye for a player, and picked the likes of Peter Beagrie and Peter Duffield up from the North East as well as a host of others who went on to make good careers for themselves in the Football League – amongst them, a young Chris Wilder. Imagine the buzz of that?

The chance to play for your club after initially passing up the opportunity when sounded out years before; it must have been a dream come true. The difference is a simple one. He was a good professional and one of those who survived the arrival of Dave Bassett. He fitted and he fitted because he understood what it took to wear the red and white stripes of this proud club, because it was a lifetime ambition to do so. For him, it was an honour. Chris goes back to a time when the Blades were different. The lack of a permanent training ground meant the use of the University pitches on Warminster Road – this, in turn, meant that the players used Bramall Lane as a base. They met there in the morning to get changed before either sharing a minibus up there or cadging a lift off a teammate who actually had a car. After training there was a race down to Bramall Lane to try and ensure that you were the one who got the warm water in the bath or the shower, and not the cold, muddy seconds.

Players had their dinner alongside fans and staff in the old Lane Social Club in the South Stand. They could be found sat in the offices in the afternoon chatting to staff, walking in and out of the shop and ticket office doing the same. Visible at all times but encouraged by the manager to do all these things. If the players were out, then so were the girls from the laundry or pools office. That sort of community creates a very strong bond indeed. The chief executive back then was Derek Dooley – Sheffield football's finest ambassador, and he loved the connectivity and camaraderie under Bassett. In fact he actively encouraged it. Why all this waffle, you may ask? Well, it is this environment that made the manager what he is. The recipe and rights of passage that shaped the man in the game.

Wilder was on the pitch for the club at Leicester in one of its finest hours, and never put in less than 100 percent any time he pulled on a shirt – for the Blades, his Blades, or beyond, when he eventually moved on, to Rotherham United and Bradford City. It seemed inevitable he would manage – as a player he had run local Sunday League side Bradway with plenty of success – but after retiring from playing, went into it from the hard side of the fence, cutting his teeth in non-league at clubs like Alfreton and Halifax when many others would have walked away.

Instead, Wilder built his reputation, taking lessons learned from over 400 league games and the managers and coaches who had shaped his career as a player. And he did well.

When the United call came, it was on the back of a record-breaking title-winning season at Northampton Town and at a point where his career needed to move on. It was nearly to Charlton, but thankfully the timing for United was spot on. A few weeks before I had shared a sociable beer with Chris, bemoaning the plight of our beloved club – or more to the point, the general feeling of malaise that had set in. In fact, I told him to run a mile if United came knocking. I'm glad he didn't heed my advice!

The thing was that – as my words have hopefully spelled out – Chris gets it. He understands how the place ticks; the way it needs to be, to all pull in the same direction. Football clubs seldom go wrong from the outside in. By the time it becomes evident out on the pitch that all is not well, it has probably been going that way behind the scenes for a fair period of time. Disconnected. He has brought back the unity. The staff see the players around the club, not just on match days. They dine as one before the game – upstairs in the 1889 Suite – they mix with the cleaners, the ticket office staff. The manager takes the time to pop in, sit down, have a brew and find out what is going on in the street. Old school. He knows people's names, what their wives are called, what their kids are called. It's simple, really, but it works.

The days of cold, post-training baths and chip butties have been replaced by the state-of-the-art training complex that is Shirecliffe, but the values of old still stand firm. Chris lifted the whole place when he arrived – not just the fans and the team but the behind-the-scenes foot soldiers. He played at a time when that link was everything, and has brought that very much to the table once again.

3

A new era begins

Dressed smartly in his new club suit and red, white and black Blades tie, and flanked by his new boss Kevin McCabe, one of Chris Wilder's first commitments as the new Sheffield United manager was to face the media for his unveiling press conference – but it wasn't long before he was making his mark behind the scenes at Bramall Lane. His predecessor Nigel Adkins had, at considerable expense, installed motivational signs and posters inside the tunnel leading from the home dressing room to the pitch and although a workman was booked to remove them later in the day, Wilder couldn't wait so, screwdriver in hand, obliged himself. It was, perhaps, an early indication that the new Blades boss was intent on doing things his way.

Ten players, including Adkins' skipper Jay McEveley, were released and Wilder wasted little time appointing Billy Sharp, another Sheffield lad, as his replacement. In his younger days Sharp and his dad Steve had waited outside Bramall Lane for Wilder, then a United player, and persuaded him to give young Sharp his shin pads after a game. Around two decades later, the two were now working together at United and Sharp's appointment as skipper of his boyhood club gave the Blades the unusual distinction of having a fan, born in the city, in three key positions: captain, manager and co-chairman.

Another homegrown player, goalkeeper George Long, saw the terms of his new deal offered by Adkins renegotiated by Wilder, who was keen to regain control of United's finances and wage structure which had previously spiralled out of control. Relations between Long and Wilder remained cordial throughout negotiations and the youngster signed the revised agreement, but a marker had been laid.

Tightening United's financial belts also extended to transfers in and out. Wilder admitted his budget "wasn't a blowaway one" and he had to generate revenue, so essentially was prepared to listen to offers for all of his players. Wilder rated Paul Coutts, the former Derby midfielder, highly but took a financial decision to transfer-list him, as one of the highest earners in the United squad. Coutts' partner gave birth to twins on the first day of pre-season training and neither he nor Kieron Freeman, who was also made available, were ostracised from the first-team group. "I had to have the conversation with Couttsy because I had to generate some money and see what interest was out there. Basically, there wasn't a lot," Wilder said.

"That maybe showed that the players weren't highly rated by anyone else – because if they were, they'd be gone." Two who did attract interest, forwards Che Adams and Dominic Calvert-Lewin, were sold after making it clear they wished to move on. Their combined fees of around £3.5m helped to fund key signings like Simon Moore, Jack O'Connell, Leon Clarke and Daniel Lafferty, while John Fleck and Mark Duffy both arrived on free transfers. Both must surely rank as two of the best-value United arrivals in recent years.

Crucially, all fitted Wilder's policy of signing players whose careers were on an upward trajectory rather than on the way down, after seeing countless pounds squandered by his predecessors. Now, all prospective new recruits were judged by a multi-point checklist, covering technical and tactical aspects as well as a psychological analysis.

It is little coincidence that many members of Wilder's successful United squads have 'real-life' experience on their CVs, or rejection in their memories – Duffy had spells as a scaffolder and a sports coach after being released by Liverpool, Chris Basham worked in McDonald's after leaving Newcastle and defender Jake Wright's time in the Conference with Oxford ensured some raised eyebrows when he linked up with Wilder once again at Bramall Lane.

But of all Wilder's early transfer business, at a time of real upheaval, only Chris Hussey proved a real disappointment. Even then, there was no indecision; Hussey and former fan favourite John Brayford were hailed by the manager as the 'best full-backs in the division' shortly after he took over but between them, played just 15 games and were soon shipped out on loan. "We had to make quick judgements on players, and there were some that we had made statements about who didn't work out," Wilder admitted. "But from our point of view, the more ticks you can get in the box, the more chance there is of success. I had to grab the club and give it a shake; I wanted to bring everyone together.

"There were a couple of contracts that needed amending to bring the power back to the club, and I signed players who wanted to run around, wanted to care about the club and forge a career for themselves. I knew that if they did that, they'd enjoy their time working for me and have a great time living in the city, and playing for a great club. When it gets going and gets a bit of momentum behind it, it's a powerful football club."

One unwanted item in Wilder's new in-tray was the Dean Hammond situation; the midfielder's loan deal, sanctioned by Adkins, contained a clause loaded in his favour which entitled him to a 12-month deal at United if he wanted it. The clause was designed to protect United's interests if his loan spell in South Yorkshire proved a success, but it turned out to be anything but and when Hammond decided to exercise the option, it gave Wilder an unnecessary distraction as he got to grips with life at Bramall Lane. In the same press release that confirmed Hammond had taken up the option, he was named on the transfer list and eventually, a deal was agreed to cancel his contract by mutual consent. The decision was purely a business one, rather than anything personal for Wilder, but it was certainly the only time in many fans' memories that a club has paid a player *not* to join them.

United's players found Wilder's methods a breath of fresh air, but that was nothing compared to the relief sensed by local journalists who had grown weary with Adkins' clichés. Wilders press briefings were mostly delivered weekly at United's Shirecliffe training base, in the media suite; a glamorous-sounding description of a fairly basic room, with sponsor boards, a few chairs, some folders in a filing cabinet and little else, apart from a gold bell by the door – one of few remnants from the building's previous incarnation as Forgemasters sports and social club.

Wilder delivered refreshingly-honest press conferences with what he calls an 'annoying twang' to his accent after a spell living in London between the ages of six and ten, and often gave off the impression of a man simply in his element talking about football. Eventually, though – after what seemed like an eternity since his appointment – the time for talking came to an end, although it was a measure of Wilder's impact that – considering how the previous campaign had ended – United fans began the 2016/17 season in optimistic mood.

Despite initial plans to boycott their first game of the season, away at Bolton Wanderers, in protest at some tickets costing £30, United eventually sold out their allocation and over 4,000 fans backed them at the Macron Stadium. Wilder's new-look Blades dominated the game but lost 1-0, to a stunning volley from Jay Spearing, and the disappointment was to become a familiar theme throughout the first few weeks of the campaign.

United bowed out of the League Cup at the first hurdle, to Crewe at Bramall Lane, and then drew 1-1 with Rochdale before a defensive capitulation, and three goals in the first 15 minutes, saw them lose 3-0 at home to Southend. Local newspaper *The Star's* match report from the game was damning, including such reflections as "the manner in which United capitulated afterwards ... was unforgivable" and "United improved after the interval ... but given their chaotic showing beforehand, it was probably impossible to get any worse."

Centre-half O'Connell, one of Wilder's summer signings from Brentford, scored an own goal and gifted Southend another in the defeat and Wilder, *The Star* writer James Shield mused, must have been "wondering exactly what he has got himself into" at Bramall Lane as the hangover of the season previous loomed large. Alan Knill, Wilder's No.2, remembers seeing his granddaughter in tears at half-time because she was so accustomed to enjoying victories from the season at Northampton and the only real positive from a United perspective was a 45-minute cameo from Coutts, who had impressed Wilder with his attitude in pre-season after being transfer-listed.

The Scottish midfielder was rewarded with a start in United's next outing, a difficult trip to Millwall and after Stefan Scougall had cancelled out Shaun Williams' early stunner, United were heading for a confidence-boosting point before O'Connell inexplicably handled a cross in the 89th minute, conceding a morale-sapping penalty. As the smell of marijuana drifted across the press box, Steve Morison stepped up and scored from the spot and United were bottom of League One with just one point from four games. Although no-one could blame Wilder when he took issue with a television reporter questioning his position after the game, the pressure was undoubtedly beginning to mount. Wilder's response, when asked how he planned to arrest the poor start, was simple. Work harder.

"I still had confidence through that run," Wilder said. "Okay, people can look back at that period and the results we had, and Southend wasn't a great evening for the football club, but the performances were nowhere near as bad as the results were. We could easily have won at Bolton on the opening day, Rochdale were an established League One outfit and the draw was a fair result. And against Southend everything that could go wrong, did go wrong.

"Look at Jack that night. If you asked, after 20 minutes of that game, if he'd go on to be a fans' favourite, have the United career he did and be worth what he is now, it'd be a no. At Millwall, I thought we did okay with a couple of injuries and got done in the last minute."

As United's team bus set off from the Den and snaked through the streets of South Bermondsey, the mood on board was almost at rock-bottom. The moment that many credited with turning around United's season came when Wilder ordered the coach driver to pull over, gave Sharp £100 and sent him into an off-licence, to buy as much beer as he could physically carry. At the time, Wilder joked he was tempted to keep it all to himself but added: "I am a bit old-school and I could see the lads were down. They care. We had lost the game in the last minute but had played all right. They were down on that bus and I wanted to change the mood."

"Performance-wise, we felt there was light at the end of the tunnel," he later reflected. "Getting the beers on the bus is something I'd do at any level … I'd do it at Premier League level if I thought it was the right thing to do, and I thought it was. The players were still running around and although we thought one or two things needed to change, we thought it'd come sooner rather than later. I spoke with Mikey Allen, our analyst, and asked him if our side was the worst over the last six years. No way, he said. We needed something to go for us, really, and eventually it did."

Their break came away at Gillingham's Priestfield Stadium, after a 2-1 victory over former club Oxford had given Wilder his first win as Blades boss. United, who had persevered with Wilder's preferred 4-4-2 formation thus far, switched to a 3-5-2 with wing-backs with new signings Moore, left-back Lafferty and centre-half Wright, who had worked with Wilder at Halifax and Oxford, in the side. Crucially, the formation allowed Duffy more freedom in the 'No.10' role, helped Coutts get on the ball and dictate play and also made United more solid at the back. But as it evolved throughout the season, a rather unprecedented tweak in the formation proved successful; overlapping centre-backs, with O'Connell and Chris Basham tasked with joining in attacks in an attempt to break down stubborn, opposition defences.

"It was a formation we often switched to if we were losing at Northampton," remembers Wilder's No.2, Knill, "and we'd worked on it a little before going to Gillingham. Then one day, Chris walked in and said, 'we're changing the shape'. We were all a bit taken aback but he said 'we're going to change it'. Couttsy had come on against Southend and did well, and we felt it suited the players, like Fleck and Duffy and Freeman. But we tweaked it a little. Duffy wasn't a traditional No.10; we gave him a free role to find space and it worked because he's a really good learner. The key thing for us is that we have to enjoy what we're watching, and the big change was the overlapping centre-backs.

"We walked onto the training pitch and I said today, we were going to have a go at getting the right-sided centre back around the right wing-back. There were a few puzzled looks but I told the boys that everyone we played seemed to sit in and try and catch us on the counter-attack, and the only overload we could really get is with the centre-halves. We put it to the test on the training pitch and Bash liked it straightaway, but it wasn't natural for Jack immediately. I told him it would make him a better player and make people look at centre-halves in a different light. A defender and a footballer as well.

"They both took to it really well, although there were murmurs of changing it after we played Walsall and got done on the counter four times. I put it to Chris, and he said no chance. That's how we play and we were sticking with it. It's so good. We speak to people and they say it's amazing because no other team plays that way. It's risk and reward, of course, but it's exciting to watch. That's the big bit for us. We're excited to watch it and we think there's more that we can do with the system."

United actually went behind at Gillingham, in front of the Sky Sports cameras, when the impressive Bradley Dack curled home a well-placed free-kick. But the new formation enjoyed its first success when right-back Freeman poked home the equaliser from all of two yards out and in the last minute, Basham's cross from the byline was handled, almost as bizarrely as O'Connell's at Millwall, by Gillingham defender Josh Pask. Skipper Sharp powered home the resulting penalty for the first away victory of the Wilder reign, and United were up and running.

"We needed to change one or two things," Wilder reflected. "A few lads had to be moved around and a couple needed to go out. We changed the goalkeeper and brought in Lafferty and Ethan Ebanks-Landell, and we wanted to get Jake in the team because of his leadership qualities. It would have been easy for people during the early results to look at it and go 'same old Sheffield United' but it wasn't. The players in the previous group weren't running around – fact, because I saw it with my own eyes – but we never had that problem."

Indeed, Wilder's approach remained consistent in good times and bad. Paul Mitchell was another Wilder signing, after joining as

United's head of recruitment from Chesterfield, and remembers the manager bounding into Shirecliffe the day after the Southend debacle. "He said 'come on, why's that telly not on?'" Mitchell told Alan Biggs' *Sheffield Live TV*. "'Get that telly on. Nowt's gonna change around here'. That's when I said to myself: 'This guy's good.'

"He never flinched, never panicked. You sometimes find out more about people in a trough than you do in a peak. I've worked with some good coaches and managers, seen a lot of coaching evenings and studied managers in-depth, and Chris is way ahead of all that I've seen. His work ethic is second to none and everything is spot on, from top to bottom.

"I think he was born to lead. He delegates really well but gives really good direction on what he expects, and he opens up things to debate amongst the coaching staff, too. He's really good like that. He listens to what people have to say, and then he makes his decision. With a bit of luck, because everyone needs that bit of luck, I think he could go all the way and maybe the only thing holding him back could be that he's British.

"When we took over and we didn't start very well, as a staff we weren't too shocked – we had a lot of new players and Chris had implemented a different style that the players we inherited weren't used to, with the high press. The new players had to knit with the group. But he never stopped doing what he thought was right, and that is when he was at his best."

In addition to the successful triumvirate of Wilder, Knill and Mitchell United could also call on the expertise of coach Matt Prestridge, who has a background in sports science and was working at Spurs before linking up with Wilder and Knill at Northampton and joining them at Bramall Lane. "One of Chris' mates did some work at Loughborough and met Matt, who was living in Watford so it was ideal for us at Northampton," said Knill.

"He interviewed really well and fitted in brilliantly with us. He's more football-based, which we are, and the dynamic is really good. He's a good lad and good at what he does. We work closely together and one day I think he'll be a really good coach.

But I'm not letting him, in case he's better than me! When there's a decision to be made he's in the group and he's just one member of a great staff at United."

They belong to a different era, and have some way to go to assemble a similar trophy cabinet, but in more than one way – both collectively and as a duo – Wilder and Knill remind Blades fans of a certain vintage of the legendary managerial pairing, Brian Clough and Peter Taylor. As Clough had done some years earlier, with his superb Nottingham Forest side, Wilder built a side in the club's and the city's image, as well as his own; good players, and good blokes. Both managers knew that results on the field would ultimately define them, but an added responsibility was felt, too; to entertain.

Bums on seats, and smiles on faces. Wilder knew how many Blades fans, including his pals and family, head to Farm Road Club or London Road before the game for a few beers, pick the team and then pull it apart again before heading to the Lane. Blades fans, Wilder feels, are intelligent enough to understand that his side won't always win the game. But if they have enjoyed what they have seen, and felt their side has 'had a go', then they'll consider that a decent day all told.

Like Clough and Taylor some years previous at Middlesbrough, Wilder and Knill first encountered each other as young apprentices at Southampton – a spell which taught both men life lessons they still carry today – and both Knill and Taylor, the eldest of the respective duos, tried their hands at management in their own right. Knill, who had spells at Rotherham United, Bury, Scunthorpe and Torquay, now concedes that, in hindsight, management wasn't for him and coaching, what he and Wilder both call 'being out on the grass', is his calling.

Where Wilder and Knill are different to many others, though – and perhaps again similar to Clough and Taylor – is that they very much come as a pair. Wilder is undoubtedly the main man, the manager, but to the pair titles are almost irrelevant. They come as a package and the silverware that has followed suggests that together, they are worth arguably more than the sum of their parts.

Knill, though, always tends to be cast as the good cop to Wilder's bad, which will come as little surprise. Again in similarity to Taylor, Knill doesn't always appear wholly comfortable being the centre of attention and although he is nevertheless a popular and very likeable bloke, he doesn't keep a huge circle of friends. Wilder, though, is almost a polar opposite in that regard and although it would perhaps be wide of the mark to say he covets publicity in the way Clough revelled in it, he is certainly much more content to be 'front and centre'. Born, Knill says, to manage.

Wilder and Knill have different personalities, and rarely socialise away from football, but share the same philosophy – and the results speak for themselves. After his remarkable first season in charge at Bramall Lane, many United fans felt that Wilder could walk on water just as Clough metaphorically had decades earlier. The only difference? It would be the River Don, rather than the Trent, below Wilder's feet – which probably runs too closely to Hillsborough for his liking.

Wilder even proved one step ahead of Clough in one instance. While Clough and Taylor had prepared themselves for management by pushing salt and pepper pots around tables in a local café, Wilder got involved with running a Sunday League team. He was just 19 years old at the time, and on the books of United as a young professional, but many of the principles that shaped Bradway's success in the Meadowhall Sunday League carried over into professional football.

One such prerequisite is training standards. For those few players left over from the Adkins era, like Sharp, Basham, Coutts and Freeman, the intensity of Wilder and Knill's training sessions at Shirecliffe was remarkably different from the mannequin-based approach of their predecessors. To play Wilder's high-pressing game, the players had to be fit enough – and the difficulty at times came in trying to calm players down, rather than gee them up. "Jack's the worst, by a mile," smiled Coutts.

"We all try and avoid him if we can … he just smashes everyone! Before, there was no intensity and a lot of passing. It was quite bizarre. I remember speaking to Chris in pre-season and he asked about how we'd trained before. He was in disbelief when I told him. The season before, we'd go up against training dummies all week, get to Saturday and the other team would press the life out of us. Our next plan was to shell it to Billy, up top on his own."

Instead of just going through the motions between games, training was increased in intensity under Wilder and after a boxing session at Sheffield's English Institute of Sport, United flew to La Manga in Spain to continue their pre-season preparations. One day, as temperatures crept up, the players were surprised with a run in the heat, led by skipper Sharp and that night, were rewarded with an evening off and allowed a few beers. "As long as they were all back by 11 and didn't abuse it," Wilder said, "we didn't see the harm."

Wilder is not offended by the "old-school manager" tag which such methods have predictably attracted – especially considering the Prozone trackers, GPS vests and video analysts at his disposal at United – because his values have barely changed since his early days in management, even if so much else is different.

Ryan Hindley, who played under Wilder at Alfreton and Halifax, hailed him as a "genius" and remembers the manager likening him to Limahl, from 1980s pop group Kajagoogoo, when Hindley had blonde streaks put in his hair. Wilder warned him to remove them before pre-season began, or he would be sold.

"He wasn't joking either, so they were straight out," Hindley recalls with a grin. "Chris was one step ahead of other managers, but us as well; he'd know if you'd been out the night before because he'd done it in his career, or if you'd not got eight hours of sleep or had argued with the missus.

"But he knew how to manage it, too – when to put an arm around you if it hadn't been your day. I remember making my debut, and he rang me up and said 'I thought you were outstanding'. I felt ten feet tall but I've seen him destroy people and make them feel two feet tall, too. He was just ahead of his time … he surrounded himself with the right people and put his own stamp on it."

Echoing his own approach during his career, Wilder's players must, first and foremost, outwork and outrun the opposition and then, when they win back the ball, look to outplay them too. The key, he believes, is playing without fear; although he twice won promotion with United, playing in the top-flight at places like Anfield and Highbury, the most enjoyable season of Wilder's career actually came in the Northern Counties East Premier League.

"I was player/manager at Alfreton, there was no fear and I loved it," he remembers. "It was then that I started to realise that players produce their best performances when there is no pressure, and the only expectation from the manager is to go out there and enjoy it … play freely within the team structure."

So, he instilled that in his players and despite admitting he feels he should have done more with his playing career – "It's something I look back on, because I got caught up having a good time" – he was determined to follow his own path in management, taking influences from good, and bad, habits of bosses he had played under – including Dave Bassett and future England boss, Sam Allardyce.

"I'd never follow or copy anyone. It's important to go your own way, and I manage on gut and experience. Every manager has their own methods and you pick up things from good managers and from mistakes, too. I just like to treat players the way I would have wanted to be treated, as much as possible, and go about it the right way. Create a good environment, but a serious one. We definitely have a giggle and want players to enjoy coming to work, and then when they step out on a matchday: don't be fearful … go and enjoy the challenge."

Wilder's United did just that, embarking on a 15-match unbeaten run to climb to third in the league. And on the rare occasion that their skill and ability wasn't enough to win games, their battling qualities and team spirit made sure they didn't lose them either. Trailing 2-1 at Glanford Park against early pace-setters Scunthorpe, with ten men and only eight minutes remaining, United recovered to earn a point and after giving away a goal at Fleetwood, Wolves loanee Ebanks-Landell sparked jubilant scenes in the away end by scoring a last-gasp equaliser.

"We work the players very hard during the week and they

have to go to the end, and sometimes take themselves out of their comfort zone," Wilder said. "There's a lot said about sports science and the like but there comes a time when they have to push themselves, and those goals at Scunthorpe and Fleetwood were celebrated as much as winners in the last minute at the time. You can dress it up however you like – they're good players, good characters, good team spirit – but we thought we could get something out of every game, and those were important psychological goals for us just as well as the points."

The origins of which could be traced back to the plush resort of La Manga. "We wanted to create a fit, athletic side that could play," Wilder added, "and I believe we did that. We knew we had talented footballers, of course, but they can't show that if they're not able to run around and they get outfought, outbattled and outrun by inferior players every week. We had to have all those aspects, individually, to produce a decent team. In that first pre-season we tested them physically, possibly more than I have ever tested a group as a manager, and we saw the ones that were the leaders, who pulled themselves and others through the tough times.

"So it was about character as well as fitness. We wanted to create a group that pulled each other out of tight positions, had each other's backs and drove each other on. Those couple of sessions really showed that, and we rewarded them with a night off and a few beers. Every manager goes about things in their own way, and I won't be changed in my outlook or dictated to on that. It's really important that they have their downtime and relax … they have a long hard slog together through the season, up and down the country and in hotel rooms and on training pitches and out there on a Saturday or a Tuesday, so I've no issue with that. And they were made to earn it."

Some who worked with both at Bramall Lane suggest that there are almost as many differences as similarities between the management styles of Wilder and Bassett, who the United manager still regularly speaks to, but both share a deeply-held belief of the importance of the group above any individual. 'You're either in or you're out' is Wilder's mantra, which not only stretched to winning battles on the pitch but giving time for charity visits and community initiatives too. In March 2017, with one of those poetic twists of fate that often crop up in football, O'Connell was outstanding, and scored, in United's victory over Millwall at Bramall Lane, less than nine months after his lowest point in the return fixture at The Den.

That week, with no game until the following Wednesday, United's players gathered in the Sheaf Island, a Wetherspoons at the bottom of Sheffield's trendy Ecclesall Road, to celebrate O'Connell's 23rd birthday. Photos on social media taken by fans suggested that alcohol was very much permitted and more importantly, at Wilder and skipper Sharp's behest, attendance was compulsory.

If I could turn back time ...
By Kevin Gage, former Blades defender

First thing's first ... I would absolutely love to play as a wingback in Chris Wilder's Sheffield United side. It was a role I fulfilled for United, amongst other great clubs, in my playing career but Chris' system would suit me right down to the ground. When you consider the stats on the amount of crosses United's full-backs get in, I would love to roll back the years and give it a go. I reckon I'd get 20 goals a season and be player of the year for three seasons on the spin! I'm joking there, of course, but it's a fantastic style of play.

I originally started off my playing career as an attacking midfielder, in the No.10 role if you like, before Dave Bassett converted me to a right-back during our time at Wimbledon. That gave me two things: a knowledge of Bassett's methods, and an appreciation of playing right-back. Under Bassett, we rose through the leagues before I joined Aston Villa and played under Graham Taylor, who was excellent. We won promotion to the top flight and then finished second the following season when Graham left for England, and Ron Atkinson took over. He wasn't my cup of tea and we didn't get on, simple as that, so Bassett brought me to United in 1991.

Now, there's a common myth going around that I ended Chris' career at United, and I would like to nail it once and for all! John Pemberton was in the side at right-back when I joined and I remember Bassett talking to me about the players in the squad who played in my position. He thought Chris was great technically but wasn't quite strong or quick enough to play there long-term, and that Pembo was quick and strong but didn't have the technical ability he was after. Ideally he'd have mashed the two together, which is apparently where I came in! So I didn't replace Chris. I think when I joined he was already out on loan and I don't actually remember training with him ... I certainly didn't play alongside him, unless there was an obscure pre-season friendly or something.

I knew he was connected with the club and used to come back and watch games when he wasn't playing, and at the end of my first season he left for Rotherham. So it's now on the record that I didn't ruin Chris' career at his boyhood club! Technically, Chris was far better than he perhaps gets credit for, but he didn't fit in with Bassett's style of play. If I played under Bassett, it wasn't because I was a fantastic defender but because I can take a touch and land the ball 40 yards, accurately, down the channel for someone else to run onto.

I'm asked often if Chris is similar to Bassett and I'd say he was actually closer to Graham Taylor. I wanted to play for Graham because I found him fascinating, and I get the feeling Chris is more akin to that than the raw emotion Bassett used to have. For all Chris' tubthumping, 'we're all doing it for the club' stuff, there's an awful lot of technical thought and planning that goes into it as well.

Where they are similar is their values. Anyone who signed for Bassett knew what they were in for and must have fitted the brief he wanted, and I can't see Chris ever signing a player who isn't going to fit into the mould. Chris is a deep thinker, he knows what he wants, he's ruthless in who he wants and how he wants to play. The players have bought into it, and how can you not? Everything is geared up for them to do well. I know from personal experience that it can be a special place and we seem to be having the upside of our near neighbours, too, which helps. We're now top dogs in the city, which is a huge thing because it feels like a long time since that happened.

The first game I was involved in for United was actually against Wednesday; I'd signed on the Thursday afternoon and the derby was on the Sunday. I was on the bench so sat and watched it unfold as we beat them, and by the time the return leg came around I was in the team and we beat them 3-1. Because I'd only just joined, it didn't feel massively significant at the time – I understood the rivalry, of course, but it meant more to me to win 4-2 at Hillsborough in September 2017 because I feel more attached to the club now, as a fan.

Bassett's methods were successful, so I bought into them but if I had a problem I don't think I could go to him. It was purely a business relationship and I didn't agree with the way he treated people sometimes. I thought he could be extremely harsh with some players if we'd lost a game, or not won one he thought we should have. I'm sure he'll agree he didn't give out praise very well ... it was very much tough love, and Chris had first-hand experience of that. He was part of the sides that won promotion to the top flight but was jettisoned through no fault of his own. So if he's learned one thing from Bassett, I think it'll be that ruthlessness to cull players if need be.

When he came back as manager, I was lucky enough to meet up with Chris, along with Keith Edwards and Andy Pack, because he wanted a little flavour of what life was like at United. There wasn't much tactical analysis from what I can remember – it was more like mates talking in the pub – but one thing I picked up on was Chris' insistence that he'd play 4-4-2! Soon enough, he changed that formation and the rest was history. The same with changing his mind on Paul Coutts and Kieron Freeman. Many managers would stick to their guns but Chris was willing to have a bit of egg on his face, for the good of the team.

Personally, I wouldn't mind having a bet that Chris will be England manager in ten years. The pool is minimal anyway, beyond people like Alan Pardew and Roy Hodgson, and you can make a case for Sean Dyche and Eddie Howe but have they done it continuously, at every club, including non-league? It's the perfect fairytale, really. There's no reason whatsoever to think Chris wouldn't be a success at a Premier League club and from my point of view, I hope he stays at United for the next five or ten years because the football is great, and I think he'll get us in the Premier League. He's ambitious and the sky's the limit.

I can't see why he shouldn't get the top job one day. He's not exactly a young, up-and-coming manager but he's been around and done his apprenticeship. Put it another way, he can certainly manage players and that's what the England job is all about. You don't have to coach them or tell them how to play ... just encourage and motivate them, get them believing in themselves and one another. Give them a formation and say 'away you go lads'. You heard it here first!

4

The Blades start to believe

As the weeks ticked by and the wins stacked up, it was becoming more and more apparent by the game that Sheffield United, and Chris Wilder, were destined for the Championship. But it was a hard-fought victory back in September, over AFC Wimbledon at their claustrophobic Kingsmeadow ground, that set the tone for much of what followed. United prevailed 3-2 that day, against a spirited Dons side, and as they applauded their fans after the game supporter Lee Burgon tweeted a picture with the caption: "Finally a team that actually give 100 percent. That's all we ask for." Far from a prolific *Twitter* user, Wilder was shown the tweet and had it mounted on the wall of United's dressing room at Bramall Lane. A further reminder to the players what is expected of them when they walk out in a red-and-white shirt.

On a remarkable afternoon in October 2016, United hammered Port Vale 4-0 at Bramall Lane but also had four goals disallowed. A similarly breathtaking 3-3 draw away at Bradford City, one of Wilder's former clubs, followed with a superb atmosphere generated by the 20,972 fans inside Valley Parade, and spurred on Wilder's men to six wins on the spin in all competitions. In the 89th minute at Charlton, a club Wilder and his No.2 Alan Knill almost joined before an eleventh-hour approach from United, the Blades were 1-0 up and looking set to make that seven when, with rubber footballs and London taxis strewn around the outside of the pitch after an earlier supporter protest against Charlton owner Roland Duchâtelet, Patrick Bauer bundled home a 90th-minute equaliser to ruin Wilder's mood … and his cousin's big day.

"He was a bit disappointed because it was his birthday, and

I had a mask of his face that I said I'd wear after the game if we won," Wilder remembers. "We were really disappointed to only get a point from that game, and afterwards gave the boys a bit of a talking to, reminding them that we couldn't afford to chuck points away. We stayed down in London for his birthday and went into Greenwich, and bumped into a load of United supporters! There were times when they lifted me. I was feeling a bit down after a game we should have won but they were walking around delighted with what we were producing, so it was good from that point of view.

"We all had a weekend off after the Charlton game to clear our heads and there were Blades fans all over. Not that I was surprised. I've been in those pubs loads of times before, before games ... the difference now, I guess, is that they were seeing their manager in there with them! But looking back, there were some great games over that period, like Bradford away from home and scoring at Fleetwood late on. It was an incredibly tough division, as we knew because we had been in it for six years, and maybe even more so for these big powerful teams, like United and Leeds who'd had it before.

"It's cup final time for every other club, home and away. When they walk into their home ground and see three or four thousand United fans in the away end, it gives them a boost. I'm in the fortunate position to have played the game, as well, so I know the psyche of professional footballers. The pressure was taken completely off these teams when we played them, so for us to handle that as well was especially pleasing."

In August, when a 2-1 defeat at Millwall sent United to the bottom of League One, early pacesetters Bolton and Scunthorpe were 11 and nine points ahead of Wilder's men respectively. But Kieron Freeman's last-minute winner, on New Year's Eve against Wilder's former club Northampton, sent United to the top of the table and from that point, they were there to be shot at. "We just went from strength to strength throughout the season and just ended up blowing teams apart," forward Mark Duffy remembers. "Eventually teams started coming to Bramall Lane, we'd kick off and they'd just physically retreat, hoping for a draw.

But the gaffer just told us to find a way, and we often tended to.

"As a midfield of me, Flecky and Couttsy, we'd go into any game thinking we could get the better of the other team because we had an unbelievable understanding. We'd think 'if they go 3v3, we're better individually than them, so that's fine and if they go 2v3, they just don't have a chance'. That was just our way of thinking, because we complemented each other so well. Couttsy went deep to dictate the play, Flecky was a bit of a mixture of both and I'd be further up the pitch, trying to create. It seems so simple but other teams would always comment how well we played together, and it probably helped that we have a great friendship between us and trust each other with the ball."

Blips occured along the way – Walsall curiously registered their third victory over United of the season with a 4-1 win at the Banks's Stadium, and Fleetwood triumphed 2-0 at Bramall Lane – but United made a big statement of intent to their promotion rivals by taking four points from their home double-header against Scunthorpe and Bolton, who were also still in the hunt for Championship football. After Billy Sharp scored United's equaliser in a 1-1 draw against his former club Scunthorpe, the build-up to the crunch clash with Bolton was dominated by former Sheffield Wednesday striker Gary Madine and a video which emerged on social media, of him calling Sharp 'a fat pig'.

Unsurprisingly, the video did little to assuage the ill-feeling towards the former Owl from Blades fans and he noticeably took his time to leave the Bolton coach outside Bramall Lane, to a chorus of boos. When the teams were confirmed an hour before kick-off, his name was absent and he was sent back over the Pennines in a taxi, with the official explanation of illness attracting some raised eyebrows on the United terraces. Fittingly, it was Sharp who scored both United's goals in a 2-0 win and celebrated by rubbing his belly in front of the Bolton fans, and holding a finger to his lips. The message clear.

"We really had the bit between our teeth going into the new year and we were grinding teams down," Wilder said. "It did become a matter of time until we scored in games, and I think everyone looked at the two games against Bolton and

Scunthorpe as really pivotal ones. They'd been pushing right the way throughout the season and Fleetwood had enjoyed a good run, too, so we knew it'd be two teams from four and we were delighted to be in that pack, playing well and knowing they both had to come to our place.

"I remember Chris Basham making a tackle against Scunthorpe, sliding through about three of their players, and there was an enormous roar. I said when I came to the club that sometimes a big tackle, a chase or a header gets as much reaction as a flick, a dribble or a good pass. We knew we had good players, but that was a moment when we said 'if you want to come and mix it with us, we won't have the mickey taken out of us'. Some people look down on a tackle a bit in football but for me, that was a bit of a marker for both of the games that we weren't going to roll over.

"We were disappointed not to beat Scunthorpe when they went down to ten men, but we fully deserved to beat Bolton. I've come across Gary a couple of times and always got on with him, I know Bolton's staff really well, and of course there's history there with his connections. There are a few things he'll probably look back at and say were a bit daft. But I can't say anything … I did daft things as a player too! There's a fine line, but I don't want people coming to our ground and being comfortable. We, whether it's players or fans, don't get that at grounds like Millwall or Birmingham, and it's part and parcel of football, as long as it doesn't overstep the mark. I said in an interview that I didn't want people throwing petrol bombs at away supporters coming out of the station, but I didn't want anybody to get a free ride and teams had come to Bramall Lane in the past and felt a little bit comfortable. The atmosphere against Bolton was great … and Gary not playing benefitted us, as well, because he was a big player in the division."

As a youngster, Wilder lived a decent goal-kick away from Bramall Lane following a spell in London and one of his first memories was seeing United relegated to the old fourth division in 1980/81, after losing to Walsall at Bramall Lane. United won a late penalty and scoring it would have kept them up, but regular taker John Matthews declined the opportunity and Don Givens missed. To a young Wilder it reinforced the point; no-one follows United for the glory of it. "I've found that clubs sometimes do have a bit of a hold or a hoodoo over you," said Wilder, with a wry smile as he remembers disallowed goals and a late saved penalty, "and sometimes it's hard to explain and get your head around! They beat us three times over the season and the one at Bramall Lane ... I've never been involved in a game like that, with some of the decisions by the referee.

"We have an obligation to do a report on officials after games and unlike other managers, I've never been one to try and influence decisions but some of the decisions on that night ... I was just proud of my players, the way they kept going. We missed a penalty and some nights it's not to be ... and home, away and in the cup, they proved that more than once."

'Proper football'
By Sam Parry, Kop

Less than a year after the Nigel Adkins era ended with *that* defeat to Scunthorpe United – when only a cheer to celebrate Dean Hammond's substitution managed to lift the crowd – the Blades were crowned champions of League One, and Chris Wilder and Alan Knill negotiated a hurdle that Danny Wilson, Chris Morgan, David Weir, Nigel Clough and Adkins could not. In the aftermath, Wilder was not slow in coming forward and proclaiming that United was a "proper football club." Proper coaching. Proper players. Proper fans. Proper football.

Proper people, too, beginning with Wilder and Knill and the minor distinction: that Knill is the coach to Wilder's manager. Sometimes you can see this on the pitch. Complex free kick routines against Scunthorpe and Charlton both led to important goals. The more you scrutinise this relationship, the more you get the impression that Knill and Wilder are the package, not to be sold separately – and at the same time, this is something of a moot point.

Does it matter who came up with this routine, or that tactical change? I think not. The 3-4-1-2, the blood and thunder pressing, the overlapping wingbacks, the overlapping centre-halves and the clinical finishing all add up to success. Between them, Knill and Wilder have coached the Blades out of a low ebb and with no plateau in sight. Proper coaching, however, only adds up to on-the-field results if the players have the quality to get the job done. Bottom of the table after four games, it is a testament to the players, as much as it is the manager, that they had the wherewithal to take 99 points from the remaining 42 games.

Firstly, the players that were brought in throughout the course of the season were of great quality and great character. Wilder prides himself on the homework he does to ensure any potential signing is the right fit. Here, Mark Duffy is a case in point. Skill in abundance, tricks in abundance and a good guy who had previous with Knill at Scunthorpe. Secondly, the players that Wilder was left with by his predecessor Adkins were given a chance. Billy Sharp, who Wilder immediately made club captain, was the perfect foil for the rest of the squad to provide a common thread between fans, management and players. This decision brought a proper sense of connection for the fans. And, of course, Sharp himself brought 30 goals.

However, no players quite typify the results of Wilder's excellent man management like Kieron Freeman and Paul Coutts. Two players signed by previous managers who were both placed on the transfer list at the start of the season. Some managers choose to sideline players they expect to sell, but Wilder clearly acknowledged that how he treats players, whatever part they are playing in the first-team, reflects upon him as a person. After being loaned out to Portsmouth by the previous regime and now given the chance to impress, Freeman went on to score 11 goals from right-wing back. But it was Coutts, more than anyone else, who demonstrated the transformative powers of Messrs Wilder and Knill. Having become a figure of derision under Adkins, partly due to results and partly due to his nonchalant style of play, Coutts became the exemplar of what Wilder's 'proper football' is all about.

The centre-point through which all of United's good play

travelled, Coutts inspired confidence in his peers. Confidence to give him the ball and get it back; confidence to pull out of position knowing that he would cover and confidence that he would, as his terrace song goes, "never give the ball away." Most of that comes down to Coutts' natural ability, but coaxing consistent performances from him, and resultantly the team, comes down to Wilder's ability to create a team ethic – a togetherness. In isolation, camaraderie doesn't automatically bring success.

The Blades team that last played in the Premiership had camaraderie, no doubt, but it didn't prevent their relegation. Nevertheless, a team that works for each other is always discernible to fans that watch week in and week out. Chris Wilder brought a touch-feel sense of togetherness. Oftentimes you hear people saying that the fans 'bought into' Wilder's style of management. Yet that belies a more nuanced observation; Wilder enabled the players to buy into what the fans wanted.

United fans want to see themselves reflected in the players on the pitch. Wilder knew this when he took the job, that hard work and motivation is implied by wearing the shirt. Hard graft is a given; any latent success only comes about because of it and failure comes about due to a lack of it. Culture is the watchword here and Wilder's culture is United's culture is the supporters' culture. Observing the Kop's reaction to a striker, who has just lost the ball, only to track his opponent all the way back and into his own half and regain possession, illustrates the basic expectation of the supporters.

Taken in isolation, proper coaching, proper players and proper fans do not necessarily add up to a 100-points haul and promotion. It must be acknowledged that Chris Wilder alone is responsible for re-joining the dots in S2 to make a very successful, very passionate and very Blade-shaped constellation. With him in charge, it does feel as if the sky's the limit – he has something special that many managers do not.

The hipsterisation of football has led to fans salivating over 'tiki-taka', 'the gegenpress' and Total Football – but these can be reduced down to tactics. The Pep Guardiola-zealots will tell you that he is a philosophical manager, a genius. No doubt, he is an incredible – and an incredibly successful – manager. But proper football exists within spaces that cannot be boiled down by observational analysis or statistics. Wilder's proper football is probably only recognised, in the truest sense, by Blades fans who have seen the club in its lowest ebbs. Perhaps this is why, as a fan himself, Wilder has been able to enjoy the highs, as he puts it, twice as much.

To contrast the Great Man with Guardiola for a final time, it's amusing to look back at Wilder's reaction to promotion. It differs somewhat to Guardiola's who – after winning the Champions League with Barcelona, the team he supported since childhood – is said to have felt disappointed, and even admitted to a friend that he "got it wrong." Where Guardiola struggled to enjoy the moment, Wilder certainly did not.

In fact, he (and the players, staff and fans for that matter) treated United's title-winning season almost as if it were a Friday night after a week of hard graft – we all certainly deserved that elongated Happy Hour. Where Guardiola sought intangible tactical perfection, Wilder did not. When there are no games left to play, then you can – and should – celebrate success properly. Proper football, if it is a philosophy at all, is a simple one.

It is people-focused. Good characters and square pegs in square holes. It balances hard work, professionalism, skill and tactics in equal measure. He's brought a lot to my club – pride, togetherness, the best football I've witnessed in years, Duffy, promotion – but what distinguishes Wilder's short spell in charge from almost everything else that has come before, is that all of those things function smoothly. Almost as if we were always this United. That is proper football.

5

Pitch-not-so-perfect

After surging to the top of the table on New Year's Eve, Chris Wilder's Blades looked well-placed for a promotion from League One that had eluded them for six years, but they weren't having it all their own way. Walsall firmly cemented their place as United's 'bogey team' with a deserved 4-1 victory on their home soil – their third win over Wilder's men of the season – and after Gillingham frustrated by earning a 2-2 draw at Bramall Lane, future Blades target Devante Cole scored for Fleetwood as they triumphed 2-0 in South Yorkshire. By that point, though, United were still top of the division, seven points clear of third-placed Bolton, and their unique system of using overlapping centre-backs was still causing teams problems.

In some games, however, opposition sides often camped men in their own box to negate United's overload and although their system had been far from 'found out', Wilder knew United needed a Plan B. So, in January, they spent £130,000 on James Hanson, the former Co-op shelf-stacker who later turned professional with Bradford City and was considered, by Wilder and his coaching staff, as the best 'target man' in League One. The signing of Hanson enabled United to play in a more direct fashion when the situation demanded, while fellow new-boy Samir Carruthers always threatened to light up a game with a spark of brilliance. But it was the character of two more impressive performances on the road that convinced Wilder that his Blades were destined for success.

"I remember we went to Southend in early January – who'd been a tough side to play on their own patch – and getting the teamsheet before, and thinking 'wow'. We reckoned they had eight or nine lads at six feet tall, and thought 'they're going to try and beat us up here'. But we physically dominated them, played football and won 4-2. We were having a drink afterwards with Phil Brown, who I have a lot of respect for, and he told us that no-one had done that to them for a long time. We told the players what was coming, and they stood up to it. There are always different ways to win games – if it opened up, we'd outplay teams and if it was a tight or a physical one, we wouldn't be dominated or intimidated.

"Then there was Oldham away, on a terrible pitch. Myself, Knilly and Paul Mitchell had all gone to watch them and said the same thing … 'wow, the pitch is gonna level it right out', and it did. They were fighting for their lives with a good manager in John Sheridan, and teams at the bottom want to stay in the division as much as teams want to get out of it by getting promotion. But we matched them, Jay O'Shea came up with a moment of magic and I went out afterwards and said 'this is a good point. Don't think it's anything but'.

"A few of the lads were a bit down but I reminded them that Bolton and Fleetwood had still got to go there, on that pitch, and I'd be majorly surprised if both of them came away with three points. It's a division where you have to overcome all challenges and different hurdles, and that was a result I felt was bigger than a few victories we had around that time."

They kept coming. The draw at Oldham was the only time United dropped points in the final 11 matches of the season and as the weeks ticked by, and the wins stacked up, it became more and more apparent that United, at last, were destined to escape League One's clutches. Wilder, in his dealings with the press and the players, remained calm enough as he repeated the 'one game at a time' cliché but, on occasion, the elation proved difficult to contain. United could have been promoted as early as April 5, if they overcame Coventry at Bramall Lane and results elsewhere went their way.

The game brought back memories of the first meeting between the two sides that season which descended, frankly, into farce as Coventry fans took the opportunity that a Sky

Sports-televised game offered them, to ramp up their protests against the club's owners Sisu. Home supporters blew whistles throughout the game and invaded the pitch with anti-Sisu flags, leading to a delay as players and officials left the field. When the game eventually restarted, Billy Sharp hit an injury-time winner which did little to enhance the mood around a sparsely-populated Ricoh.

By the time the Sky Blues visited Bramall Lane, there was a feeling amongst their supporters that the trip could be their last – with the club marooned at the bottom of the table, relegation imminent and their longer-term future even more unclear. United, though, were only looking up and won 2-0 to hold up their end of the bargain, but Fleetwood beat Oxford to delay the promotion party for another week. That didn't stop Wilder enjoying the moment, though, when Coventry old boy John Fleck scored United's second after dancing through the visiting defence and finishing in front of the Kop. Fleck, Kieron Freeman, Leon Clarke and Chris Basham celebrated with a Jurgen Klinsmann-esque 'dive' and Wilder couldn't resist, racing onto the field and sliding to join in before jogging away to hug the fourth official and apologise to opposite number Mark Robins.

"It was right in front of me, so off I went," Wilder remembers. "I grazed my chin on the slide and thought afterwards, what am I doing there? But the emotion just took over me. It wasn't premeditated or anything like that. It was right in front of me and I thought 'I'm having a bit of this'. I can't erase it, unfortunately! But that's just the euphoria you feel when your team has taken a massive step towards getting out of the division.

"I won't apologise for being like that. It's ridiculous how football clubs can take over your life and I wear my heart on my sleeve, I always have done. I stood out there, when we were 3-0 down after 15 minutes against Southend in August, and I didn't run back into the dressing room. I stood out there on the touchline. That's how I manage and my players take things on the chin."

Chin patched up, Wilder had little time to reflect on United's next shot at securing promotion, which came just three days later. The date was April 8, 2017. And, in a fittingly-poetic twist to the fairytale journey of the former Northampton Town manager so far, the stadium was Sixfields.

6

One day in April

It simply had to be Northampton. Almost a year to the day since Chris Wilder, Alan Knill and Matt Prestridge had helped the Cobblers to promotion at Sixfields, the trio were back again – different colours, same circumstances. Promotion was within touching distance but they were now on the other side of it; arriving at Sixfields as visitors, not custodians. Wearing the badge of Sheffield United, Wilder knew everything in his managerial career had led him to this point; the early, trophy-laden days at Alfreton Town, meeting with triumph and disaster at Oxford Town and treating those imposters just the same when working through near-financial crisis at Northampton, when he and his staff weren't being paid and funds to build a new stand had gone missing. Just one more game. Another win. Three more points, and the Blades – *his Blades* – were up.

Officially, around 1,500 Blades packed into the away end of Sixfields behind the goal, with many more dotted around the home stands and even a hardy few that had travelled to Northampton to watch the game from the hill overlooking the ground, which offered a decent enough view of three-quarters of the pitch. It was enough for them, just to be there and be a part of the day, and thousands more Blades fans were back at Bramall Lane, watching the game beamed-back on giant screens. The city was buzzing in the build-up – Northampton was to be this generation's Leicester, talked about in the same breath as the 1990 promotion decider at Filbert Street when United, with Wilder on the pitch, won 5-2 and clinched promotion to the old Division One. Their joy that day was compounded when Wednesday were also relegated but almost 27 years later, it was a day that belonged solely to United.

The players arrived at Sixfields in relaxed mood; Mark Duffy, Kieron Freeman and Jake Wright posed for selfies with fans while on-loan Middlesbrough youngster Harry Chapman entered the ground drinking strawberry milk through a straw. Wilder remembers a "ridiculous" demand for his complimentary tickets in the build up and Gary Sinclair, the matchday announcer at Bramall Lane, ended up sponsoring the matchball on the day to ensure his seat at Sixfields. The boss experienced Leicester as a player and the aftermath of Darlington in 1982, when around 10,000 Blades joined the promotion party at the old Feethams ground, as a fan but was now in that position as a manager. Possibly in an attempt to calm his own nerves as much as those of his players, Wilder called an impromptu huddle on the pitch before kick-off – although skipper Billy Sharp admitted it didn't quite do the trick. "I was more nervous for that game than any other," he later revealed.

Needing only to equal Fleetwood's result at Oldham, Wilder sprung something of a surprise an hour before kick-off when team news filtered through, and Sharp had been left on the bench, with Jay O'Shea and Samir Carruthers supporting lone striker Leon Clarke. Carruthers hit the bar early on and loanee O'Shea curled wide before Blades all around the ground, on the hill and back at Bramall Lane received news that Oldham had gone ahead. Then, almost out of nowhere, Marc Richards put Northampton in front with a stunning strike into the top corner, right on the stroke of half-time. The Cobblers clearly hadn't read the script.

"I knew Justin Edinburgh, their manager, and a lot of their players and they didn't want someone else to come into their backyard and have a party," Wilder said. "Just like I wouldn't. I'd always do it out of respect but I don't want to be the side giving a guard of honour to a promoted team, or having to get off our pitch quickly so another club can celebrate. We made the call to leave out Billy because of the fixtures around that part of the season and knew we could bring him off the bench if we needed him, along with James Hanson.

"The bench had been key for us because we had players who

could come on and affect the game and enable us to change the way we played. To be successful, people talk about the strength of your bench – and we certainly had a strong one."

Sharp did indeed get the call to go on at half-time but it was the introduction of former Bradford City man Hanson eight minutes later that helped change the game. Clarke, the former Wednesday striker, wrote his name into Blades folklore with the equaliser from John Fleck's sublime pass, and the little Scot then scored a late winner after Hanson and Sharp had combined. Cue pandemonium all around the ground, another pitch invasion and memorable scenes involving one fan charging onto the field armed with the corner flag and another shoving the matchball up his shirt, a souvenir of promotion for years to come. One supporter even headed back to Sheffield with a sign from Sixfields.

All Blades fans present that day will have their own memories but few will rival those of Richard Glossop, who saw out the final few minutes of the Northampton game from surely the best vantage point possible ... the Blades dugout. After Fleck scored the winning goal, Glossop raced to embrace Wilder and his staff but as the pitch was cleared, he had a decision to make. "Obviously I've had an insight into scenes like this from Darlington away and Leicester in 1990," Wilder said, "but the players hadn't. They were asking what to expect and I told them there would be Blades fans all over the stadium. One of the biggest things I can remember is a fan sprinting to the dugouts and jumping all over us after Flecky scored ... but then they cleared the pitch.

"If he went back to his seat, he was going to get nicked by the police. He looked at me and said 'Chris, what do I do?' and I told him to stay where he was. I had to look after him because he could have been any of my mates ... or me, if I wasn't the manager! So I kept him in the dugout and the cheeky get even asked me for a selfie! But I had to make sure he didn't get nicked, on probably the best day of his life following United.

"When Leon scored the first, I thought it was going to be our day but I was still in the zone a little bit, wanting to win the game. Afterwards, we had five minutes in the changing room where I thanked everybody, and it was quite an emotional time. It was a tight group who had to put up with a lot of pressure through the season, and I was proud of the way they handled everything from start to finish. We had a couple of low points during the season but kept going, and the journey back will live with me forever.

"I remember the journey back from Leicester was huge, Dave Bassett getting off the bus and the car park being packed and everyone going into the old Bramall Lane social club and then into town. We wanted to make our own memories. We'd taken some crap over the last six years in League One, so it was great for the supporters and the way we did it was a credit to everyone involved. Blades fans talk about Darlington and Leicester as the iconic moments in recent years and hopefully people will now talk about Northampton in a similar breath. I remember being stood outside Filbert Street, with my mum and dad and a few pals, and some more coming round the corner and saying Wednesday had also gone down. Just when I thought the day couldn't get any better."

Despite the result, Northampton also showed a touch of class of their own by allowing United supporters from all four stands, and even up on the hill overlooking the ground, into the stadium to join the celebrations and offered their congratulations to their visitors on the big screen. A champagne soaked Wilder was cheered by fans of both clubs after climbing on the dugout to make an impromptu speech but it was the sight of Sharp being chaired from the field, holding a red and white scarf above his head, that became one of the defining images in United's long history. At one point, Sharp had to wipe his face with it as the emotion took over and amidst the jubilation, his voice could be heard over almost all others; singing with the fans, as one of them.

"And now you're gonna believe us … the Blades are going up."

The best view in the house
By Richard Glossop, Bramall Lane Corner (and Sixfields dugout)

Saturday, April 8 will be a day that stays with me for the rest of my life; the day that Sheffield United, *my* Sheffield United, finally gained promotion from the abyss of League One to the level, at least, that they belong. But what made it even more special, as thousands of Blades fans celebrated on the pitch and Billy Sharp was chaired off the pitch, was that I wasn't even supposed to be there. It took a chance text message on the day of the game from my mate to even travel down to Northampton and when the final whistle was blown, and promotion was sealed, I had the best view of any Blade in the house. Well, maybe apart from Sharp and our manager in a million, Chris Wilder.

I've been a Blade all my life and, like many people, it runs in the family. My dad brought me to Bramall Lane for my first game when I was about eight years old and I sat on the Kop, until I got a bit older and moved away to the Westfield Corner to get a better view. And the football we've played under Wilder has looked very good indeed! The memories of that day at Northampton still feel a bit surreal today. I got a message at 8.30am on the morning of the game, asking if I wanted to go down. I remember it being a lovely day, the sun was out, and we couldn't get a ticket but Sixfields is quite famous for the hill overlooking the ground, so I thought 'yeah, why not?' My mate drove down while I urgently scoured *Facebook* and *Twitter* looking for a ticket. It felt like the whole of Sheffield was doing likewise at one point but we both somehow managed to get one. We were absolutely buzzing.

The only snag was that they weren't with the Blades, but were in the home end with the Northampton supporters. We sought the guy out straightaway to make sure we had them secured, and it turned out that we were in different stands; my mate was behind the dugouts, while I was opposite him, and it was quite a scary moment knowing we'd be on separate stands. But still, we were there – and a quick glance at the number of Blades on the hill suggested that not everyone had been quite so lucky. As it turned out, a Northampton fan was in a hospitality box so had a couple of spare tickets. It worked out well for everyone – he got a few quid for them, and we got to see one of the biggest days in United history in decades.

I will never forget what followed. During my time following the Blades, there have been a lot of downs and only one real up, the promotion to the Premier League in 2006. I've been to Wembley three or four times and seen us lose each time, but that day was a different kind of nervousness; mainly about actually getting into the ground, past the security and police who would surely know I was a Blade. I did my bit by keeping my mouth shut, nodding at everyone instead of actually saying anything, but I'm sure they knew what would happen … I know Chris remembers that day at Leicester in 1990 when Filbert Street was about two-thirds full of Blades!

A few of my friends had secured tickets for Sixfields in the Blades contingent, which was behind one goal and in a little area on one side stand; my side stand. A few Blades were also in the home section with me and I remember when the ball came towards me in the first half and I started doing kick-ups with it – getting some abuse from my fellow Blades in the process who thought I was a Northampton fan, trying to waste time! I was trying to keep my head down and there I am doing tricks, but it was all part of the fun of the day.

It wasn't much fun, though, when Northampton went ahead and it was just a case of clapping politely. I just remember thinking that it might not be our day but the attitude we showed all through that season, when we'd gone behind in games and seemed to come back so many times, made me think it could still happen. Then, when Leon Clarke went through on goal, the finish was inevitable. He was on fire at that point and from there, there was only going to be one winner. Almost before I knew it, I was on the pitch after Clarke's goal and when the field was cleared by the stewards, I ended up in the stand behind the net – the away end, where I had tried so desperately to be earlier. My mate, James Raistrick, also ended up in there with me – in hindsight, we should have agreed to meet on the penalty spot if United scored – and from there, we could see John Fleck up close as he bore down on goal to score what turned out to be the winner.

Now, in my mind, from Bryan Robson to Nigel Adkins, there had been disappointment after disappointment managing my club since it came down from the Premier League and finally, Wilder had got it right. The fact that we were all down at Northampton, in the stands or up on the hill, celebrating one of the best seasons in the club's history was, for me, all down to him and so I wanted, in a silly kind of way, to just say thank you for bringing back the good times. It was down to him and his staff, getting the players to believe in him and his methods, so I decided to sprint to the dugout and tell him. I must admit I didn't think I'd actually get there. I started with a bit of pace but the pitch was bigger than I thought and I was tiring by the time I got to Wilder and the Blades bench. By then, the pitch was clear.

He's mentioned me in an interview since and said that he took pity on me because I could have been one of his pals, or even him if he wasn't United manager, and didn't want me to get arrested or thrown out on the biggest United-supporting day in many years. Perhaps fortunately, I'd chosen to wear a black adidas tracksuit top on the day – the same kit supplier as United – so I kind of blended in with the coaching staff, and Wilder told me to stay in the dugout for the remaining few minutes of the game.

It was absolutely surreal. Clarke, one of the heroes of the day, was on the bench by now, as were Samir Carruthers and Mark Duffy. They were all really down-to-earth people, too, which made it all the more special. Wilder then came over so I thought I'd try my luck and ask him for a cheeky selfie! I can't imagine that happening with many other managers but with him being a Blade and enjoying a day like this before, I think he could see the day from my perspective a little.

So from there, on the bench surrounded by players and staff, water bottles and bags of footballs, I watched history unfold. In hindsight, I should have put some shorts on and gone for a warm-up! I've thought since that I should have done things differently, maybe ask for a shirt as a souvenir or something, but I was so caught up in the moment and to be a small part of the day is something I'll always remember. The spell in League One was forgettable for many reasons but at the moment it ended, I was right there in the thick of it.

I remember Wilder, even on the verge of promotion, still shouting at his players and urging them to keep going right until the end but when that final whistle went, it was pandemonium. There were just bodies everywhere, jumping over anyone and everyone they saw, fan or player. I picked up Duffy as he'd ran on the pitch with me and we stayed behind for the players to come back out and celebrate with us … it was just an amazing day. I'm just thankful that my phone battery lasted as long as it did. I'd been all over social media on the day of the game, trying to find a ticket, and if it had died before I could get the selfies on the bench, I doubt anyone would believe what happened on that day! I know my mates wouldn't.

It's a day that I'll remember as long as I live and especially after originally planning to watch it from the top of the hill overlooking the ground, I had the best seat in the house. After Sharp and Wilder, of course. And the good times didn't stop that day. Adkins had led us to the lowest position in the league since before I was born, and the entire club was down. The job that Wilder and his staff have done in such a short space of time really is incredible; to turn it around from the position Adkins left us in, and then be bottom of the league after four games and then win the title with 100 points … phenomenal.

Blades fans are a pretty easy-to-please bunch; all we ask for is honesty and hard work and we're getting that in abundance, with great football too. As long as the players keep working for him and believing in him, we can go all the way. I said it that day and I'll say it again; thank you, Chris Wilder, for bringing the good times back.

7

Celebration time(s)

The joyous scenes continued in the away dressing room at Northampton Town after Sheffield United's six-year spell in League One officially ended but Wilder, along with Steven Sylvester, the renowned sports psychologist who worked with United that season, was still looking forward. With champagne still dripping from his brow, he remembers sitting the players down and telling them: 'This doesn't end here'. Promotion was one goal ... winning the title was next.

Wilder admits he was surprised that his only real outpouring of emotion, as the season climaxed so spectacularly, came at Northampton but he was still not willing to pass up an opportunity to celebrate. John, United's regular coach driver, was unavailable for the trip to Sixfields so a temporary one was drafted in and Wilder gave him the ominous warning ... "Get ready." His wife Francesca, a lifelong Blade, managed to sneak onto the team bus somehow and Wilder's only regret was that they weren't coming back from somewhere like Plymouth, to prolong the celebrations even more.

"The scenes were great going back," he said. "We had a player of the year do at Bramall Lane so as we were coming back the police told us to go around the back way, round Shoreham Street, but nah. That wasn't happening. The poor driver had the police in his ear saying 'you must take a left' and the manager in his other ear saying 'you must go on'.

"I think he maybe felt, at that point, that I'd elbow him out the way and drive the bus myself if he didn't listen to me, so we ended up going along Bramall Lane and the scenes there were absolutely incredible. I knew what it was going to be like but it was more important for the players and the staff, who don't have the history with the club that I have, to witness it and see what it meant to people."

Thousands of supporters had gathered to welcome the players home – hundreds, gathered outside the Railway pub just opposite the ground, stopped the coach for an impromptu sing-song – and skipper Sharp's voice broke with emotion as he addressed fans with an emotional speech outside Bramall Lane. "Last year [under Adkins] was embarrassing … I felt ashamed," he said. "This year, I'm so proud to be a Blade and the gaffer has done something that no-one else will ever do."

The skipper then disappeared under a crowd of teammates singing his name after United's players got off the coach one by one, each greeted by their own chant. Chris Basham sprayed champagne everywhere and just to further underline the bond newly-forged between manager and fans, it was Wilder who led a rousing chant of United's timeless 'Barrel of Money' chant which references three more Lane legends: Alan Woodward, Tony Currie and Eddie Colquhoun. A distinguished pantheon of greats, alongside whom Wilder had etched his own name.

But still, he wanted more. By this point United had 88 points with four matches left to play and the target was clear; win the league, win every game, break the 100-point barrier. Even the manager, ruthless to the core, was amazed that his players got anywhere near after also making sure they drank in every moment, literally and figuratively. Wilder remembers bringing his players together and attempting to draw a line under the boozy celebrations, with games still to play, before walking into the Copthorne Hotel and seeing a group of them sat at the bar. Sharp later admitted he feared the worst; Wilder knew, deep down, that he'd be doing exactly the same.

"I wanted us to make history and leave a mark on the division, because the club had never won 100 points before and there was an individual honour of 30 goals to chase for the skipper, too," Wilder said. "I wanted us to go right to the end and we owed it to ourselves to squeeze every drop from the season. I heard a bit of criticism that I should have played some other players once the title was won, but did the players who had played 43 or 44 games of the season not deserve to play in the big games?

"There's no sentiment here. I want to win games of football and I can't change that mentality. If I did, the players will start changing theirs and the dynamics of the whole place will be altered. I don't think you can ever get tired of celebrating … I've been in football so long and seen players play 500 league games and never experience that feeling. There are only so many medals that can be handed out every year so if you win, you've got to get the maximum out of it. And I think we were world champions at that."

But, in a season of champagne moments, the culmination was almost an anti-climax as United sealed the League One title without even playing a game. A clinical 3-0 victory at Port Vale on Good Friday, backed by 4,330 Blades fans in a crowd of 8,999, was as memorable for Leon Clarke's stunning volley as it was for outbreaks of trouble between the two sets of fans but if Bolton failed to win at Oldham the following day, the title was United's. United regrouped at their training base in Shirecliffe, an old Forgemasters sports club around a mile from Wednesday's Hillsborough stadium, for a recovery session and waited. Bolton hit the bar twice in the second half and Oldham were reduced to ten men, but it was the Latics who prevailed 1-0 and as news filtered through to Shirecliffe, the bubbly was out again – although, with a game 48 hours away on the Monday, more ended on the carpet than down the throats of the players.

No such worries for the manager, though; that afternoon, as he made his way into his cousin's house in Frecheville with two cases of Stella Artois and one of John Smith's under his arm, friends and family formed a guard of honour to welcome him and Francesca. The Blades were champions. "I'd called at Tesco on the way back," Wilder smiled, "and it was brilliant. A friend of ours tweeted the video and a few neighbours saw it and did a bit of detective work, realising it was only two doors down from them! All of a sudden there were half a dozen neighbours in the front room, thinking 'we'll have a bit of that'."

Monday's game against play-off chasing Bradford brought a

guard of honour from the visitors, three more goals in a ruthless performance and another lap of celebration around the Bramall Lane pitch, but it was the following weekend's trip to MK Dons that proved the most memorable of the run in for many Blades supporters. Officially, 7,000 Blades had bought tickets for the game and many more were in the home areas of Stadium MK, after the home side turned down a request for 3,000 more tickets on the back of a #10ktoMK *Twitter* campaign.

Wilder remembers pleading with everyone he thought could increase the allocation, believing United would have taken 15,000 if they could. Still, after making the trip south in their droves and in all manner of fancy dress attire, a large section of fans moved en masse just after kick-off from the home end, over a dividing sheet and into the away section with their fellow fans. They were determined not to miss out on the biggest title-winning party so far.

A customary strike from the in-form Clarke put United ahead before Sharp scored his 200th and 201st career goals to seal another 3-0 victory and move them to 97 points. Another lap of honour saw Jack O'Connell, a somewhat reluctant hero for United and freshly shaved after vowing to grow his ginger beard until United won the league, serenaded by his now-ubiquitous 'he wears a magic hat …' song, while Alan Knill enjoyed his own reluctant moment in the sun when United fans chanted in his honour. Wilder was determined to ensure he soaked it up, too, pushing his trusted No.2 out into the technical area when he tried to retreat and taking a rare seat on the bench to give Knill his moment. In a season of so many highs, it was particularly pleasing to see one of the good guys – and a vital cog in the United machine – get the credit he deserved.

"That was really good of him and you do appreciate it," Knill said, "but I do find it a bit awkward. It's great that the fans appreciate what we do but at the end of the day, it's my job to do that isn't it? I've never been one of those who likes the limelight but in football, you have to try and enjoy it while it lasts! The relationship that the manager and his staff have with the supporters is something different to most other clubs, and he's good at pushing us out into the limelight. We just push him back out there again!"

The final chapter in a season to remember came on the final day, when United hosted Chesterfield in front of 31,003 fans needing three points for a club-record 100. Sharp was also one goal away from 30 and both were not to be denied, although already-relegated Chesterfield certainly tried their best to spoil the big day by twice levelling the scores. The unlikely hero was Danny Lafferty, the Northern Ireland international left-back, who netted the winning goal to send Wilder's men into the history books after Sharp had earlier nodded home his landmark goal – becoming the first Blade since Keith Edwards in 1983/84 to reach 30 in a season.

United's players, including reserves Jake Eastwood, Louis Reed and David Brooks, were introduced onto the pitch one by one with the loudest cheer, as expected, reserved for Wilder and skipper Sharp. Flames erupted around Bramall Lane as the boyhood Blade lifted the trophy above his head, self-appointed chief champagne sprayer Clarke continued his own personal struggles with opening bottles despite weeks of practice and the players were joined on yet another lap of honour by their families, with some youngsters stealing the show with some skills of their own – cheered on by a Kop in jubilant mood.

"I think we managed to drag the celebrations out for about four or five weeks but I wanted to get the 100 points, because we'd achieved 99 the season before at Northampton and there were three or four games we drew when we shouldn't have," said Wilder. "Ironically, the poorest performance of the last six weeks was against Chesterfield. I think everyone maybe thought it would be a foregone conclusion and perhaps we were a bit fortunate that day, because a few out there were running on empty after the celebrations! But the gods smiled on us … Billy got his 30th goal, and we reached that 100 point mark."

With history made, the league won and the trophy secure, the next commitment for Wilder and his Blades was an open-top bus parade, followed by a civic reception hosted by the Lord Mayor at the Town Hall. With the players told to report to Bramall Lane at 4pm on the day, Wilder had made a somewhat earlier start to proceedings around lunchtime on Ecclesall Road and an open bar at Bramall Lane, with chip butties – what else? – prepared the players for the parade and the scenes that followed.

Hundreds of fans had gathered in the Cherry Street car park to wave the players off and again, each player emerged one-by-one with Wilder last out, trophy in hand, in typically exuberant style. Members of the local media who had covered the club all the way through the season were also invited on the bottom deck of the open-top bus and were allowed up on top in groups of two or three, but the parade was compelling viewing from either vantage point; especially when reserve goalkeeper Eastwood rushed downstairs, praying to find a bathroom, and realised how far away the coach was from its destination. Every crate of beer and cider that had been loaded onto the bus was consumed less than halfway into the journey.

Jake Wright, who had joined United in pre-season as back-up to O'Connell after working with Wilder at Halifax and Oxford, finished the season as Bramall Lane's 'Mr Invincible' after playing 30 games without tasting defeat. Wright had also avoided losing in his last eight for Oxford in their League Two promotion-winning campaign and said: "It was definitely my most enjoyable season in football and to go so long without defeat, setting a record for a club like this, is a brilliant achievement. It makes me really proud.

"I remember getting to about 22 games unbeaten and someone asked me to do an interview because they said the record was 25, but I didn't want to jinx it! It's a record that can never be taken away from me and I guess will take some beating, although I was a bit fortunate to never play against Walsall when we lost to them three times! I always try and stay level throughout the season whether we've won or lost, but I think players should enjoy their successes at the end of the season if they win something."

For the evening, as the bus snaked through the city centre, Sheffield was transformed into a sea of red and white and it seemed at one point that the whole city was involved – of all ages, genders and even species. One Blade held his dog, dressed in a red and white shirt, in the air as proudly as Sharp had the trophy, and became a cult hero for the duration of the journey as Wilder and his squad chanted 'Billy the Dog'. Just past Plug nightclub, fans hung out of windows and in between levels of a multi-storey car park to get a glimpse of their heroes and there was a fantastic moment when a Chinese student, on the top deck of a bus going the other way down Arundel Gate, looked up from her book and saw a tipsy Wilder waving at her. She promptly picked the book back up.

Seeing buses travelling in the opposite direction gave Wilder a brainwave and before long, the club doctor Subhashis Basu's shoes were on the top of one after the manager ran out of patience with his choice of attire. By now, Wilder had also acquired an O'Connell scarf and as the bus pulled up next to the Town Hall, he almost fell off it; rescued only by strength and conditioning coach Lee Rickards. Later Wilder nearly sent the trophy over the edge after slipping, no doubt on a puddle of Peroni, but was in no mood for slowing down.

Once the Blades were inside the Town Hall, the famous old walls reverberated to the sound of the O'Connell song – x-rated lyric included – and Wilder stole Lord Mayor Denise Fox's hat for a photo on the steps. Outside, Wilder threatened to make Brooks, a shy but unbelievably talented young man, give a speech to the thousands of assembled Blades fans and jokingly threatened to release him on a free if he didn't. "Free me then," a startled Brooks replied. Thankfully for United, he wasn't.

Back upstairs, each member of the United squad was again introduced on the balcony and inside, an almost-speechless and beyond-tipsy Wilder gave an emotional live interview to BBC Radio Sheffield in which he name-checked almost every business within walking distance of the Town Hall, remembered the time he threw former United teammate Mark Todd – then head of the club's community foundation – in the fountain outside old Sheffield nightclub Josephine's and described an intimate, private moment with just his players and staff in the Bramall Lane dressing room as one of the best half-hours of his life.

"This is how my head is, right," he said. "Every three weeks, I need my hair cutting and I park in Cole Brothers [now John Lewis]. I get a ticket and walk past the City Hall, past Hotpants where I used to go on a Saturday every two weeks – best night ever – and walked past Josephine's, thinking how many times I've been in there and how many times I've been refused entry, and then past the Town Hall and looked up, and thought what might happen in May if we produce. How mad is that? Every three weeks I've done that."

With that, and a mention for Lynne's Pantry and Taylor Taylor barbers and the revelation that he'd also tried to 'borrow' the Lord Mayor's ceremonial chain, Wilder was off to continue his night. But if ever an interview with a football manager summed up both him as a person and his relationship with the club and fans, it was this. Wilder and Sharp led the chants on the Town Hall balcony as if they were sat on the Kop themselves and the thousands of Blades fans below lapped it up. For this night, at least, the city was theirs.

Next up for United's players, who had kept the party going through a gruelling schedule of end-of-season dinners and other commitments, was another challenge, as Lafferty revealed – 100 beers in Las Vegas, where they spent four days to continue the celebrations. Splitting their time largely between The Cosmopolitan and MGM Grand, every member of United's squad apart from Chris Hussey, who felt he hadn't been a part of the achievement, joined the celebrations and were pictured at pool parties and nightclubs, where Sharp had organised videos of United's goals and wins the previous season to be shown on big screens.

It was described as the trip of a lifetime by more than one player, but Vegas' strict minimum drinking age of 21 caused issues for the younger members of the party like Brooks, Eastwood and Reed. The latter was challenged for ID by bouncers while lounging by the pool, almost as soon as the squad landed, and Brooks remembers the trio struggling to buy a bottle of water in the Nevada heat while their teammates enjoyed themselves elsewhere.

Eventually they resigned themselves to playing golf and watching magicians Penn & Teller at The Rio while receiving Snapchat messages of pool parties from their teammates, and Mark Duffy revealed the squad offered to club together and buy the three tickets for Saúl "Canelo" Álvarez's fight against Julio César Chávez Jr. at the T-Mobile Arena, on the Vegas strip.

"We went to the pool and couldn't even get a Coke because we weren't 21," Brooks remembered. "So we were having a nightmare, walking around shops trying to get bottles of water while the boys were having the time of their lives! But it was a magical time and just unfortunate we couldn't get more involved. But that's the gaffer's style – at the right time, go out and socialise and become a tight-knit group. That means you'll likely play better because you're doing it for each other, not just yourself. I've only properly been involved in this team so can't compare too much but from what I've seen, it does work. When we're close as a team, we work a lot better together."

The celebrations continued when, as United players relaxed and some detoxed, city rivals Wednesday lost in the play-offs to eventual winners Huddersfield Town. But difficult decisions also had to be made. Stefan Scougall and Marc McNulty, who had served United well since making the trip south of the border from Scotland, were released as their contracts expired and Matt Done, Hussey and James Wilson, who had helped kickstart the season's momentum with the winner against Oxford to give Wilder his first win as United boss, were transfer listed. McNulty, who had a spell on loan at Bradford City during the promotion season and subsequently won the League Two play-offs with Coventry City in 2018, said: "I think Chris is a top manager … I loved working under him every day in training. But he's also a great guy. For players who don't play it can be difficult, but right throughout the season he was great with me."

As the champagne dried, the hangovers cleared and the days wore on, attentions began to turn to the next challenge; the Championship, derbies against the likes of Wednesday and Leeds United, locking horns with the likes of Aston Villa, Derby and Wolves. A challenge to be relished rather than feared, and the message from Wilder and Co. was clear: they were there on merit. As the history makers, the trailblazers, the champions. They had spent too many years in the footballing wilderness, but now the Blades were back.

The Blades against the world
By James Beighton, Lee Woodhouse and
Reece Woodhouse (aged six), Kop

We liken it to that friend that you haven't seen for years, but who knows you inside-out, and appears at a family barbeque. Once the "Ey up mate, what have you been up to?" questions are out of the way, it's like you've never been apart. From day one, Chris Wilder understood this club. It's his club, he's one of us. He knows what makes the Blades tick because he is one. He lives and breathes it with us. Fresh from enduring Nigel Adkins' 'Bladeacoaster', which ironically contained many downs without many – if any – ups, we were about to embark on arguably the greatest journey in the club's history and all because someone had stripped things back to basics.

Wilder and his team are fantastic coaches and have adopted a system which is exciting to watch but aside from tactics and training, his most effective strategy is hard work and passion. There is no secret to what Wilder did immediately after setting his stall out at Shirecliffe and it was obvious that the lads knew it; graft and earn your place, and you have a future at our football club. We sit in the heart of a proud, northern city where people see reward in hard work and there was a return of the Warnock-esque mindset; the Blades against the world. Safe to say, we're still winning the battle.

The difference can almost be felt, from the players down to the club shop staff and every single one of us fans. The Lane has continued to have a positive feel about it and we are heading in the right direction – but most importantly, we're on the journey together. There is a genuine connection between the players and the fans. We've come from booing players for touching the ball to scenes where our manager strides across the pitch to kiss the badge and raise his arms to salute travelling Blades fans at Swindon and Ipswich.

The memories will live forever. The scenes at Northampton, for those not old enough to remember Darlington or Leicester. Hordes of Blades who descended on Milton Keynes, and sharing a beer with Pamela Anderson and the entire Jamaican bobsleigh team. Who knew they were Blades? Grown men were heading foam bricks, Wilder and Billy Sharp stood arm in arm at the Town Hall, singing the Greasy Chip Butty song with thousands of fellow Blades fans. Priceless. What had Wilder done to our football club?

Beyond all that, though, football is about many things for fans, including having fun on a Saturday afternoon with their mates. Footage of a few of our goals last season shows exactly that; fans stage diving across the away end at Bradford. Players hugging fans on the pitch after Billy grabbed a late winner at Peterborough. The gaffer himself Klinsmann-diving into the players after Fleck bagged a quality goal in front of the Kop. United, together.

So soon after a season of apathy under Adkins, we're now going into games knowing that Wilder expects every inch as much as we do in the stands. We'll take that. I'll take 3-5-2, a belief that we're always in every game and a sense of leaving Bramall Lane knowing that our players have left nothing out on the pitch. That feeling I first felt as a kid on Cherry Street is back. As a six-year-old myself, I'll never forget Bassett leaving the pitch at Leicester in his pants and things like that are starting to happen again. It's enjoyable to go to the Lane again – safe in the knowledge that we're well and truly on the march with Wilder's Army.

8

A summer break ... of sorts

As Sheffield United's entire playing staff decamped to Vegas, Chris Wilder and his family opted for the more serene surroundings of Spain in the summer but football still wasn't far from the United manager's thoughts ... or indeed his phone. Agents, attracted by United's newly-recovered status as a second-tier football club, offered him all manner of players and characters despite being given strict parameters, but every call was taken just in case it did throw up a gem. Despite the calls and contact, however, it was a signing from eight miles across the border with Derbyshire that kicked-off their Championship recruitment drive – and made front and back page news, in local and national media.

Ched Evans, the Welsh international striker, joined United from Manchester City in 2009 in a deal which could have risen to £3m. His first two seasons at Bramall Lane were solid, rather than spectacular – he scored only four goals in his first and nine in his second, as United were relegated to League One – but he exploded into life in the final year of his deal, netting a remarkable 35 times in 42 appearances. Under Danny Wilson, and with Evans in scintillating goalscoring form, United looked destined to bounce back to the Championship at the first attempt but in April 2012, the Welshman was convicted of raping a 19-year-old woman in a hotel room and jailed for five years. Without their talisman, United couldn't get over the line and surrendered their automatic promotion place to bitter city rivals Wednesday, losing on penalties in the play-off final at Wembley just to compound the misery.

Evans, who was visited in prison by United co-owner Kevin McCabe, was released from HMP Wymott, on licence, in October

2014 after serving half of his sentence and the following month, United agreed to a request from the Professional Footballers' Association for Evans to train with the club, to regain fitness. On the back of a 170,000-strong petition urging them against signing Evans, and with high-profile patrons and sponsors quitting or threatening to, United performed a high-profile U-turn on their decision, with then-co-chairman Jim Phipps admitting he was "angry and upset" and calling the "influence of mob-like behaviour ... a defeat for principle."

Hartlepool United, Grimsby Town and Oldham Athletic all experienced similar opposition when considering signing Evans – with staff and sponsors at the latter club subjected to death threats, according to chief executive Neil Joy – but there was a chink of light for the player, who had always maintained his innocence, when his legal team submitted fresh evidence to the Criminal Cases Review Commission. After a ten-month investigation, and citing new material that the original jury had not accessed, they referred Evans' case to the Court of Appeal and his conviction was quashed, with a retrial ordered. Evans was then found not guilty.

In between his original conviction being quashed and his retrial, Evans returned to professional football with Chesterfield – then managed by Wilson, with Evans' former Blades teammate Chris Morgan as first-team coach. Evans, who described every day in prison as a "nightmare" but worked in HMP Wymott's gym to maintain his basic fitness, scored on his return to professional football in a 1-1 draw at Oxford and caught the eye when Chesterfield hosted United later that season, before he was forced off with injury. Then, days before the two sides were set to meet again at Bramall Lane on the last day of United's title-winning season, news broke that he was on his way back to United. Just over a week later, on May 8, the move was official and Evans was a Blade once more.

There were some reservations, albeit now of a footballing nature rather than a moral or legal one; Evans had, at this point, played less than 30 games in five years and joined United on the back of a frustrating, injury-disrupted season. But Wilder had seen enough in his 66-minute cameo against the Blades back in November 2016, when Evans gave the normally-infallible Chris Basham a torrid time, to take another look and after meeting with the striker in person, his mind was made up. "His attitude to me was one of the most positive I've had with a player coming to this club," Wilder said at the time. "Let's be right, he's moving from a club that's gone out of this division one way to one that's leaving through the front door. Lots of people will say he's bound to be like that. But this was a little bit different. There was a real glint in his eye."

Nathan Thomas, the talented Hartlepool United winger, joined Evans at Bramall Lane after turning down a more lucrative offer from his boyhood club Middlesbrough, and Wilder linked up with another familiar face when left-back Enda Stevens – who had played under him on loan at Northampton – signed on a free-transfer after helping Portsmouth win the League Two title. George Baldock, who became Wilder's fourth summer signing when he arrived for an undisclosed fee from MK Dons, enthused about United's 7,000-strong support at Stadium MK and admitted it was a huge draw and Richard Stearman, the former Wolves and Fulham defender, brought a much-needed wealth of Championship and Premier League experience when United paid up the remainder of his Craven Cottage deal to bring him to South Yorkshire.

After getting back into the swing of things on the pitch with a 9-0 victory over local non-league side Stocksbridge Park Steels in their opening friendly – Caolan Lavery netting a hat-trick – United jetted off to the Costa del Sol for a five-night stay at the state-of-the-art Marbella Football Centre. United's squad played golf, enjoyed the odd San Miguel or two and even shared a boat ride with co-owner Prince Abdullah but were made to earn their time off, after being put through a punishing training schedule in the baking Spanish sun. The trip also gave United's players and staff the chance to observe a Premier League club going about their business, too, with AFC Bournemouth sharing the Marbella facilities.

Eddie Howe, the Cherries' manager, guided his club from

League One into the Premier League, without spending huge sums and instead focusing on character over cash. Top flight riches may have changed the landscape a little – amongst Bournemouth's delegation were three ground staff and their own overzealous security guards, while United were represented solely by their operations director, Dave McCarthy, for the entire trip – but as far as inspiration goes, United could hardly have had any better working away on the next field. Envious glances were cast the other way, too, when Wilder allowed his side a night off and a few beers while on tour. Bournemouth, in contrast, had been hit with a booze ban for the entirety of their 12-day trip and the gesture, of the Blades being let off the leash for an evening, is still talked about regularly in a desirous manner at Dean Court.

United subsequently topped off their tour with a 1-0 victory over La Liga side Malaga, who had reached the quarter-finals of the Champions League four years earlier and beat Barcelona at the end of the previous season. "Sheffield United were in Europe," laughs Wilder. "We thought we'd beaten one of the real giants of Spanish football and it was only the following season when we realised they were the worst team in La Liga! But that was an eye-opener for the new players, especially. They got off the bus for the game and there were four or five hundred Blades fans outside the ground, queuing to get in. And it was only pre-season! I think that surprised them a little but it gave them an idea, if they didn't already have it, of the kind of club they had joined."

Back in Blighty, United completed a 100 percent pre-season schedule – with youngster David Brooks enriching his own reputation with goals against Chesterfield and Premier League side Stoke City, fresh from winning the Toulon Tournament with England over the summer. Brooks capped off the success in France by being named the competition's best player and United reneged on a deal to send him on loan to Chesterfield for the season, with Wilder instead preferring to assess him at United's Shirecliffe training base. "It was a tough call to make," he admitted.

"I pondered about it. I want really good relationships with those clubs. They're good clubs, and we're a down-to-earth football club. We know it's a difficult industry and that all clubs are trying to do the right thing for themselves. But we knew, as soon as we walked through the door, that Brooksy was a player. And we got him up with the first team straightaway. A lot of managers talk about doing this and that to players, but the biggest thing was him training every day with the lads here, who have really high standards. We try and help him with bits and pieces but too many managers take credit for a player's development, and the environment they are in is so important. That's what happened with Brooksy."

Wilder, continuing to focus his recruitment drive on young, hungry and talented footballers with careers on an upward trajectory, raided old club Oxford United to sign their captain John Lundstram. Wilder's No.2 Alan Knill described the young midfielder as 'the outstanding talent' below the Championship after Brentford signed Ollie Watkins from Exeter for almost £2m, and Southend midfielder Ryan Leonard had been identified as another target. With just one season remaining on his Roots Hall contract, many considered the Leonard deal to be a formality but Southend refused to budge, rejecting United bids in May and July.

One player that did arrive at Bramall Lane before the start of the season was Chelsea goalkeeper Jamal Blackman, a giant of a man with a big reputation and Champions League and Europa League winners medals in his trophy cabinet. Simon Moore, United's No.1 throughout much of the title-winning season, damaged his knee in pre-season at Rotherham United and with goalkeeper George Long dispatched to Wimbledon on loan, young stopper Jake Eastwood deputised between the sticks before Blackman arrived. Wilder saw forging links with top Premier League clubs as a productive way of attracting young, talented players on loan, to fit with both his budget and recruitment policy, and top-flight sides who studied the way United approach the game were happy to oblige.

Mauricio Pochettino, the highly-rated Tottenham Hotspur boss, hailed the atmosphere during Spurs' League Cup semi-final second leg at Bramall Lane in 2015 as the best he had ever experienced since coming to England and it was a personal recommendation from the Argentine that saw Cameron Carter-Vickers, the Southend-born USA youth international, join United on loan from White Hart Lane.

Carter-Vickers revealed Pochettino told him "this was a really good opportunity at a good club, a big club, and a club he believes plays football in the right way. A club with the right work ethic. He's a great manager and so when he tells you things like that, you trust him." Perhaps more importantly, United also tied down four key men from their promotion season – Basham, Billy Sharp, Paul Coutts and Kieron Freeman – to new contracts, with John Fleck and Jack O'Connell later following their lead. Three months after their glorious coronation on the last day of the season, and 2,290 days after their relegation from the Championship was confirmed in 2011, the long wait was over. And Wilder was determined to seize the opportunity.

Buses, beers and Bradford City
By Richard Sutcliffe, chief football writer, The Yorkshire Post

The Chris Wilder celebrating promotion by almost dropping the League One trophy from the top deck of an open-top bus wasn't too dissimilar to the Chris Wilder I had first met two decades earlier. Not in terms of how inebriated he was at the time, even if many of my favourite memories of Chris over the past dozen or so years involve enjoying a pint or nine in his company when attending the traditional Yorkshire managers' Christmas jolly-up that is put on by the press.

No, the Chris Wilder from those promotion celebrations in 2017 that so reminded me of the defender I had first met all those years earlier when at Bradford City was more to do with the passion etched across his face moments before giving way to panic as he stumbled and then fell to the floor, still clutching the precious trophy. A passion that he carried regardless of club or colours but burned brightest of all when it came to Sheffield United. I realised that much 24 hours or so before transfer deadline day in March, 1998.

Chris had been at Valley Parade for almost exactly a year. I had got to know him reasonably well since taking over the City 'beat' at the *Telegraph & Argus*, Bradford's evening newspaper, the previous summer. We had spoken a few times over the course of a season that had started with Chris Kamara as manager and the Bantams setting the early pace in what is now the Championship. Despite those infrequent chats for the 'paper, Chris and I were on little more than nodding terms when our paths crossed. But I did have his home telephone number.

So when, totally out of the blue, the Blades came in for Wilder that March after chairman Geoffrey Richmond had admitted all offers for the club's players would be considered, I was able to flick through my contacts book and put in a call. At first, he was cagey. The transfer was well advanced but he hadn't signed and didn't want to do anything that could scupper the move. Nevertheless, a couple of entries from the footballers' book of cliches were agreed on between us and I ran them both the following day.

To be fair, Chris wasn't my main focus as Peter Beagrie and Eddie Youds were also heading through the exit door that deadline day. And these two were, with all due respect, much bigger news to supporters. Nevertheless, what remains etched on the memory more than 20 years on is the 'off the record' chat I had with Chris after those initial banal comments for publication had been agreed upon as he explained why he just had to go, as he called it, "home". This wasn't the cynical 'always wanted to play for my boyhood club' drivel that Robbie Keane trotted out about four or five clubs. Or the badge-kissing antics by far too many players who every fan knows is loyal only to the size of his wage packet.

No, this was genuine, pure unadulterated love for Sheffield United. Sure, Chris had already spent six years at Bramall Lane and fulfilled his boyhood dream of sporting those famous red and white stripes. But, if there was to be a second chance to do it all over again, he wanted to take it. And no-one, not even a chairman such as Richmond who could belligerently hold out for a bigger fee if the fancy took him, was going to stop Chris.

Watching with an open mouth as Chris came so close to tumbling off that bus during United's promotion parade all those years later, I couldn't help but smile at how his career had panned out. Neither of us could have imagined, during that 1998 phone call, a moment such as this. I was pleased for Chris but not surprised. I had followed that season's success, sometimes at close quarters and sometimes from afar, on behalf of *The Yorkshire Post*. Having ten clubs on a patch can make prioritising what game or club to cover each week a tricky business. Focus on Leeds United, for instance, and there will be complaints from Huddersfield and Sheffield. Likewise, give Rotherham United's quest to escape League One prominence and Bradford City fans will demand to know what they have done to be ignored. Some go even further, a club official from South Yorkshire once bemoaning the amount of coverage Hull City, then of the Premier League, were getting within the pages of the YP as a travesty due to "Hull not even being in Yorkshire". With an added swear word or two.

Striking that balance can be hard and is why my own visits during the 2016/17 season were sporadic. In the *YP's* defence, my colleague Richard Hercock did cover all United's Saturday home games en route to promotion being clinched. What I did find, though, on these trips to the Lane was a club totally together. Fans, players and management were all pulling in the same direction – in stark contrast to how it had seemed the previous season. This, of course, doesn't happen by accident and it had been a feature of every club where Chris had managed. Halifax Town, Oxford United and Northampton Town had all benefited from the kind of spirit that, by then, was well on its way towards ending a six-year absence from the Championship for his beloved Blades.

United's stunning promotion success does not need recapping here. This book's author has done that exhaustively elsewhere. So, let's instead focus on the period that I believe made Chris the manager he is today. Halifax Town, a club that had struggled for more years than anyone in Calderdale cared to remember, fell out of the Football League in 2002. Chris took over a few weeks later to start what proved to be a priceless six-year apprenticeship in dealing with all that can go wrong at a football club.

Training was a lottery, mainly because the Shaymen owed so much money in their hometown that facilities had to be begged and borrowed all over Yorkshire. This led to the sort of challenges that, say, Sir Alex Ferguson or Jose Mourinho have never had to overcome. One Friday, for instance, Chris and his players were turfed off one training pitch because the lines had to be marked out for an important Sunday League game. Then, there was the time the Halifax squad turned up to find a dog show being held where training had been planned.

Travel wasn't always straightforward, either, with unpaid bills meaning the team bus might not turn up for an away game. Other trips would see the players asking for the bus to pull over at the nearest High Street bank to pay wage cheques in, fearing they would bounce come the following Monday. Chris even once suffered the indignity of his wife getting to the checkout at Sainsbury's and only then discovering his Halifax wage had not been paid in.

No wonder Chris, when speaking privately to his staff, would liken the quest of leading the Shaymen to promotion as 'like trying to win Formula One in a Ford Escort'. He gave it a damn good go, though. Just ten minutes stood between Halifax and a return to the Football League in 2006 only for Hereford United to hit back with two goals to triumph 3-2 after extra-time in the Conference play-off final.

That heartbreaking defeat at Leicester City's Walkers Stadium came two years after I had first resumed contact with Chris. My arrival at the YP was the reason and an early visit to The Shay, complete with a main 'stand' that consisted solely of exposed steelwork due to the money having long since run out, underlined what he was up against.

"Do you like our new main stand?" he asked with a wry smile, as we walked round the pitch to the club offices on the opposite side of the stadium. "It gets a bit drafty in winter but we don't notice it." This ability to keep smiling even when things are going sour has been a feature of a managerial career that now boasts four promotions. It is why even the Blades' slow start to the 2016-17 campaign did not faze him. Instead, a bit of 'old school' psychology on the trip home from a 1-0 defeat at Millwall – when he bought £100 worth of booze at an off licence in south London and then passed it out among his players to enjoy on the journey home – brought the lift that, nine months later, led to the lifting of the League One trophy and a club-record 100 points.

Success had been achieved by a combination of not only being able to lift spirits at times of adversity but also a tactical acumen that, once in the Championship, would bring those hugely satisfying wins at Hillsborough and Elland Road, plus a place at the top of the table. Things fizzled out after Christmas but Chris and United will be back. A glance at his career, both as a player and a manager, proves that. Which brings me back to his departure from Bradford as a player to re-join the Blades. "Wilder is 31 next September so the fee is a good one," I wrote in the following day's *T&A* about the £125,000 transfer, "but I believe his accomplished passing game will be missed by City. This will be particularly apparent if they decide to use the three-man defence again, as Wilder has proved able to slot into the centre with ease from his usual wide role."

Such a glowing assessment didn't prevent me from subsequently giving Chris a six out of ten in the end of season *T&A* review. Even now, it feels harsh. And had I been asked to give a similar verdict on his managerial career – not just at the Lane, but elsewhere too – then amends would be made via a much, much higher mark. Not that Chris would be unduly bothered. He has already had the only verdict that matters, from those supporters who serenade him on a weekly basis during Blades games ...

He's one of our own.

9

Back where they belong
August 2017

Sheffield United's 2017/18 Championship adventure got underway on August 5 at Bramall Lane, against Brentford, and the opposition gave Blades fans a decent yardstick for life in English football's second tier. The Bees, owned by a supporter of the club in Matthew Benham, had won automatic promotion from League One in 2014 and in their first season in the Championship, finished fifth and lost to Middlesbrough in the play-off semi-finals. And although Chris Wilder's approach to transfers could not be likened to Brentford's 'Moneyball' approach too closely, the similarities were there; future Blades target Scott Hogan, the former Stocksbridge Park Steels striker who Brentford later sold to Aston Villa for around £12m, cost them £750,000 from Rochdale and Andre Gray, now an established Premier League star with Watford after impressing for Burnley, arrived at Brentford from Luton Town. Crucially, Brentford had shown that the gap between League One and the Championship could be bridged comfortably enough, with clever investment, belief and ability.

Their starting XI at Bramall Lane on the opening day was packed with quality – former Chelsea man Josh McEachran, the impressive midfielder Ryan Woods and Spanish forward Jota all started, while Neal Maupay and Ollie Watkins, understood to have cost almost £2m each, were on the bench – but after ex-Brentford centre-half Jack O'Connell had hit the post with a shot from 30 yards, United began the new season as they had ended the last, as skipper Billy Sharp rose to head Leon Clarke's cross past Daniel Bentley for what proved to be the winner. Clarke had earlier had a strike of his own disallowed and Sharp saw what would have been his second goal ruled out for offside in the second half after John Fleck's free-kick came back off the post, but United had a let off when Lasse Vibe somehow headed over with the goal at his mercy before debutant Jamal Blackman pulled off one of the saves of the season. Substitute Maupay had almost rounded him and looked certain to score, but the Chelsea goalkeeper thrust out a hand from nowhere and somehow kept it out.

"It was right up there in terms of atmospheres," remembers Wilder of the game, watched by 26,746 fans in the Bramall Lane sunshine. "This wasn't little old Brentford ... they're an established football club in the Championship and it was a great reward for the supporters that had stuck with the club throughout the six years in League One. We've had it tough in this city, a football city. That is a reward for the outstanding support, loyalty and love of their football club that they've shown through thick and thin. Maybe we all had a point to prove ... whether we've not managed in the division or been a part of it, as players, coaches and staff, were we good enough?"

By extending their unbeaten run, which stood since January, United had gone a small way to proving they were – not least 6ft 6in goalkeeper Blackman, who drew special praise from skipper Sharp after the game. "I'm pleased for Jamal," he said. "He's been a quiet lad up to now but no-one is going to tell him to be louder. He's about three feet taller than me! He commands his box well. Going into the game, he's not stupid – everybody will have been thinking: 'Let's see what you can do.' He did well."

Wilder's No.2, Alan Knill, knows members of Brentford's coaching team well and remembers asking them after the game if the Championship was always so tough. Every game, was the reply. "We knew in League One that if we didn't turn up as a team, but some of our players had a good game, we still had a good chance of winning because we had the best players," Knill said. "In the Championship, we knew we had to be at our best just to give us a chance of winning. It's a brilliant league, but there was a proper belief that we could do something. Because we were promoted so early, I went to watch Leeds against Reading at Elland Road the season before and I think it was fourth against sixth, so a massive game for a play-off place. It was so dull.

"I rang Chris afterwards and told him I'd just watched the most boring game. Teams seemed to take no risks at all – it's a league where managers get sacked all the time, so they'd rather not lose. Chris and Paul Mitchell watched some games too and felt the same. There were good players but the way they play wasn't great, and a lot of players were bang average and just going through the motions to pick up their money. We said we were going to go about things exactly the way we had in League One. The last thing we say often is 'be us'. Be really good at being us and it will take care of itself. Don't worry about the opposition."

With optimism levels around Bramall Lane arguably as high as they had ever been, August also gave United a chance to right a rare wrong from the previous title-winning campaign and get one over their 'bogey team', Walsall. In winning 100 points and securing the league title, United lost just six games but curiously, two of those defeats came at the hands of Walsall, who eventually finished 14th in the table and beat United at Bramall Lane in the Checkatrade Trophy for good measure. As a fan, Wilder had also seen Walsall relegate United to the old division four as a boy and let out a wry smile when the EFL Cup first-round draw paired the two sides together once more. Almost true to form, Walsall took the lead through Amadou Bakayoko's fourth goal in four games against United but the introduction of substitute Ched Evans changed the game, the Welshman setting up two goals on his second Blades 'debut' to secure a 3-2 win.

An emotional Evans kissed the United badge on his shirt after believing he had scored with a deflected effort from an acute angle – which was later credited as a Kory Roberts own goal – and Wilder said: "Ched came back and said: 'I'm back and I am going to make the most of this opportunity' – and he did. He gave everyone a lift. We were delighted with the reception he got and his contribution to the game was great. Players need to grab opportunities and that's exactly what he did, while some others didn't. Some players had to do better, to force their way into my thoughts and give me selection problems. I wanted what I had off Ched from all the players and I told them that."

A 1-0 defeat at recently-relegated Middlesbrough followed, with the scoreline not even telling a fraction of the full story. Chairman Steve Gibson promised that his Boro would 'smash the league' after dropping from the top-flight – sanctioning around £50m worth of signings to back up his words – and when Rudy Gestede put the home side ahead at the Riverside in the first half, many thought the floodgates would open. At half-time, Wilder reminded his side that they were not in the Championship simply to make up the numbers, and an improved second-half showing saw O'Connell head home a deserved equaliser in front of the Sky Sports cameras – only for the assistant referee to incorrectly flag for offside. Sky blurred the lines a little further by showing a split screen of the moment Mark Duffy took the free-kick and O'Connell straying offside at different moments, seemingly to justify the incorrect decision, and Wilder was left understandably frustrated.

"Jack started off in an offside position but moved back into an onside position and then impeded their centre-half from heading the ball," he said after the final whistle had blown. "Are we going to just let their centre-half head it clear in the last minute at Middlesbrough when we're after a result when we've been unbeaten for about ... three years? You just can't get those decisions wrong. I'm not saying we've come here and dominated the game, as this is and will be a tough place to come with the players they've got and a new manager in place. But when we play like we did in the second half I think it was a just reward to get something from the game and that's been taken away from us by a very, very poor decision."

Reflecting on the game some months later, Wilder's mood had thawed over that offside flag but he remembers the trip to the Riverside as something of a watershed moment for his Blades. "We'd just stepped into the division and we were looking at their team, the players they had paid good money for that were fresh out of the Premier League," he said. "For the first 45 minutes against Boro, that was probably the first time we looked at ourselves and thought, 'this is what Championship football is all about'. We were on the back foot, they got themselves in front and were comfortable, but we shook it up at half-time and we came storming back. We deserved a result on the day which we were denied by that poor decision. But maybe that was a start for us, we saw that the bigger boys were there to be taken down. And that had to be our attitude throughout the season, to show that we could compete at the top end of this division."

If defeat away at Boro was controversial, then a 2-0 reverse at Neil Warnock's Cardiff City three days later was more straightforward. Cardiff, the early pace-setters with three wins from their opening three league games, were comfortable winners as United were outfought and out-thought, goals from Sean Morrison and former Bramall Lane loanee Nathaniel Mendez-Laing doing the damage as Sharp had a decent-looking penalty appeal waved away by the referee. Wilder was encouraged by the effort and commitment levels of his players, even with the game slipping away from them, but back-to-back defeats gave United a stark wake-up call as to the harsh reality of life in the Championship. Although the manager conceded there would inevitably be what he described as "tough nights" to come, he was honest enough to acknowledge that they needed to be better.

"That game was a bit of a reality check for us," Wilder reflected, "and reminded us that we had better learn, and quickly. They were stronger than us, better at set-pieces, more direct, had more pace and generally better players and deserved to win that game. We had to quickly get over that disappointment. But I thought after the second half at Boro, we showed we'd arrived. They had a bit of a moan about a decision in the return leg later in the season, but we were justified in complaining about the decision with Jack's header. I thought we did well second half, David Brooks looked bright after coming on the pitch and I thought we deserved something from the game.

"Their chairman talked about smashing the league and at the time our record signing under me was about £700,000 and they'd just bought Britt Assombalonga for £15m. They had similar players on the bench and on the pitch, but the game was live on Sky, proper football in a brilliant division, at a great ground in front of good support, against good support and players. Myself and Al had had a couple of seasons in League One and League Two and, with respect, this was the level we were wanting to work at. We just had to get on with it pretty quickly."

The tide turned when United returned to Bramall Lane, for a South Yorkshire derby against Barnsley perhaps best remembered for an off-the-ball incident that saw Leon Clarke and Reds skipper Angus MacDonald sent off just before half-time.

By then, Sharp had put United on the way to victory and Reds goalkeeper Adam Davies, formerly of Sheffield Wednesday, made fine saves to prevent Brooks and O'Connell from further extending the Blades' lead. Wilder's only criticism of his side was that they didn't take their opportunities to put the game beyond their neighbours, and his Blades certainly took the advice on board when they faced much-fancied Derby County at Bramall Lane a week later. Sharp, written off by some observers as not good enough for the Championship, opened the scoring after being presented an absolute gift by Rams goalkeeper Scott Carson and the visitors' defensive horror-show continued when Johnny Russell finished beautifully in the bottom corner – of his own net – just before half-time. Derby managed just one shot on target all game before substitute Craig Bryson's header ensured a nervy finish. Or rather it should have done, but for Sharp killing off the game with a late third and sparking jubilant scenes in front of the Kop – with goalkeeper Blackman sprinting the length of the field to join in. It was a sweet moment, too, for Jake Wright, who had worked with Wilder at Halifax and Oxford in the Conference and helped keep Derby's £8m man Matěj Vydra, who later won the Championship's golden boot, and former England striker David Nugent quiet all afternoon.

"I've never looked at it like that, to be fair, or been too preoccupied with people's roles or reputations," Wright said. "To me, they're just strikers. I do my own analysis on players and I like to know what they are like, whether they're big or strong or fast or will they try and run in behind or go short? But I don't think 'he's won this or he's worth that'. To me, we're just going up against 11 players and have to do our jobs, win our individual battles. If they're getting paid more than me, then that's good for them but it's irrelevant to me. I just see the man."

Wright's long, proud unbeaten record in a United shirt was finally ended in the EFL Cup, in a 4-1 humbling at home to former Premier League champions Leicester City. The Foxes fielded £29m striker Islam Slimani alongside impressive young winger Demarai Gray and former Blade Harry Maguire, who received a good reception on his homecoming. Slimani scored twice, with Gray and Ahmed Musa adding the others, but the Blades would end the month of August fifth in the Championship table, with three wins and two defeats – a wholly respectable start to the season for the newly-promoted side. But, as ever, Wilder wanted more.

With a break in league commitments due to international games, the thoughts of Wilder and his staff then turned to August 31 – the final day of the transfer window. Anticipating a frantic day of activity, with five possible incomings and three players lined up to leave the Lane, Wilder's day began at 7.30am when he assembled No.2 Knill, head of recruitment Mitchell, football administration supremo Carl Shieber and media chief Kevin Cookson, plus a team of coaches, medical staff and analysts, at United's training base at Shirecliffe.

For the day they were joined by journalist Ed Hawkins, who Wilder knew well from his days at Oxford and was given unprecedented behind-the-scenes access for *Bleacher Report* over the course of what turned out to be an extraordinary 15-and-a-half-hour day. Wilder's wishlist was topped by a trio of attack-minded players: Fleetwood Town's Devante Cole, the son of Manchester United legend Andy; Birmingham City forward Clayton Donaldson and Watford striker Jerome Sinclair.

Domingos Quina, the teenage West Ham United midfielder, was also lined up to move to Sheffield but the first order of business for the day was a deal for Ben Heneghan, from Motherwell, after Wilder called a former teammate to inquire about the giant centre-half's character. One down, although deals for Quina and Sinclair had already hit stumbling blocks; both players, who share an agent, were due in Sheffield a week earlier. "Today is gonna be mad," said Wilder, prophetically.

In front of a whiteboard, a trusted Wilder accessory of planning and delivery, the manager addressed his staff and discussed their options. Names, or rather initials, of all five prospective incomings were on the board, in their positions; Heneghan will deputise for Richard Stearman in the centre-back position, Quina would compete with Paul Coutts and Cole, Sinclair and Donaldson were pencilled in alongside Sharp and Clarke, with James Hanson earmarked for a move away and Ched Evans facing ankle surgery. Deals with West Ham and Watford, for Quina and Sinclair, had been done and Quina was to undergo a medical in Portugal. John Brayford, the right-back who cost United £1.5m in 2015, agreed to terminate his contract and left on a free while Wilder focused on Donaldson, whose deal went from a loan, with an option of a permanent, to a £200,000 transfer, to a £50,000 move. The striker worked with Wilder during a loan spell at Halifax in 2004 and the manager tried to sign Donaldson four times in the intervening years since.

Wilder moved three times on three successive deadline days towards the end of his playing career and got married on the last one, the previous January, but this one promised to be more fraught than any. Cole's price went from free, to £500,000 and then, remarkably, to £1.2m. Wilder walked away. Then, 25 minutes before deadline, Fleetwood wanted to get a deal done. It proved too late.

Similar issues punctuated the moves for Quina and Sinclair, who Wilder spoke to at just past 2.30pm and found out he was still in Hertfordshire. Wilder gave him the lowdown on United, how they like to play, and promised him he'd enjoy his football up north. He hung up the phone, puffed out his cheeks and waited. Shieber told Wilder about a previous story of Sinclair arriving late for a move to Birmingham, blaming a puncture. It did little to improve his mood. Then, just before 4pm, Sinclair and Quina's agent called, demanding an extra £5,000 a week wages for Sinclair and a 20 per cent increase on his own fee. Wilder refused, and was told that Sinclair was sat in Sheffield train station waiting for the thumbs-up from his agent. He sent Wilder a text: "Train just getting in now. Wish you and the lads all the best for the season ahead."

Wilder admitted he felt "gutted for the lad. He wanted to play, he wanted to come here. So did Quina. That's two lads who wanted to be here but who have been messed about by the system. We walked out in front of nearly 30,000 at Sunderland the week after; they played in front of 400 at under-23 games. Crazy." After targeting five new signings, Wilder was forced to be content with just two and lamented the deadline-day madness, thinking of what might have been.

"Players have got to take more control of their own careers, in my opinion," he said. "It is their career. I've always thought that football, playing football, is the biggest driver. I'm not alone, I spoke to Harry Redknapp about it, in a general sense. We talked about players taking ownership, 'manning-up' and making decisions for their own career. I totally understand it's a big decision; I've had to make big decisions myself.

"Do I sign for Sheffield United at 14 or do I go to Southampton? I know how the industry works more than any young footballer, more than any agent and possibly more than a lot of other people at clubs. I've been in it since I was 14. I've managed at non-league, Conference level and to the Championship. There's been a lot of stuff I've had to go through. I've started out at the bottom and possibly seen and done pretty much everything."

Bleacher's footage of Wilder on deadline day, and his stance against agents dictating terms to the players rather than the other way around, went viral on social media. Sinclair had his say, too, via his *Twitter* account, posting: "This footage is one-sided and very misleading. I was approached, but nothing was agreed. I am very happy at Watford and am looking forward to the season. Don't believe everything you read or watch!" But instead of spending the majority of the campaign with United, Sinclair played just 45 minutes of senior football for Watford, across five games.

"I'd known Chris since he was at Oxford," Hawkins, a U's fan and a respected betting writer, said, "and I felt he was doing a good job there in difficult circumstances. Fan criticism was out of hand because there was a belief that he should have been doing better than he was. In fact, on budget – that word which was so irrelevant 30 years ago when I fell in love with the game – he was doing well. But it seemed people sniped because he wasn't over-achieving. So I started to question what I thought the game was about and what I was watching.

"And I talked about this with Chris, saying: 'It would be good to do a piece together where fans could understand better what exactly goes on ... what the pressures are.' And we were going to do that at Oxford. But it didn't fall right timing-wise. And then he left. And then he went to Northampton and we talked again about sorting something. And, by the way, I was the one who couldn't organise myself! Chris, I think, seemed a bit baffled, thinking: 'Why doesn't he just turn up?' He had an open door for me. So, finally, we arranged it. I told him exactly what I wanted to do. I would be a real pest. I wouldn't leave him alone. I'd be snapping at his heels like a terrier. He said: 'fine'.

"From a journalist's perspective, the main thing I took away was that I couldn't believe what terrific access I got. It was unbelievable. I thought that Chris or some of the other staff, at some stage, might get a bit weary and ask for 30 minutes off. But no. It was every second. And it was a great tale. From a football perspective what struck me was the duplicity of agents. This was exposed by the Sinclair deal. The agent was saying he was coming up, he was signing, he's on the train. He wasn't. He never was. And from that you saw the ebb and flow because another deal had to be given new life and it was frantic.

"Brows were furrowed and cheeks were being puffed out. There was a tension there at those times but it had always been present, really. At the beginning it was nervous excitement, then a low-level hum was there until the Sinclair collapse. But no-one switched a hairdryer on. It was an acceptance of 'this is how it works'.

"Chris was very hands-on with deals, and I guess he's old school in that regard. Always has been from his days when he started at Oxford. No doubt he had to be the same at Halifax, too! He was pretty level throughout the day but there was no doubt he was disappointed about the Sinclair deal, and then Cole. I think that came from an annoyance at the structure of the deadline day – 'Why does it have to be like this?' – and a desire for the authorities to set something up so that it isn't as crazy.

"I think his opinions on agents came across pretty well, but it was like a parent might scold a kid – 'I'm not angry, just disappointed'. It was just a weary acceptance of the nonsense of the day, but he was pretty relaxed throughout it. And then there'd be bursts of energy when something was happening. He was playing everyone at pool. We'd be sitting down watching *Sky Sports News*. Or having a cup of tea in his office.

"I've always found Chris approachable, fair and someone with a good sense of humour. You can have a laugh with him. Or you can ask him a 'tough' question and he won't take it the wrong way, like some managers will. And he is always keen to talk about the game at any level, give his views on that player or this team. So it's hard not to respect him tremendously as a bloke.

"Professionally he's a fantastic manager. Has any boss got three clubs promoted in their first three proper jobs? I'm not sure, and I asked the LMA to check that stat for me. They never got back to me! But he's had more promotions than some managers who have been doing it three times as long. Again, 30 years ago he would probably have been snapped up by a top-flight club this season when the various vacancies have come up. But the game has changed. The English manager doesn't have the same currency any more, although arguably he is the best of the bunch. But that's not a bad thing for Chris or Sheffield United. I've no doubt United will keep building steadily and will make a very strong run for the Premier League under him in the next two or three seasons."

The Wright move
By Jake Wright, defender

I never had any doubts whatsoever about my ability to play in the Championship, and I fully believed I could make the step up. Before coming to Sheffield United, I had spent four seasons in the Conference, six in League Two and one in League One, with United, and I just tried to not think about it too much and just enjoy it – experiencing the great stadiums, playing against good players and seeing how well I could do.

It's mad, really, but for a few of the games I found playing in the Championship easier than in the Conference. In the Championship, you have a lot of time and breathers when teams have the ball and pass it about, and no-one really wants to stretch you and run in behind. They seem to want to come to feet a lot and with me playing in the middle of a three, I found it comfortable. In the Conference I often played in a four and had big, strong strikers looking to elbow me in the face and run past me and work hard. They might not be the most talented, which is why they're down there, but they'd be relentless and work hard for 90 minutes. So from that perspective, I found the Championship easier!

I know that I'm never going to be a 10/10 every week or score 50 goals a season, but my aim is to be a seven or eight consistently and I think that's why Chris brought me in. We didn't have the greatest start when I arrived so it played into my hands a little; the gaffer had to make changes, and the good run started when I came into the team and continued throughout the season.

After working with Chris at Halifax and Oxford, I obviously didn't have to prove myself to him but players can sometimes be a bit wary. They knew I'd been with him before, so were maybe thinking 'is he a snake or going to tell the gaffer everything that's said?' So I had to keep my head down, work hard and prove to the boys what I was all about. Most of them probably hadn't heard of me before and thought 'we've just signed a player who's been released from Oxford?' so a few maybe weren't too impressed, but hopefully I've proved that I've been a good signing. With the league title in my first year and a good showing in the Championship, it's been a good two seasons.

My first taste of life under Chris came when I was a third-year trainee at Bradford City, and I spent a bit of time with his Halifax Town side down in the Conference. We did really well and I think we were about fourth in the league when Bradford called me back, which I was gutted about really. That year, Chris took Halifax to the play-off final and when my Bradford contract ran out he asked if I wanted to go back. I signed straightaway. It was men's football, playing against experienced older professionals and young lads, and I really enjoyed it. I was playing left-back for him then, but it was a very different position to the Enda Stevens role ... there wasn't much overlapping!

There was a spell at Halifax when we weren't getting paid for months and it was tough because my missus was pregnant, but Chris was brilliant in making sure we were all okay. We were docked points for going into administration and still managed to stay up, but then a few weeks later he took us all out for a drink and said the club had folded.

I went to Crawley, he went to Bury as Alan Knill's assistant and tried to take me there, but I couldn't get out of my Crawley contract. I stayed in touch with him when I moved to Brighton and that didn't work out, so I rejoined him at Oxford on loan. We got promoted in the play-off final at Wembley, which was an emotional game for me because my grandad had cancer and came to watch me in a wheelchair, before passing away a few months later. We knew he didn't have long left to live and that was an emotional occasion but a brilliant one that I'll never forget.

The gaffer actually tried to take me to Northampton when he was there and then, after we'd won promotion with Oxford, Michael Appleton – who I got on well with, and still do – said I could leave and he wouldn't stand in my way. My name went on the transfer list, Chris called me and said 'how much do I have to pay for you?' I told him nothing, and the deal was on. He knew my agent, Tyrone Thompson, from the Halifax days and we travelled up, did my medical and got it sorted so quickly. I didn't bother speaking to any other clubs because I knew I wasn't going to get a bigger one than this and, ironically, my first game was against Oxford at Bramall Lane.

So Chris has either taken me, or tried to take me, to every club he's been at but it's not just because he knows me; I've done well for him over the years, so it's a two-way relationship. It's been a good one over the years, and I hope it continues. He knows I give everything for him and for the team, but when I signed he explained that I was cover for Jack O'Connell and I had to fight for my place. That didn't faze me. He knows that, whatever the situation, I'll give him everything. I did that at Halifax when we were struggling in the Conference and not getting paid, and I did the same when United were top of the Championship. I've not changed as a person but I've improved throughout my career, just as the gaffer has.

The change of shape in the promotion season suited me well. I'd played in a back four for the majority of my career but a three wasn't unfamiliar either so I knew I'd enjoy it ... especially with how Jack and Chris Basham go about it! It's entirely different to the way most teams play it and often left us one-on-one at the back, but I quite enjoyed that, and the lads in midfield helped us absolutely dominate games. It was by far my most enjoyable season and to go the whole season unbeaten, setting a record for a club like this, is brilliant and makes me really proud.

Then came the celebrations! They were hard work by the end. The gaffer kept telling us to meet wherever at 1pm, and I'm thinking 'we need a day off ... give us a rest!' But he was right to do that. Seasons like that don't come around too often, and when you have success you have to make the most of it. I played with players who had long careers and never won anything, so when that happens you should enjoy it. And it can't harm the spirit, either. You can't force that togetherness if lads don't get on, but the gaffer's always done well on that front by signing the right type of people as well as good players.

I think I've probably played more games for Chris than any other player, and personality-wise I don't think he's changed at all from the days in the Conference. He's always liked getting involved and has never done things from the outside. He takes fewer sessions now, because he has a brilliant assistant in Knilly, but he's always involved with the banter just like he was in the Conference. At Halifax we had a tight-knit squad with lads who used to drink together, and that helped through the tough times when we weren't getting paid or training in local parks, dodging all the dog mess.

He's brilliant at getting a team ready for matchday, physically and psychologically, and the shape work on a Friday is the same as it was at Halifax 12 years ago. We've had our fall-outs over the years, of course, but by Friday everyone is bouncing and bright for the game. The biggest compliment I can pay him is that he's very enjoyable to play under, because we're not outside for hours in training and sessions are short and sharp, and hard. He's enjoyable to be around, when he's not in a bad mood, and I'm sure that one day he'll manage right at the top. His past experiences have helped him when times get tough, and he's been very consistent in his approach since the early days.

And, of course, whether it's training or a friendly, he loves winning. He's been good for me and hopefully, I've been good for him as well.

August 2017 – Football's back
By Pete West, South Stand

There is no better month of the football season, surely, than August? A time when every football fan can look forward to the new season with some degree of optimism and wonder what it may bring. Some clubs will have failed miserably in the last campaign, others will be still on a high but either way, interest from the fans is piqued at a high. After what seems like months of no football, the game is back. There's something to do again on a Saturday afternoon! The start of the new season is equal, in excitement terms, to what I used to feel as a child on Christmas Eve. It is a fresh start. A clean slate. A new bill of health. We are going into the unknown – and that's exciting!

In Sheffield United's case we entered August coming off the back of one of the most successful seasons in the club's history, preparing for our first taste of the Championship for over six years. Chris Wilder had recruited a handful of new players, using his formula that had proved successful in the promotion season; few big names, no big egos, but everything to prove. How would we fare? Well, according to one sports journalist, we were destined to struggle. Every time, the words "Sheffield United" were following with "survival" or "relegation battle" which I found very, very strange. For me, this guy's view on United's prospects for the coming season were pessimistic, to the point of being totally unrealistic. Of course, football is all about opinions. That's what makes it a great game.

But from my perspective, United didn't just win promotion by some quirk or fluke or lucky break – they did it by absolutely steamrollering just about every team put in front of them. It was like some huge efficient machine, sweeping across the pitch from one end to the other, gaining yards on the opposition with every pass, until eventually they reached the danger zone, the opposition finally cracked under the relentless pressure and victory was gained.

I was fortunate to see the great 1970s side, with Alan Woodward and Tony Currie and others, and that, to this day, is still the best team of individually talented players I've ever witnessed in a United shirt. But, I would rate the quality of football produced by the League One-winning United side ahead of that produced back in the golden era of the 1970s. We really were that impressive. To my mind we were already playing Championship standard football, in League One. Trapped in the wrong football body.

So, I could not understand where the negativity about our prospects for this season was coming from. Apart from S6, of course, where our bigger city betters, as they like to think of themselves, were warning us how difficult the Championship was and how we would most likely be going straight back down again. They, of course, were certainties to be promoted to the Premier League, having come close, but not quite close enough, in the past two seasons. So, it was now time to find out. The first match of the season was upon us. Brentford – at home.

In some ways I felt this was the ideal fixture for United to ease themselves back into the Championship after such a long absence. Brentford finished a respectable tenth in the second tier in the previous season, so it would be a good, but not extreme, test of how we may stack up against a team that more than held their own at this level. In the opening few minutes of the game I felt we were going to be taught a painful lesson.

The most noticeable thing was the speed, and accuracy, of

Brentford's movement and passing. It was a different tempo to what we'd been used to seeing in League One and I feared it would overwhelm us for a while. But in a game low on chances, club captain and legend-in-waiting, Billy Sharp, plundered a single goal to decide the game in our favour. We were back! We had won! And we were delighted.

The big test of the month arguably came away at Middlesbrough, who'd just dropped from the Premier League, with big name players on big salaries and a war chest of parachute payments at their disposal. I don't think many people, myself included, expected us to get much from this game; a little step too far, too soon. United started the better of the two sides, Boro got into their stride and about 20 minutes in, the Blades defence finally cracked. From there on, for the rest of the first half, it looked like we were going to be overrun. I could hear the journalist's words echoing around my head. Survival. Relegation battle. Maybe the gulf in class was too great after all? Braced with a Bovril, I hoped for better in the second half. I needn't have worried.

The Blades found it within themselves to pick themselves up again, off the floor, and come back fighting to gain a foothold in the game. A splendid second half performance saw United bossing one of last season's Premier League teams. Then, up popped Jack O'Connell to head home the equaliser. Amazing. But ... offside! TV replays later showed that he wasn't, but by then it was too late. The 1-0 defeat was our first in the league since January – but we came away with heads held high.

The games didn't get much easier. Cardiff, managed by ex-boss and lifetime Blade Neil Warnock, were top of the table and flying. Warnock, in true Warnock style, had assembled a team of physically strong players with experience and United were beaten with ease. The Bluebirds just looked too strong and too good for a fledgling United team still looking to find their wings at this level. A bit of respite came with a run of games at home and I fancied we would be too good for Barnsley, given the unfamiliarity of their squad and the strong bond enjoyed by ours. In a fiesty derby, that proved to be the case. Leon Clarke and Angus MacDonald saw red, for the type of offence that wouldn't have even merited a telling off in days gone by, and United cut through Barnsley, who had "survived" the Championship before, with ease. It gave me every hope that we could survive it, too.

As good as United were, Barnsley were very poor; probably the worst Barnsley performance, in a derby, that I've ever witnessed. So I tried to keep the result in perspective, and was pretty sure the next home game would be much tougher. Many tipped Derby for promotion this season; they were a very good, established, Championship side, one that has been knocking on the door for several years now. This would be a far better indicator of where we were at.

What followed was one of the finest home displays of progressive football that any fan could wish to see. United were like a team possessed; hunting down every ball, closing down every pass, winning every tackle. If Derby dared to try and get on the ball United took it back off them, like a parent scolding a naughty child. They hassled and harried and pushed and pressed Derby in every quarter of the park. The United machine was in full, relentless operation now. Attack after attack after attack. We were 2-0 up when Craig Bryson scored for Derby in the last minute. We checked our watches. We knew how this one was going to end. We had all the play, all the possession, played them off the park, but now they were going to undeservedly sneak another one in injury time.

But this United team is a different animal. Derby won a corner with seconds left on the clock, Carson went forward, United broke away. Sharp rolled the ball home for 3-1, lancing the boil of a late Derby revival and sending us into the top six. I came away from that game, the last in August, feeling highly satisfied; not just with that one result, but with the way our season was shaping up as a whole. Despite the soothsayers in the media and S6 predictions of doom, I was witnessing quite the opposite; a team that had come out of League One, in some style, carrying on where they left off. Yes, the games were tougher and we weren't having it all our own way. But in no game so far had we embarrassed ourselves or failed to give any opposition a difficult time.

That's all we ask of our United team, actually. We don't expect a great deal, but we do expect 100 percent effort and we got that in spades. Win, draw, or lose, those lads always do their very best for us. We may have surprised some people by our start, but there was nothing surprising about it for those who had followed them closely since Wilder took over. The Blades were back. We were not there to make up the numbers and were looking up rather than down. Roll on September!

10

The heroes of Hillsborough
September 2017

Chris Wilder strolled into the packed media suite at Bramall Lane, dodged around one of the many television cameras waiting for him and let out a chuckle. Pre-match press conferences, usually conducted at United's Shirecliffe training ground, were typically unspectacular affairs with a handful of local reporters but today, a room full of national media and Sky Sports cameras greeted him, days before his first Steel City Derby as Sheffield United manager. As ever, Wilder met each one with a hello, a handshake or a nod of the head; business as usual for him. "Big game on?" he grinned, as he took his seat.

Just a bit. Wilder, it transpired through the next hour or so, thought United v Sheffield Wednesday was the best of the lot; the biggest, in fact, there is. "Liverpool versus Everton, Arsenal against Tottenham or Newcastle and Sunderland? I've got to say, they don't do a lot for me. This is the big one. This is the one that matters. It's bigger and better, in my eyes at least, than everything else." The Steel City Derby, after a five-year absence, was tagged as 'The Game English Football Forgot' in a *YouTube* preview video bringing together fans of both sides, but it was rarely far from Wilder's mind – especially after promotion to the Championship was secured the previous season. Wednesday's subsequent failure to overcome Huddersfield in the play-offs meant they were in the second tier for another season. And the big game was back on.

Wilder's first experience of a Steel City Derby was a fairly inauspicious one, although he concedes it could have been worse. After missing the first meeting between the two bitter rivals in 1979/80 – a 4-0 defeat at Hillsborough dubbed the 'Boxing Day

Massacre', which both sets of fans still sing about – a 12-year-old Wilder saw his heroes draw 1-1 with the enemy at Bramall Lane the following April. The names of those who wrote themselves in Bramall Lane folklore with goals in victory over Wednesday – Davison, Whitehouse and Brown, even D'Jaffo, Asaba and Akinbiyi – were more than familiar to him and although he didn't get on the pitch when United did the double in 1991/92 – a season Wednesday finished third in Division One, seven points behind winners Leeds – the memories are still as vivid as ever.

Like most other United fans, the first games Wilder looked for when the 2017/18 Championship fixtures were released towards the end of June were the ones against Wednesday, closely followed by big hitters in the division like Leeds United, Aston Villa and Sunderland. "When the fixtures came through, it really hit home for everyone what a fantastic competition it's going to be – one we knew we could bring something to and were really looking forward to," he said. "We knew we'd be a dangerous outfit." Just for good measure, the first Sheffield Derby since 2012 was scheduled for Saturday, September 23 – the day of Wilder's 50th birthday. The game was eventually pushed back a day for Sky Sports coverage – clashing with a 10km race in Sheffield city centre – but the countdown had begun many months earlier.

Born almost 200 miles north of the border in Scotland, Neill Collins made his United debut against Wednesday as a loanee from Sunderland in 2006, in a 2-1 victory at Hillsborough, and then played in both derby games in 2011/12 after returning to Bramall Lane for a second spell. United, 2-0 up and cruising after 20 minutes of the first game at Bramall Lane, were rocked by two late Wednesday goals to take just a point and Chris O'Grady scored the winner in the return leg at Hillsborough as United, rocked by the loss of top scorer Ched Evans, struggled to get over the line for automatic promotion and were pipped at the post by their bitterest rivals.

"Players and fans feel that extra sense of nerves as they know what is at stake," Collins recalls. "Players realise that a winning goal makes them a lifelong hero. A mistake? A villain for eternity.

"As a fan, the desire for your team not to lose to your closest rivals is so strong it makes you anxious. The thought of losing and having to face your neighbour or workmate gloating for the foreseeable future is enough to make your skin crawl. The dislike and hatred for your rivals is indescribable; so deeply ingrained from battles experienced over a number of years, that you can't shake it.

"I remember the first game when I was on loan, which came about 48 hours after I was lying in a hospital bed on an IV drip with an infection spreading up my leg. Neil Warnock, who was in charge of United at the time, rang me and the conversation was simple. 'How are you doing son?' he asked. 'How would you like to come and play in the Sheffield Derby tomorrow?' I rushed down to sign the papers before the deadline on the Friday and was feeling as you would expect after three days in the hospital, but was quickly jolted out of any lethargy as I boarded the bus.

"My new mates were all arriving and I was greeted by the formidable figure of Ade Akinbiyi, who shook my hand and asked if I was ready. I nonchalantly replied 'yes' before he gripped my hand tighter, gave me the death stare and repeated 'ARE YOU READY?' It was his way of making sure I knew this was for real. Do or die. They didn't want a young lad coming in on loan and screwing it up for them. If I wasn't quite ready before, I certainly was now. I didn't want to let this guy down.

"The team was full of experience and I was going to play beside team captain and no-nonsense centre-back Chris Morgan. My only previous dealings with him had been the previous season, when I faced him with Sunderland and he punched me square in the gut at a corner. That afternoon, I was delighted to have him alongside instead of opposite me. We went 2-0 up with quality goals from Michael Tonge and Akinbiyi and in the second half, missed three absolute sitters and the chance to turn it into an absolute rout. As we came back out for a warm down afterwards, the Blades fans were still in the ground and the delirium was evident as they went through the full repertoire of songs. Then, a half-cut Sean Bean came on the team bus to congratulate us at the end. Perhaps if we had played his *When Saturday Comes* character, Jimmy Muir, upfront, then he would have stuck one of our chances away."

Remarkably, in the eight games against Wednesday since, United had won just one – even that was by no means a certainty, after racing into a 3-0 half-time lead and eventually holding on at 3-2 – and the landscape in Sheffield football had changed off the field, too. While United languished in League One under a succession of managers pre-Wilder, Wednesday had been taken over by Dejphon Chansiri, a Thai tuna magnate, and were throwing unbelievable amounts of money at players in an attempt to return to the Premier League for the first time since relegation in 2000.

Under Portuguese head coach Carlos Carvalhal, they had twice finished in the Championship play-offs and reached the final in 2016, losing to Hull City. Striker Jordan Rhodes then arrived at Hillsborough from Middlesbrough in a deal worth at least £8m and Wednesday's wage bill ballooned to an extraordinary £30m a year. The *princes and the paupers* description placed on the two clubs by a local journalist may have been a bit of a stretch, but the basic premise wasn't far wrong.

Perhaps a little predictably, that influx of cash and relative success of twice finishing in the play-offs had further inflated egos amongst Wednesday fans, and the prospect of their city neighbours joining them in the Championship didn't fill too many with dread. Wednesday fans had christened League One 'the pub league' and even United's storming start to life in the second tier was dismissed as merely down to momentum. But many United fans followed their manager's lead and viewed the derby as something of a 'free hit' – not just another game, as Wilder's predecessor Bryan Robson had once infamously dubbed it, by any stretch but one they could approach as the underdogs. The pressure was very much on Wednesday.

Especially so given United's build-up, when everything seemed to conspire against the men in red and white. The month had started promisingly, when deadline-day signing Clayton Donaldson bagged a brace on his debut at Sunderland's Stadium of Light, but the striker damaged a hamstring just as he was sticking his second goal in the top corner.

Cameron Carter-Vickers, the on-loan Spurs defender, then marked his Blades debut with the winner in a battling display at Bolton, but United went into their weekend game against Norwich at Bramall Lane with strikers Donaldson, Billy Sharp, Leon Clarke, James Hanson and Caolan Lavery all missing through injury. In their absence, Evans – rated by Wilder as 50 per cent fit and playing "through constant pain" – stuck his hand up to play, but was unsurprisingly ineffective as Norwich returned to East Anglia with a 1-0 victory and all three points.

Wilder, to put it mildly, was not happy. Norwich's time-wasting tactics began as early as the half-hour mark after Yanic Wildschut had put them ahead, with goalkeeper Angus Gunn particularly guilty, and only centre-half Timm Klose showed any interest in playing football after a day of antics so blatant and unwelcome that even Alan Partridge, Norfolk's favourite son, wouldn't dare petition for a second series of it. In his post-match press conference, a visibly-aggrieved Wilder criticised Daniel Farke's visitors for being late to the ground before the game and not handing the teamsheets in on time, accusing them of lacking respect for him, United and the game.

Wilder's frustration boiled over during the match when the ball ended up amongst a pile of water bottles in the dugouts and, keen to get play back underway, he scattered them all over the technical areas with a solid boot. Wilder was sent to the stands by referee Scott Duncan and after his side lost a game in which they had almost 70 percent of the possession, said: "There were some time-wasting issues that were ridiculous.

"Referees have to do something about it. It breaks the flow of the game up when you're in the ascendancy. I went in their technical area, that was the problem, but there was a bit of frustration with us having five strikers out. But I thought my team were outstanding for a new team in the division. I thought we deserved something from the game."

With Wilder facing the possibility of a touchline ban from the derby at Hillsborough a week later and tasking a half-fit Evans to once again lead the line, his plans were disrupted further when it emerged that Paul Coutts, his influential midfielder and vice-captain, was being investigated by the Football Association for an alleged off-the-ball incident involving a Norwich player. The incident, missed by Duncan, would be examined by a panel and if found guilty, Coutts faced a retrospective three-match ban – which would rule him out of the derby.

But, on the eve of the game, both player and manager breathed a sigh of relief; the FA, after considering Duncan's report, would not be issuing a touchline ban to Wilder and the three ex-referees assigned to examine Coutts' case could not agree that a red-card offence had been committed. Both would be free to face Wednesday at the weekend. "I didn't really hear about it," said Coutts. "The first I heard was when my dad rang and asked if I was banned for the game! I didn't really know what it was all about because it was a bit of a nothing incident. I put my arm out and their lad ran into it. He sprung to his feet about two seconds later so I'd have been disappointed to get punished for that. I'm just happy that common sense prevailed."

Coutts, who faced the press before the derby alongside his manager and defender Jake Wright, was in relaxed mood and revealed that he'd just found out his window cleaner was a Wednesday fan, so would be soon looking for a new one. Wright revealed his son played for a football team coached by an Owl. This was a game that divided more than a city. "For some it was their first derby and we wanted to make good memories for our supporters," said Wilder. "You'd be daft not to look at the fixture list when it comes out and identify when we play Sheffield Wednesday. Whether it's supporters talking in the boozer or at home, because there's still mixed families, this was what they were bothered about.

"We had been battered for six years by Wednesday fans talking about the 'pub league' and had the taunts about them being the top team in Sheffield. There was a lot of talk about passion, how the Meadowhall League manager was going to send his boys out there to run around and kick Wednesday's superstars, but anyone who had actually watched us would have known we had more about us than that.

"We knew we were a dangerous team and would go there

without fear. We hadn't taken a backward step since I arrived, and we weren't about to start now. There's no doubt what these games represent. They give you the extra yard, to jump a bit higher, to run a bit quicker. This was a new chapter. This was us being in the division for the first time in six years, and we wanted to make new memories and make new heroes out of the players."

On the morning of the game, a sunny Sunday in the Steel City, thousands of runners pounded the pavements around the gruelling city-centre 10k course but all attentions soon turned to the border of Barnsley for the 128th instalment of derby day drama. The early 1.15pm kick-off for Sky TV didn't prevent a large gathering of Owls fans outside the players' entrance at Hillsborough – the roof is too low for coaches to get under, so opposition players are forced to walk a gauntlet to get into the ground. Evans and Clarke, the former Wednesday striker who played 87 times for the Owls between 2007 and 2010, were singled out for special treatment.

While Clarke, a laid-back character by nature, nonchalantly strode by with earphones in and Evans, flanked by two stewards, lapped up his warm reception with a beaming smile, 20-year-old David Brooks appeared a little taken aback after only making his full United league debut the week before against Norwich. As a regular in the U23s at Stocksbridge in front of a few hundred fans, he wasn't entirely accustomed to such a welcome.

An hour before kick-off, the teams were confirmed and Brooks was to start the game alongside Clarke, who'd passed a late fitness test. As the players left the field, it was noticeable that Alan Knill, Wilder's trusted No.2, had his arm around United's mercurial young star.

"When the team got announced I was delighted, but it was a bit scary and anxious," Brooks said. "I just couldn't wait to get there and see what it was all about. I made a bit of a rookie error by getting off the bus just before Leon and Ched, who didn't get the warmest of welcomes. Neither of them were fazed but it was the first time I'd ever experienced that and it took me back a little bit. Knilly was just reassuring me, saying it was my chance and that they knew what I could do and had faith in me. That I was there on merit and had earned my place.

"We were doing a bit of shooting just before going in for the warm-up, and I remember a few of their fans shouting that I was nervous and things like that, and I shanked one over the netting behind the goal! The next one went in, though, which calmed the nerves a little bit. It was a great atmosphere to walk out to and I was a bit anxious, but I believe in myself and thought I could do well in that game. When I've got the ball at my feet and I'm running, I don't hear anything from the crowd but it's more when the game stops and the abuse comes. I can't say I don't get nervous because everyone does but at the end of the day, I'd rather be involved and nervous than sat on the bench or not be involved and be safe from having a bad game or a shocker."

Brooks was given his chance partly because skipper Sharp, a boyhood Blade, was only fit enough to make the bench … and even that was more a psychological ploy from Wilder. "Billy had no chance of playing," he remembers. "In Billy's mind, he wanted to because of what the game means to him and he was a loss, because we had big issues with our strikers. But I had a decision to make using judgement, not emotion. I suppose I could have got him on the pitch for the last minute but first and foremost, he's part of a group. He understands that.

"At the time, he was two weeks into a four-to-six week injury and there was no way he'd ever go on the pitch. But we kept it quiet and thought that, psychologically, them seeing Billy on the teamsheet would have an effect and having Billy in the changing room would give our players a lift. It certainly did. All credit to him and his selflessness, really. He was obviously disappointed but had to put that to one side to get the best result for the team."

By the time Coutts, captain for the day in Sharp's absence, led the visitors out, Hillsborough was rocking. The tunnel at Hillsborough is almost impossibly narrow so Wednesday emerged first and after agonising for hours over what to say in the pre-match huddle just before kick-off, Coutts thought he had got it spot on. He reminded the players what the fans demanded of them, what the manager demanded of them. But above all, told them to go and enjoy it. What an occasion to play football. Coutts was proud of his rousing speech but months later, George Baldock broke the news to him that, as the atmosphere reached boiling point, the players could not hear a word of it.

As the last throes of 'Hi Ho, Silver Lining' reverberated around Hillsborough, Brooks kicked off the game and then helped land the first punch. He picked up the ball from Clarke and drove at the Wednesday defence, fearlessly skipping past David Jones, Barry Bannan and Tom Lees before being brought down by the latter about 25 yards from Keiren Westwood's goal. As Coutts shaped to run over the ball, Brooks rolled it behind him and as the goalkeeper took a fateful step to his left, John Fleck smashed the free-kick to his right. Westwood didn't even move before it hit the net. Exactly 2,038 days since their last meeting with Wednesday, United were ahead – after just two minutes and eight seconds.

"We work on all that sort of stuff in training and usually, on that particular routine, it's me, Flecky and Mark Duffy standing over it, so we know what we're doing," Coutts remembers. "But I had to get Brooksy involved, and I think he was still half asleep! So I'm looking at him, shouting 'Brooksy, come over here' as he's standing at the side of the wall. I'm trying to get him over without giving too much away, and he's totally blanking me! I carry on shouting and by the time he comes over, he thinks he's shooting. Eventually we worked it out and when it counted, the two of them delivered."

If the first United goal was sublime then the second was ridiculous, from the perspective of Wednesday's defenders at least. After a lovely interchange of play involving Chris Basham and Baldock, Joost van Aken desperately cleared the ball for a corner and when Ross Wallace eventually booted the ball well beyond halfway, there seemed little danger. As Enda Stevens, United's left-back, volleyed back under pressure from Kieran Lee, home fans' chants of 'hoof' could be clearly heard. But the bouncing ball dissected Lees and van Aken, right-back Jack Hunt played Clarke onside and the United striker, from almost nowhere, slid the ball under Westwood to put his side 2-0 up inside 15 minutes. After a quick glance at the home fans behind the goal, Clarke sprinted to the bench to celebrate with Evans before being mobbed by teammates and staff alike.

"The manager had let us know in no uncertain terms how much it meant to everybody connected to United but it was an extra bit special for me," Clarke admitted. "I had a bit of a tight hamstring but there was no doubt about me missing that game. The manager let us know that it was an opportunity to show all the Wednesday fans that we belonged in the Championship. After scoring, inside I was ecstatic. I'd rank it right up there as one of the highlights of my career. To go back to Hillsborough, after not having the best of periods there, and to show that I am a good player."

At the other end, Wright showed immense bravery to deflect Hunt's well-struck shot behind for a corner but as half-time approached, Wednesday came into it and just on the stroke of the whistle, they had a lifeline when Gary Hooper got half a yard on Wright and poked home. The goal changed the entire mood of Hillsborough for the half-time interval and beyond and, as expected, they threw absolutely everything at United in the second period, throwing on striker Lucas Joao for the ineffective midfielder Jones.

"We should have been even further ahead with the chances we had, but in the end Hooper's goal gave them a boost and we had work to do at half-time because the atmosphere changed completely," Wilder remembers. "But we knew we had more in our locker than they would ever know, and it was important that we showed it. Alan and I haven't had the careers we've had by booting the ball up the pitch and having fights. I was disappointed at half-time that we weren't further ahead. We'd had Boxing Day rammed down our throats for nearly 40 years, and this was our chance to stick it back down theirs. I think we went a long way towards doing that anyway."

After the teams reemerged, Jamal Blackman showed good handling to keep hold of Adam Reach's deflected shot but then came one of the moments that defined the game, and the formative career of young Brooks as he sprung back off the ground after being shoved over by Hunt, and flicked the ball between the defender's legs in one delightful motion, before Hunt even realised what was happening. As one, the United bench rose to its feet as Brooks sprinted towards goal but his pass to Clarke was at an awkward height and after the striker brought it down, he poked it over.

It was a golden chance to quell Wednesday's growing momentum at a key time in the game, and re-establish their dominance. Brooks, lifting his shirt over his face and roaring in frustration, knew it too. The miss seemed a big moment inside Hillsborough at the time but moments later it became massive, when Joao brought Wednesday back on level terms with a confident finish into the roof of Blackman's net. With the introduction of Duffy for Wright in the aftermath of Clarke's miss, United had changed their shape and in the confusion, Reach was afforded almost the freedom of Hillsborough on the left wing. His ball inside caught out Cameron Carter-Vickers, who slipped, and Joao's devastating finish brought Wednesday level.

A photographer behind Blackman's goal almost forgot to take the shot of the goalscorer as he celebrated and by this point, Hillsborough was rocking – literally. From the press seats in Wednesday's South Stand, the foundations of the ground were shaking as Owls fans in all four stands of the ground bounced to their signature, anti-Blades song. Wilder, and more than one Blades player, admitted they had never heard an atmosphere like it before. "At that point," Wilder admitted, "I bet a lot of our fans were thinking 'here we go again'." What happened next will go down in United folklore.

With that Joao strike, United were on the ropes and Wednesday could sense blood. But so, it transpired, could Duffy, who received a header from Basham, laid it off to Clarke and sprinted in behind van Aken. Clarke's clipped ball was inch-perfect but as Duffy faced the Dutchman almost on the angle of the penalty area, there seemed little danger. Wednesday's fans were still bouncing. Hillsborough was still rocking. Duffy feinted to shoot and cut inside on his left foot, and the bouncing was a little quieter. As

Duffy chopped back onto his right foot, smashed the ball past Westwood from a tight angle and left van Aken stood with his shirt over his head, it had stopped. Almost mid-bounce.

For what seemed like an eternity, Hillsborough fell silent; both sets of fans in shock at what they had witnessed. Then, the only noise came from the top tier of the Leppings Lane end as Duffy first sprinted to the corner flag to celebrate, then ran the length of the United fans to soak up their celebrations. Just one minute and 47 seconds after Joao had dragged Wednesday level, Duffy had put United ahead again. If ever a passage of play typified a Wilder side, it was surely this one.

Duffy smiled afterwards that if he could bottle and sell the feeling he experienced for that 30 seconds or so, he'd be a rich man. But it got even better for United when Clarke added a second, and United's fourth, 13 minutes from time after Lees and van Aken again failed to cover themselves in glory. It became the first time in the club's history that United had scored four goals at Hillsborough and the closing minutes, as the home stands emptied rapidly, became an elongated celebration as Wilder was serenaded with a rousing rendition of 'Happy Birthday'. Turning 50 is rarely an occasion to treasure but that half-century weekend will be one that the manager will never forget.

"I think it summed us up as a team," he said. "We're not a team that has a lot of fighting qualities and can't play, but we're also not a team that will get bullied. We have mental, physical, tactical and technical qualities. Everyone's looking for that complete package to be successful. We had a bottom six budget in the division and were tipped by the bookies to finish 17th or 18th, and our owners would have been delighted with that. Here we were, at a team paying £30,000 and £40,000 a week to their strikers, and a lad we got for free from Birmingham, who had played for Vauxhall Motors and Prescot Cables, smacked one in. Incredible."

Aside from the obvious in a game against Wednesday, there was extra motivation for Wilder to prove a point. When he took over at United he was pointed in the direction of a demeaning message from an Owls fan, along the lines of: 'Our manager is Champions League while United have got one out of the Meadowhall Sunday League'. The author has probably long forgotten writing it now, but Wilder did not; for him, it was all fuel for the fire. "I thought it was a complete, all-round performance from Leon at Hillsborough," he said. "The only disappointment was that he didn't bag a hat-trick but he can't be greedy and I can't be critical. To take the game away from them at that period was a great feeling; it really put a dagger into their heart.

"We should have been out of sight at half-time, but we weren't naive enough to think there wouldn't be a bit of pride from the Wednesday players just because they were these superstars on big money. Duffy's big moment will be talked about forever I should imagine, and from then on, I thought we were comfortable. My players showed what good players they are individually and how good a team we are collectively. You're always going to get your nugget supporters who haven't got a clue about football, but deep down I think the majority of Wednesday fans will look back and say 'they're not a bad side, them'. And what better stage to show it than a Sheffield Derby?

"I don't think it gets any better than that. It was everything for both clubs, but I think we won it pretty comfortably. It was special; I don't think you can put it into words. We had it rammed down our throats over the last six years so it was nice to give the supporters something back. I was emotional after the game and I didn't get to the players straightaway – I wanted to take it in first. We'd made a huge statement. This is not just another game, and it never will be."

In the away dressing room, United dimmed the lights and put the speakers on to enjoy a party atmosphere but with another game against Wolves in midweek, the heroes of Hillsborough were limited to bottles of strawberry milkshake and sandwiches. In the tunnel afterwards, clutching a protein bar and the Sky Bet man of the match award that he was insistent should have gone to two-goal Clarke, Brooks looked like a boy again but there was little doubt that he was a man now. "I just try and enjoy all my football, wherever I play and whatever level I play," he said. "I try and do the same things, do everything right. It was a hostile atmosphere, the first I've been in since breaking into the first team, and it's different – being booed and stuff is all new. But I just took it on the chin a little and once you start playing, you just get on with it. I think I had a good game and, bar a goal, I thought I did well."

With that significant understatement, Brooks was off to join the team coach for the short journey back to Bramall Lane, where he and the rest of United's players were serenaded by jubilant fans. With Wolves visiting in just three days, the players had no option but to be professional but Wilder was determined to enjoy the occasion. "We'd had all the taunts aimed at us over the last six years," he said. "Carlos said he slept all right ... I didn't sleep a wink for the week before the game. It was a long old seven days. In this game, you have enough lows ... so I was going to enjoy it."

His moment of magic even earned Duffy something else he had been craving since he joined United ... his own terrace song, immortalising a late September Sunday night in United folklore. *Oh what a night* indeed. "It's about time I got one, isn't it?" Duffy smiled. "The fans sing about everyone else ... there were players who played about four games last season and got one! I wanted to know where mine was. But it's brilliant. There's a few good ones to be fair ... the Jack O'Connell one was big and Flecky's Scottish Hero one is brilliant, too. The fans still sing about Tony Currie all these years later so maybe in 50 years, they'll still be singing my song ... I'll be able to bring my girls and tell them it's about me. They won't believe me, so I'll have to show them the goal on *YouTube*!"

"Not bad for a team fresh out of the pub league," added Coutts. But if victory away at Wednesday was United's most emotional win of the season, then beating eventual champions Wolves days later must surely rank amongst the most impressive. Boasting the likes of £16m signing Ruben Neves from Porto and Diogo Jota, whose loan move from Atletico Madrid was later made permanent for over £12m, Nuno Espírito Santo's men had changed the financial landscape of the Championship but it was Clarke, the former Wolves man who cost United £150,000 from

Chris Wilder's first steps in management came at Bradway in the Meadowhall Sunday League, where he worked alongside good pal Ian Whitehorne and enjoyed almost unprecedented success. *Ian Whitehorne/Bradway FC*

Wilder, then manager of Oxford, in the Blades end at Crystal Palace, in 2009. United took around 9,000 fans to Selhurst Park and eventually lost in the play-off final at Wembley. He certainly didn't follow United for the glory! *Martyn Harrison*

Another boyhood Blade 12-year-old Regan Slater celebrates on the Bramall Lane pitch after United's play-off semi-final win over Stevenage in 2012. Again, they went on to lose in the final at Wembley and Slater went on to play for United. *Regan Slater*

United fans let off flares away at Charlton, in a 1-1 draw at The Valley. A late equaliser ruined Wilder's mood but he ended up in a London pub with fellow Blades supporters. *Mick Chadwick*

In Wilder's first game in charge, away at Bolton, United fans planned to boycott the game in protest at high ticket prices but ended up taking over 4,000 supporters over the Pennines for an undeserved 1-0 defeat. *Danny Hall*

Jubilant scenes in the away end, and on the pitch, after Billy Sharp's 87th-minute winner away at Peterborough. Sharp went on to score 30 goals in United's promotion campaign. *Tyrone Hoyland*

David Brooks in United's U18s. The youngster often had to wear a shirt from the age group below, and even that sometimes buried him too. But United's faith was eventually rewarded. *Martyn Harrison*

Oldham's cabbage-patch pitch on which they drew 1-1 at Boundary Park. Wilder thought it was a vital point and was proved correct. *Martin Stevens*

Wilder's favourite picture as manager of United. Beating the badge became a trademark gesture after important victories – this one away at Bolton. *Sportimage*

Blades fan Richard Glossop took a selfie with Wilder and his heroes after watching United win promotion from the away dugout at Northampton. *Richard Glossop*

Bramall Lane on a matchnight. "In the heart of the city", as Wilder puts it – as opposed to rivals Wednesday, out of town in Hillsborough. *Richard Markham*

Dane Shaw took a selfie with Chris Basham after promotion was confirmed at Northampton. It was Dane's birthday. "It'll take some topping, let me tell you," he said. *Dane Shaw*

Billy Sharp holding aloft his Blades scarf while singing with fans, after promotion was confirmed, became an iconic image. This is how it looked from the pitch. *Oliver Thorpe*

Joy at Northampton as United (finally) seal promotion. *Abbey Kirwin*

Dan Atkin, left, celebrated promotion at the Bramall Lane beamback – the emotion seemed to prove too much for his friend Chris Ridley. *Dan Atkin*

Francesca Wilder managed to sneak on the team coach for the journey back to Bramall Lane after promotion was sealed at Northampton. *Francesca Wilder*

Wilder and his team were serenaded when they returned to Bramall Lane, in scenes reminiscent of Leicester in 1990. And the manager enjoyed every moment!
Becky Rayson

Thousands of fans in fancy dress converged on Milton Keynes for a promotion party when United played MK Dons – and masks of Wilder seemed a popular choice.
Rob Siddall and Ian Whitehorne

Magic man Jack O'Connell was a popular figure at MK, many fans sporting their own magic hats with foam bricks to head to the left and right. *Rob Siddall*

An iconic image of the promotion season, as a Blade leads the chants from a beam high above fellow fans at Stadium MK. *Jamie Wallis*

Wilder had this tweet mounted on the home dressing room wall at the Lane as a reminder to his players what is expected of them every time they pull on a red and white shirt. *Danny Hall*

United somehow reached the 100-point mark in the season they won the league, despite weeks of celebrating. Billy Sharp prepares to lift the trophy for his boyhood club. *Jonny Buchan*

Bramall Lane was packed as United prepared to receive the League One trophy, on the final day of the season against Chesterfield. *Oliver Thorpe*

Fire greeted United onto the field against Chesterfield and they returned afterwards one by one – the biggest cheers for Sharp and then Wilder. *Ed Lambert*

A fan's view of the trophy lift, complete with flames. *Paul McDonald*

Leon Clarke gets in a little more champagne-spraying practise after weeks of celebrations for United. Wilder ensured they soaked up every last second of their success. *Sportimage*

Sharp sautes the Kop at the end of an unforgettable season, with 30 goals to his name and a title winner's medal around his neck. *Craig Dennis*

Wilder thanked wife Francesca and his pals for their support since he took over at United. *Francesca Wilder*

United's players enjoy the moment – some more forcefully than others!
Steve Hoole

Wilder's No.2, Alan Knill, gets a selfie for posterity with United's staff, with Paul Coutts sneaking on. Wilder later almost dropped the trophy off the bus.
Alex Moore

On the evening of the open-top parade, Sheffield was turned red and white – and Billy the Dog became a cult hero after joining in the fun.
Steve Hoole

After a number of awards evenings, United's players then went to Las Vegas for four nights to continue the celebrations – although the younger members of the squad missed out on some of the festivities!
Billy Sharp/SUFC

United's players took the time to meet their fans on tour in Malaga.
Daniel Oxley

United's 2017/18 campaign began with a 9-0 pre-season win at Stocksbridge Park Steels. *Anthony Sydney*

United's momentum from the title-winning campaign was damaged by back-to-back defeats, away at Middlesbrough and Cardiff. But led by Wilder and skipper Sharp, United never lost the faith. *Sportimage*

Sharp's late third against Derby at Bramall Lane sparked jubilant celebrations in front of the Kop – with goalkeeper Jamal Blackman even sprinting the length of the pitch to join in.
Matthew Colbert

Mark Duffy secured his place in history with this goal, to put United back ahead at Hillsborough and stop 30,000 Owls fans bouncing. He will forever be known as the 'bounce killer'. *Sportimage*

After their 4-2 victory over rivals Wednesday, Wilder gathered United's players in a huddle to soak up the moment before celebrating with the Blades fans at Hillsborough. *Tyrone Hoyland*

United were cheered on at Hillsborough by two former players in the away end, Michael Doyle and Marc McNulty. *Adam Smith*

Leon Clarke finished the 2017/18 season with 19 goals, and six-year-old Reece Woodhouse had a new hero – even rearranging the Christmas decorations to prove it. *Lee Woodhouse*

Clarke became the first man since Keith Edwards, in 1983, to score four goals in a game at Bramall Lane as United hammered Hull. Afterwards, the two met up for this picture.
Emma Wylie

Brooks earned his first caps for Wales in November – but there was no chance of his teammates letting him get carried away.
Sheffield United

Arguably the turning point of United's season: Coutts' broken leg away at Burton Albion. Victory sent United top of the league, but no-one felt like celebrating.
Sportimage

United's players in fancy dress on their Christmas party, in Dublin. The theme was famous duos and Clarke as Foxy Cleopatra was a particular highlight, although George Baldock made a convincing Harley Quinn. *George Baldock*

Fifty years after he signed for United, the Bramall Lane South Stand was named after Tony Currie – the club's greatest ever player. *Joe Bamford/Sheffield United*

The snowy scene at Bramall Lane as United took on Nottingham Forest in March, with the pitch markings in red to aid visibility and help the goal-line technology. *Andrew Rodgers*

Wilder wipes away tears after the last home game of the 2017/18 season, fearing it could be his last in charge of United. *Joe Bamford/Sheffield United*

John Fleck, signed on a free transfer from Coventry in 2016, was named United's official player of the season after a consistent and impressive 2017/18 campaign. *Sam Johnson*

The United manager then faced the media after signing a new deal at Bramall Lane in the summer. *Danny Hall*

Wilder and his trusted staff, including Knill, Matt Prestridge and Darren Ward. *Danny Hall*

Bury, who proved United's hero once more.

United were good value for their victory although the early sending off of former Blades loanee Conor Coady, for pulling down Clarke, undoubtedly played a part. At 1-0 behind, Neves also hit the post with a penalty after Jota had been fouled but Clarke, who began his nomadic 17-club career at Wolves, had the final say. Clarke, a thoughtful interviewee who avoids cliches almost as skillfully as he does defenders, stole the show in the media room afterwards when asked about his knack of scoring against former clubs – "I've had enough," came the deadpan reply. But Clarke was deadly serious when he reserved special praise for teammate Brooks, who was called up to the senior Wales squad for the first time on the back of his performance in the derby against Wednesday.

"Brooko is a really good player," Clarke said. "He can go as far in the game as he wants to if he listens to the management and staff and takes on people's advice. I think he is really, really good and I enjoy playing up front with him. He carries the ball well and it is important to have someone like that in the Championship. I do try and help him during games ... I tell him not to play in front of the big, muscle-bound defenders as he's not the strongest lad. His game is more playing off defenders, picking the ball up and driving at people. He really can go – providing he stays focused, which I'm sure he will do – as far in the business as he wants."

After six wins from their last seven games had seen United climb to second in the Championship, they ended a memorable month of September on a frustrating note after losing at Nottingham Forest. Wilder's men, wearing their white third kit for the first time, looked good value to extend their good run of form when John Lundstam put them ahead within three minutes, but Forest hit back through Jason Cummings and Kieran Dowell in the first half to seal victory. Carter-Vickers thought he had earned United a point in the dying moments before his header hit the post, but Wilder refused to criticise his side – instead hailing the performance as one that showed United "had landed in the Championship". "It was an outstanding performance, one that did not get rewarded with a win," he added. "I am not going soft, but some of the boys might have expected a rocket. They did not deserve one."

'The bounce killer'
By Mark Duffy, forward

I came off the pitch at Hillsborough and Billy Sharp told me that I would be a Blades legend forever, because of *that* goal. I didn't know what he was on about because Leon had scored twice, so I thought he should surely have been the legend if anyone! But I guess the timing of the goal is what made it so special. It just summed up what we're like, and what the gaffer has made us like. We keep going until the final whistle and never stop believing in what we're doing.

The derby was the biggest game I'd ever played in, by far. In the build up, the gaffer and Billy told us all about it but you don't really believe it until it happens. Then as the week went on it got bigger and bigger and then, the gaffer told me I wasn't playing. I was absolutely devastated, fuming, but knew I had to get behind the boys who were playing. I sandwiched myself between Ched and Leon when we got off the bus and they were getting absolute pelters. The atmosphere was a joke. The day just panned out so well.

We were wondering how it wasn't 4-0 or 5-0 at half-time but we gave them a lifeline they didn't deserve and in the second half, they started to gain momentum. I got sent on, told to keep the pressure on them high up the pitch so they couldn't get out. I hadn't been on the pitch long and they scored. The whole ground was bouncing. But not for long.

I remember there being a few bad passes and then I got on the end of a Bash header, and played a one-two with Leon before sort of going into my zone. Normally in that situation I try and pass when I can but in that moment, time just seemed to slow down and I just manoeuvred my way in. Because of the tight angle I thought 'right, just put your laces through it' and I caught it so sweet. The scenes were unbelievable. I still get sent videos and stuff now. After the game, I reckon I had 10,000 messages, tweets, emails ... my phone went into absolute overdrive. People have made all sorts of that moment, pictures and mugs and steel plaques and badges. I've got all sorts of stuff. But I never tire of seeing the goal. Some players go a whole career without something so special happening.

It's hard to explain what goes through your head at a moment like that. Apart from the birth of your kids it's one of the best feelings possible and even then, it's a different feeling; that ecstasy, out of nowhere. Your heartbeat goes to 200bpm in a matter of seconds. I remember looking up and seeing fans going berserk and flares going off ... it just meant so much to everyone. There's a great video of the Wednesday fans bouncing and then the camera pans to the top of the away end just after the goal. I don't know why they uploaded them all, to be honest! You'd think they'd have all been deleted.

But I'm glad they weren't. My dad has them all on his iPad and watches them when he's had a drink! He runs through it with me and asks what I'm thinking when I get the ball, but it's just instinct really. I just did what I did as a kid in Liverpool, when I was six or seven years old. It came from playing on the streets as a kid and it could have been anyone in goal or in the opposition. I'd have scored many goals like that in the youth clubs growing up, actually. Just not in front of 32,000 fans in a local derby!

Leon scored twice that day but that's brushed under the carpet because of that moment that stopped them bouncing. I'm now known as the Bounce Killer! It was an unbelievable moment. Wednesday had been in the Championship for all that time and we heard all sorts about playing in the pub league, while they thought they'd be going for promotion again. But football doesn't work like that and no team has a God-given right to be anywhere, as they found out this season with a nice healthy gap between us and them in the table. But there's a clean slate in the new season and we have to make sure we're better and achieve more from now on.

I grew up in Huyton and it was probably one of the last eras of kids who'd play football on the streets for hours, until your mum called you in at night when it got dark. Now a lot of kids stay indoors on their PlayStations – I've got two daughters myself and I don't think I'd like them to be out playing on the streets. But I had a fantastic childhood doing that and I'd encourage them to do it as much as is safe; you learn a lot of life skills out there, and I always wanted to compete with the bigger and older kids because I was talented. A lot of players came from Huyton like Steven Gerrard, Joey Barton, Lee Trundle and David Nugent, and we all actually went to the same youth club. In Liverpool you really either wanted to play football or take up boxing, and I was really small as a kid so used to get pummeled when I tried to box. Thankfully, football worked out for me. Eventually.

I'm a big Liverpool fan and I played for them until I was 16, but Gerard Houllier released me because I wasn't a 6ft athlete. It absolutely broke my heart. I didn't tell anyone for months and then I didn't play for another 18 months or so; I'd completely fallen out of love with the game. It was a big part of my life and to be told I wasn't good enough ... I felt ashamed. I started to concentrate on the real world and a couple of mates asked if I wanted to come and play football with them. I told them I didn't fancy it until they said I'd get paid £40 – I was only on Education Maintenance Allowance at college at the time, so I said yeah.

My plan was to go down the coaching side, and I became an apprentice with Liverpool Council as a sports coach, going into schools and giving PE lessons. I really enjoyed that. I'd see kids who were a bit shy and didn't want to get involved, but come out of their shell week by week and their parents would thank me. I had to be persuaded to give that up and go into full-time football, because I had experienced rejection and didn't want that again.

I then had some decent times at Southport and Morecambe and worked with Alan Knill at Scunthorpe, who was brilliant for me and brought me on as a 'thinking' footballer. I nearly ended up at United twice before, as well; once at Morecambe when Scunthorpe and United were interested, but United wanted to hold off until the summer so I went to Scunny. I always remember the unbelievable following that United took everywhere, though, and for whatever reason I always used to play well against them.

I remember one game when I scored after running from the halfway line! The second time was when they lost in the play-off final to Huddersfield on penalties, and I could have signed that summer. But I ended up at Doncaster in the Championship instead.

So this was a case of third time lucky ... and even then, it nearly didn't happen! Knilly called me and said he and the gaffer were going to Charlton, so did I fancy joining them there. I'd just had my second daughter and I live in Liverpool so I said not really, as living in London never interested me. Then he called me back and said 'what about Sheffield United?' and I thought 'yeah, that does sound good'. There was interest from a couple of Championship clubs but I always held United in high regard.

Then, after four games, I wondered what I had done! But we went from strength to strength as the season went on and ended up just blowing teams apart. Towards the end of the season teams came to Bramall Lane, we'd kick off and they'd just physically retreat, hoping for a draw. It was far and away the best season I've ever had, and that most of the boys have ever had. And then the gaffer had us on about a six-week bender! I couldn't cope. I'm not a big drinker anyway but we had awards nights on Saturday, Sunday, Monday, Tuesday and Wednesday and then flew to Las Vegas for a couple of days on the Thursday. But what a trip, with the best set of lads you could wish for.

Experiences like that make you appreciate how fortunate you are to be a footballer, but my grounding in the 'real world' helps too. At Birmingham I spent a lot of time in the U23 group and they don't live in the real world; everything is given to them and they expect it to carry on forever. Some don't appreciate it. With me being from a background of being released, I had the determination to say I wasn't going to let that happen again. You don't want to lose the privilege you have of being a professional footballer because one day, whether it's someone else making the decision by releasing you or your body saying 'that's enough', it will come to an end. So you've got to appreciate it while it's there, and give everything you can to it.

How long can I keep going? A good few years yet I hope. I love football and I think I have a good tactical brain, so I'll probably carry on doing my coaching badges and see where it takes me. The gaffer here isn't a bad role model to follow really, starting out where he did and enjoying the success he has. He's shown you can climb the ladder quickly if you have your principles, and stick to them. He's a Blade through and through and it absolutely kills him when we lose, but we've all bought into the ethos and how much it means to have put Sheffield United back on the map. It seemed as though the club had fallen so far and Wednesday fans were basically laughing at United, but we've given the club back to the fans and put it back on a level playing field. It's not little old Sheffield United anymore ... if anything, we're a better team than them, as the table showed. They've got to wrestle the rights off us to be the No.1 club in the city because at the minute, they're a long way behind us.

We go out for a beer in town sometimes and people come up to us and tell us how much it means ... you can see it in their eyes. To be in the shadows for so long and put up with the 'pub team' taunts ... they've got to enjoy it while it's happening. And long may it continue. To be honest, while ever the gaffer, Knilly, the staff and these players are around, I can't see it changing.

September 2017 – On a Sunday night ...
By Paul Commons, Kop

Regardless of what Wednesday fans say posthumously, September 24 was the day that every Sheffield football fan had been salivating over for the last six years; the return of the Steel City derby. To explain the magnitude of this already bitter rivalry is difficult enough, but it had been further fermented, from a United perspective, by six years of torture since Wednesday improbably escaped what they later termed 'the pub league', at our expense. Six years is a long time to repeatedly play Bury.

The truth is, that stuff hurts. Feelings linger and manifest. These are people that we work with, live with and laugh with, or at, every single day. For too long we had been the ones getting laughed at. Wednesday had established themselves as a force in the Championship, a division we had only dreamed of grazing for what seemed like an eternity. Going into the derby at Hillsborough, even the most mild-mannered of my Wednesday-leaning friends had suddenly found an irresistible urge to snipe at our chances. The form table told a very different story, however, and in the build-up to the match, caveats like "even if you somehow take a share of the points, it won't matter ... let's look at the table next May," were added. Isn't hindsight a wonderful thing? I have been a Blade all my life, and genuinely struggle to remember a game in which Sheffield United had come out on top when it mattered.

Multiple trips to Wembley; the Millennium Stadium; Liverpool away; Wigan at home ... the list goes on. Neutrals will argue that, over the course of a season, the derby didn't matter too much. Certainly one manager went to bed the night before believing this to be the case. The other, though, struggled to get a wink of sleep. Something felt different about this game. United no longer felt like a team that didn't turn up in the games that "mattered". Chris Wilder's United were a different beast. We knew that. Wednesday knew that. I genuinely believe that Wednesday were hoping that their imperious status, and seemingly endless budget, would see them come out on top and avoid the ultimate embarrassment against players they had belittled and derided.

All football fans are guilty of thinking their respective team's derbies are the biggest, their rivalry the fiercest. All I know is that I've never wanted us to win a game as much as I did that day. Is that strange? Perhaps. It was a game early on in the season where points mattered little. How many people though, I wonder, would disagree with me? Wednesday were expected to win at a canter. Perhaps this was a true reflection of the wider audience, unfamiliar with the standards to which Wilder holds his players accountable. But, at this point I will hold my hands up. The morning the team was announced I felt a wave of panic hit me, the likes of which I've not experienced since Steve Simonsen began his run-up to *that* penalty at Wembley.

David Brooks was starting; inwardly, I was shouting "too soon Wilder!" Two minutes is all it took for me to suspect I'd be eating my words. By the third minute I'd forgotten that they'd even been inwardly spoken. John Fleck's conversion of the free-kick set off explosions of crimson in the Leppings Lane end and in that moment of sheer class, skill and ingenuity, he had given us a foothold for retribution. The message from Wilder was there for all to see: 'get at them fast and early, quieten their fans'. The first ripple of that net brought a palpable feeling that a weight had been lifted. All of a sudden, the pedestal upon which Wednesday fans had placed themselves was looking incredibly fragile.

Then, it got even better. I don't think anyone, least of all the man himself, could argue that Leon Clarke's time at Wednesday will be remembered as his career's purple patch [which looks increasingly likely to be at Bramall Lane]. It was always going to be a tough game of mental chess for him that day at Hillsborough and his goal, to extend our lead inside the first 15 minutes, is one that will always live long in the memory. For me, it epitomised the differences between the teams that season; Wednesday were a collection of players, ones that would be hard pressed to figure out each other's first names under any sort of duress. On the other hand we were always alert, always looking to read each other and gamble on balls in anticipation of a teammate's capability to deliver when it mattered.

The stroke of half-time is either the worst time to concede or the best time to score, depending which side of the fence you're sat on, and Wednesday's route back into the derby was particularly unnerving. The whole complexion of the game was changed in an instant, from the manager's team-talk to the fans' apprehension. That sloppy goal immediately felt like it would cost us. As expected, Wednesday came out in the second half applying most of the pressure, but another moment of magic from Brooks could have easily ended in Clarke doubling our lead, and his tally for the day. His miss left many, myself included, thinking the writing might be on the wall. When Lucas Joao's effort clattered in, nearly taking the netting into row Z, I, like many, feared the worst.

Couple the palpable deflation with THAT bouncing. It has to be one of the most abhorrent scenes in football, up there with half and half scarves. I think, truthfully, I was just bitter at this point about what the bouncing meant. Wednesday believed they were going to have the last laugh at United's expense once more. Sections of Blades supporters seemed resigned to the same conclusion. We'd seen it all play out before, the script was written. Only one winner from hereon in.

Now, I've witnessed my fair share of special goals (having grown up digesting Michael Brown's pearlers on what seemed to be a weekly basis) but what I saw Mark Duffy do to that game ... the goal itself, the timing, the magnitude ... I'm going to stick my neck on the line and say that, all things considered, this is up there with the very best. I maintain to this day that there was a full second delay between the ball hitting the Wednesday net and the wild celebrations that followed. No-one could quite believe that we'd react so quickly to being pegged back, and Duffy's goal will live with me for the rest of my life. To me, that was when we sent the message to Wednesday: 'This isn't your city, you will not decide how this ends. We're here to stay and you'll no longer be having things your own way'.

I've since enjoyed videos, showing the bouncing in the home end at the moment he scored. Some of the Wednesday fans were in such disbelief about what had happened they were still bouncing, as the top of the Leppings Lane end clawed over each other to get a tiny bit closer to their new hero beneath. Our last goal represents everything about that sunny, September Sunday afternoon at Hillsborough and offers a rather fitting summary of the first Steel City derby of the season. Clarke had absolutely no right to win that ball. The Wednesday defenders were favourites. Sheer determination and a will to win got Clarke his goal. United had no right to win that derby. Wednesday were favourites. Sheer determination and a will to win got us the three points.

It was a similar story at the beginning of the month, when United went to Wearside to take on Sunderland; fresh out of the Premier League, parachute payments and all, and good players to boot. Clayton Donaldson, United's striker, cost £50,000 – less than Sunderland paid Jack Rodwell each week. Another game, on paper, that United had no right to win. On the grass, 33-year-old Donaldson made himself an instant hero with two goals to seal victory, although it was a late cameo from Brooks that left Blades fans clamouring for more after his performances with England at the Toulon Tournament over the summer.

I actually felt that the midweek trip to Bolton, who had joined us in the Championship, would be one of the sternest tests of the season and if it wasn't quite a 'must-win' game, it was certainly important to avoid defeat. A sort of mini-rivalry was developing between the clubs either side of the Pennines after Bolton chairman Ken Anderson's bizarre comments aimed at United, seemingly borne out of bitterness, and our old friend Gary Madine playing the role of the pantomime villain. To come away from the game with three points, and minus any injuries, was a feeling of relief more than ecstasy all told.

It was a vastly different feeling at the end of the Norwich home game, the week before the short trip to Wednesday. It was a bizarre game. United had a lot of the ball but never looked the most likely to break the deadlock and as soon as Norwich opened the scoring, there was a palpable sense of inevitability. 'Game management' is one way of describing how the visitors closed out the match; Wilder's less eloquent label of 'time-wasting', which he called 'ridiculous', seemed more apt.

Many fans, again including me, did wonder what the state of mind of the players would be when they faced Wolves, the league's star side, just days after the derby at Hillsborough. Wolves' wealth had seen the likes of Ruben Neves arriving in the Black Country from Porto, and I believed that one of two things would happen: either we would potentially run out of steam or momentum would carry us through and we might just continue to take scalps that no-one thought we had a right to. Despite all of the pre-season hype around many teams, I was yet to see anyone in the division who convinced me that we were out of our depth, or that we would be outclassed and unable to compete.

Wolves did start very brightly, but so did we. There seemed to be a hell of a tacticians' battle going on in the middle of the park with Paul Coutts and £15m man Neves both looking to dictate the tempo. I turned to my dad after 10 or 12 minutes and said something along the lines of "we need an early goal to settle us here. We'll most likely have to score a couple to get anything against these".

Conor Coady's early bath seemed to bring a sense of relief. We had gone all guns blazing in the first 15 minutes and Wolves had been the only team, so far, to soak up the pressure so elegantly and look to apply their own. It suddenly became clear that, at this level, fine margins cost you games and had Wolves not been reduced to ten men I believe the scoreline would have looked different. Once again, however, our no fear attitude and willingness to attack teams paid rich dividends in the form of points. I'll never get bored of watching my team go at another – just like no-one gets bored of watching two 'sluggers' in a boxing ring. Football is an entertainment business and we were certainly being entertained.

Even at Forest. After taking the lead, it felt more like a case of how many goals we would score. That's football sometimes though. Losing a game we absolutely dominated. To leave the City Ground having had nearly two-thirds of possession, with our heads down, showed just how much the expectation level had risen. For a fan, it's so refreshing to see a manager stick with a philosophy that has brought the club success. The taste of defeat at Forest was sour, but it showed one thing ... Chris Wilder only knows one way to play. The winning way.

11

Top of the tree with another derby day win
October 2017

Another month, another international break for Chris Wilder's Sheffield United; another novelty of life in the Championship. But although a part of the United manager will no doubt have been glad of the break, to refresh tired bodies and minds amongst his small squad, another part was itching to get back out there. As they entered October, United were third in the table after impressive victories over the likes of Derby, Sunderland, Wolves and Sheffield Wednesday and, after opening the scoring at the City Ground in a game against Nottingham Forest that United certainly didn't deserve to lose, John Lundstram admitted that United's focus had shifted from simply consolidating their place in the division. Backed by their manager, United were only looking upwards.

Unlike many of their divisional rivals, who elected to jet off to sunnier climes and warm-weather training camps, United opted to remain in the more modest surroundings of Shirecliffe with a particular focus placed on getting some of their walking wounded back to full fitness. Richard Stearman, their marquee defensive signing in the summer, had limped off against Cardiff the month before with a hamstring injury and Kieron Freeman, who scored 11 goals from right back in United's title-winning year, was nursing a rib injury; his fitness made all the more important after fellow wing-back George Baldock limped off with a calf problem early on against Forest.

Caolan Lavery, the former Wednesday striker, was also nearing a return after suffering a horrendous facial injury after a clash of heads against Derby County back in August. The Canadian was forced to go under the knife several times to relieve the pressure on his broken eye socket and at one stage, United feared that he might lose the sight in one eye. Broken, bruised but not beaten, Lavery posted a photo of his injuries from his hospital bed on social media and after being fitted with a mask to protect his face, was given the all-clear to resume training.

One player who wasn't to spend the international break at Shirecliffe, however, was David Brooks, who instead joined up with the senior Wales squad for the first time for their crucial World Cup 2018 qualifiers against Georgia and the Republic of Ireland. Brooks, who was born in Warrington but qualifies for Wales through his Llangollen-born mum Cathryn, became the subject of a mini tug-of-war over the summer when he was named in both England and Wales' squads for the Toulon Tournament, within minutes of each other.

After giving his word that he would represent England in France, Brooks returned with a winners' medal around his neck and the player of the tournament award under his arm – although he didn't know he'd won it until the following day, because the announcement was made in French – and was then called up to Wales' U21 squad in September, managed by former Blade Rob Page. Brooks scored a superb goal against Switzerland in a 3-0 victory and Chris Coleman, the then-manager of the Welsh senior side, was known to be a fan of Brooks' abilities – but he did not get off the bench as Wales beat Georgia 1-0 in Tbilisi, setting up an intriguing clash with the Irish at the Cardiff City Stadium. In front of a passionate, packed Welsh crowd, and backed by a contingent of his family, Brooks again didn't get on the field as James McClean's winner ended Wales' hopes of reaching the 2018 World Cup in Russia.

"I found out I was in the squad at training with United," Brooks said. "A lot of people were congratulating me but wouldn't say what for! I was doing some stretching and the TV came up with the Wales squad on, and the gaffer was keeping it a secret for me. I couldn't really contain myself. After training

I was straight on the phone to my mum and she already knew! I had a few nerves before I met up with the Wales boys because I knew all about the initiation where the new lads have to sing a song.

"I wasn't keen but it was all part of it, so I had to do it. The lads were winding me up by tapping glasses but then not letting me do it, keeping me on edge for a couple of days, but eventually I got it out of the way! I sang *Hey There Delilah* by the Plain White T's, a safe option with not too many high notes. I haven't got the best singing voice so the boys were laughing, but I enjoyed my time on the camp.

"The likes of Gareth Bale and Aaron Ramsey are chatty and make you feel welcome, but you do feel a bit starstruck and I tended to mingle with people more my own age. I made good mates with Ethan Ampadu and Ben Woodburn and that made it easier for me, as I could spend time with them. With superstars like Bale and Ramsey there is a bit of caution, because you can't go in there and try and be the best player. I just wanted to avoid having a shocker and have people looking at me thinking 'why is he here?' I just tried to train well and hope for my opportunity. It didn't come, but the experience was brilliant for the future."

Like Brooks, Lafferty also failed to get on the pitch for Northern Ireland's qualifying defeats to Norway and reigning world champions Germany, but it was the youngster's Welsh call-up, just 48 days after making his senior league debut for Wilder's side, which dominated the headlines. Mum Cathryn was good enough to give an interview just as she was leaving the house to head to Cardiff with the rest of the Brooks clan before the Northern Ireland game, and remembered her son's determination to make it in the game after he was released by Manchester City as a youngster.

"Playing football is all he ever wanted to do," Cathryn remembers. "He just dealt with the news from City as if it was the next step, to be honest. He's very level-headed but was still determined that he was going to make it. He didn't have a plan B in case it didn't work out; he just kept his head down and kept up his dedication to the game. So it was lovely when Sheffield

United came in for him. He's loved it there, in digs since he was 16, so credit to United for giving him the opportunities they have."

Howard Dean was the man who spotted Brooks at City's Platt Lane training base before their new owners changed the landscape in Manchester, and brought him to United after he was released. "I always knew it was a matter of when, not if, Brooksy would become available," Dean, United's former national academy chief scout, said. "City had their Arab money and their recruitment dynamic changed completely. I first saw Brooksy at 14 and thought, this kid can play. If there was any grass on the mudheaps at Platt Lane, he glided across it and I knew he'd be a player for United. A lot of people, including Travis Binnion, John Dungworth and Chris Morgan were instrumental in developing him, but Chris Wilder also deserves a huge amount of credit for having the bravery to give him a chance in the first team.

"At the time, my missus, Karen, and I were a sort of home from home for United's marquee young players and we had kids from all over the world stay with us. David came for a few months, so we helped with his personality too. He was a very shy, introverted lad and we helped him with that integration into the football club. It's an important thing, really. Lots of different pieces have got to click in place with young players. They're humans, not robots, and that personal touch is vital. But when I'm scouting, I always tell people to look beyond the obvious. There'll be a group of 14 and one or two will be virtually men; they'll be shaving. But there'll be one at the back, a little technical player, who will often eclipse all others. That was Brooksy.

"I had no doubts he'd make it, but my final question was: can he play on the bigger stage? Can he handle it? And I remember watching the Sheffield Derby, when he stuck it through Jack Hunt's legs and was man of the match. Well, that's when he answered me. There's no bigger stage than that. To me, that was like Wayne Rooney's goal against Arsenal at 16, or Ryan Giggs' run and finish against Arsenal. The day he arrived. He'll handle everything that comes his way, without a doubt. I don't have a worry about Brooksy, whatsoever. Not one."

Brooks' rapid rise continued when he returned to South Yorkshire, and put pen to paper on a new and improved four-year deal at Bramall Lane – just months after signing extended terms following his success in Toulon. As Carl Shieber directed the various bits of paperwork under Brooks' nose to sign with Wilder almost protectively looking over his right shoulder, United live-streamed the surprise announcement on social media and the response from their supporters spoke volumes about Brooks' new-found status as a key player. "If you ask my mum or dad, they'll tell you that I'm quite a chilled character and I just feel that whatever happens, will happen," he said. "So being called up by Wales and training with the likes of Bale and Ramsey, or playing for United in big games, didn't faze me.

"Obviously, it's always nice for fans to see a player come through the system and represent the first team and I like to hear them singing my name, of course. I've got a job to do for the team when I play, but I just try to go out there and enjoy myself. I think that's important, because you never know what's around the corner."

It was a whirlwind few weeks for Brooks but the youngster was back on the bench when club football finally returned on October 14, although he did get a run-out after replacing Billy Sharp in the 68th minute of United's 1-0 victory over Ipswich Town. Leon Clarke was inches away from continuing his white-hot run of goalscoring form when he hit the crossbar but it was the unlikely figure of Chris Basham who was the hero of the day, with a bullet header to settle the game. Basham was operating at right wing-back after Kieron Freeman, making his comeback from a rib injury, dislocated his knee in a tangle with teammate Cameron Carter-Vickers but rose highest to head home John Fleck's deep cross four minutes into the second half.

Barnsley boy Mick McCarthy, the visiting manager, was scathing about the goal his side conceded and admitted the result made him "bloody angry" but bubbled with praise for United. "They're a good side and I think they'll finish top six," he said. "I don't see them falling away. They've got momentum, which is a powerful thing, but they've also got good players."

The next side to succumb to Wilder's Blades were Reading; another week, another victory at Bramall Lane and another well-placed opposition manager talking up United's top-six hopes. The Royals' luminous away kit with random half-hoops was far from regal, they had lost the previous season's play-off final on penalties to Huddersfield at Wembley – a feeling United were more than familiar with – and had struggled with the hangover under Jaap Stam, the former PSV Eindhoven, Manchester United and Milan defender. The CVs of the two managers could hardly have been more different, but it was the ex-Rotherham United, Notts County and Bradford right-back who won the tactical battle on the day as United swarmed all over Reading and remained level on points with second-placed Cardiff.

A rare Paul Coutts goal was a collectors' item in more ways than one, the midfielder sweeping a superb strike into the top corner on his return from suspension, and Sharp tapped home Mark Duffy's excellent cross to double their advantage. The introduction of John Swift, a player who caught the eye at Bramall Lane before while on loan at Swindon, gave the visitors a lift and Roy Beerens pulled a goal back in the 85th minute, but United held out for a victory that Stam, with 67 Dutch caps and four league titles on his professional CV, admitted afterwards was well deserved.

"The gaffer is a Sheffield United fan," man of the match Duffy said. "It means a lot to him and also to Billy, who is a supporter, too. They leave nobody in any doubt what it means to represent this football club and the fans are right behind us – because they can see everyone trying their hardest and giving 100 percent. Put that together with the quality we've got, then it's a good blend. I've been at places before where the dressing room wasn't great, where there were little splits and divides in the group but here, we've got each other's backs and if we haven't, then it's not tolerated. Everyone is together, everyone has bought into the club and everyone loves it here. We just enjoy coming into work."

There were more good times to come, but it was the way in which United had taken so comfortably to life in the Championship which created some debate when Phil Brown, a guest on the *Football on 5* highlights show, hailed Wilder as the 'manager of the century' but then used the word 'momentum' liberally in an attempt to describe United's second successive push for promotion. Some Blades agreed – after all, they had won 30 of their 46 matches in League One, every game in pre-season and more than their fair share in the Championship – but others felt it did a disservice, both to Wilder and the damn good players at his disposal. Their momentum, for example, would have been largely eroded back in August when United lost back-to-back games, against Middlesbrough and Cardiff, for the first time in almost a year. Of their next ten games, they won eight.

That became nine from 11 on the following Friday night, when United beat Leeds just up the M1 at Elland Road and went top of the Championship in front of the Sky Sports cameras. Not that Wilder was in any rush to use that as motivation – publicly, at least. "We're not talking about going top," said Wilder before the game. "But we won't fear it if we do. We won't all of a sudden think 'whoa, what are we doing here?' – that didn't happen last year and it won't now. If three points takes us top of the league, then that's all it means. Just that we've won more games at this point in the season. Nothing more."

By Wilder's reckoning, United's status as by far the biggest team in League One equipped them to deal with many things that the Championship would throw at them and also avoid them buckling under any pressure that might come their way. It helped, too, that United had *the messiah* in charge – at least, that was the description afforded to Wilder by Prince Abdullah, the club's co-owner, in a rare interview, with James Shield of *The Star* on the eve of the Leeds game. "Chris loves Sheffield United," the Saudi royal added. "He is 'one of us' as they say. But I am not daft enough to think Chris is not an ambitious guy. He is loyal but ambitious, and so are we. We must match those ambitions. I say to my friends: 'I want him to be the next Sir Alex Ferguson.' I want him to be here for 15 to 20 years."

The last five minutes or so of games were often christened 'Fergie Time' during the Scot's hugely successful 26 years at

Manchester United – which included an out-of-the blue call to Wilder to offer support and advice during a particularly difficult period at Oxford United – but it was a quick start that was beginning to define Wilder's era at the first and original United. And they were quick out of the blocks once more at Elland Road, going ahead through former Leeds striker Sharp in just the second minute after good link-up play between Clarke and Duffy.

Leeds goalkeeper Andy Lonergan then denied Sharp with two superb saves in the first half as the visitors imposed themselves on the game, but they were rocked ten minutes before half-time when Kalvin Phillips levelled the scores with a well-taken volley that gave Jamal Blackman little chance. Samuel Saiz hit the post for Leeds before Phillips was extremely fortunate to pick up only a booking for a dangerous late challenge on George Baldock – the referee, Scott Duncan, was the same official who sent Wilder to the stands for kicking water bottles against Norwich. But United had the last laugh in the 81st minute when substitute Brooks picked up Duffy's perfectly-weighted pass, slid a superb first-time finish past Lonergan and sent his side top of the Championship table.

To the press, however, Wilder was in conciliatory, rather than celebratory, mood. "It's a win," he said, "and we're made up to come here on a night like tonight and get three points. But I didn't think the performance was anything special. We turned the ball over too much and made elementary mistakes in possession. We were okay in our box and better in their box, but the bits in between disappointed and frustrated me because we should have had more control of the game. They are the standards that the boys have set for themselves. We've got a target on our back now so we have to be a little bit better. Every game is more significant now because we are top of the division. We don't have any egos in our dressing room and we won't be taking any backwards steps. We want to keep the hammer down now."

Duffy remembers seeing the game rather differently. "I thought we were unbelievable at Leeds and we were expecting a pat on the back, but he was raging! We'd just gone top of the league and I thought 'oh my God'. I'd got in that position a few times without getting the ball and eventually I got it, saw Brooksy's great movement and slid him in. It was his first goal and came at a perfect time really, although his celebration needs work. I think Baldock was celebrating for him in front of the fans! But it was another derby success in a season of them."

Wilder's warning was to prove prophetic, however, when the target on United's back was found just four days later by Queens Park Rangers at Loftus Road, albeit in slightly freak circumstances. A hopeful punt from QPR's back line, in just the fourth minute of the game, stuck slightly in the West London air and Blackman came out to claim. QPR striker Idrissa Sylla had given up his chase and Blades defender Carter-Vickers attempted to get out of the giant goalkeeper's way, to no avail; the two collided, Blackman came crashing down from a great height onto the turf and spilled the ball straight into Sylla's path.

Baldock's reaction, hands on head in disbelief, just about summed it up and after five minutes of on-field treatment, Blackman was carried off on a stretcher. Clarke had a second-half strike ruled out for offside, but Sylla wasted enough chances to have sealed a hat-trick on a rare off night for the Blades, who slipped back to third. "Our start wasn't the greatest, with the injury to Jamal and the goal, but I just didn't think we deserved anything," Wilder said. "I'm disappointed with my team. We've been out-fought and out-battled and didn't show enough quality. It was a deserved defeat."

At half-time, United's greatest ever player Tony Currie was inducted into the Hall of Fame of QPR, another of his former clubs in his home city of London. It was perhaps the only memorable moment for anyone of a Blades persuasion all evening.

'A breath of fresh air'
By Tony Currie, Sheffield United's greatest ever player

Sheffield United is my club, without a doubt. After so many years, it couldn't really be any other. I have an affinity with QPR because they were my first club and I was desperate to sign for them at 15, but United is a phenomenal club and the support is fantastic. It said a lot that United were at Leicester on the night that the club put on a special dinner for me, and Kevin McCabe came to that instead of the game! I like to think I've done a job for them, in the community and as an ambassador as well as a player. The amount of people that come to me and say 'you're the reason I support this club' is unbelievable and people are still saying it to this day.

Gary Sinclair sometimes announces me onto the pitch and starts bowing to me. I tell him to get up, the bloody fool! He always introduces me as the club's greatest ever player before each game when I'm with the sponsors, which is always lovely to hear, but I don't take it in an arrogant way. I was a big-head on the pitch, of course, but that was only because I was confident in my ability. To be fair, we haven't had a lot since my day – Brian Deane, Phil Jagielka ... Jimmy Hagan's lot will have passed away and Joe Shaw was a fantastic player, so it's a great honour. After the special night at Bramall Lane I phoned up Radio Sheffield and ended up taking over the bloody show! I only wanted to say a few words but from then on it was the Currie show. Even a Wednesday fan called in and said I was the greatest, and I was choking up listening at home.

It all started for me on New Year's Day in 1950. I was a Chelsea fan as a youngster but my dad left when I was four, so my uncles Bert and Jim followed me all over the country watching me play. Jimmy Greaves was my hero as a youngster and I had trials with Chelsea, as a centre-half, but they knocked me back so I got a job with a building firm called Roberts Brothers and played Sunday League in Regent's Park for a side called Kiwi United. We played a lot of away games at Hackney Marshes and it was hard to know which goal you were aiming at sometimes; there were hundreds of pitches, back to back, with about six yards between them!

There are hundreds of kids who don't make it and there is a part of you that thinks 'this isn't going to happen' but I kept plugging away, and Watford came in for me. Then on February

1, 1968, at 18 years and one month old, I moved to Bramall Lane. It was a big move for a Londoner who'd never been out of the capital and I remember it being dark and dingy up in Sheffield when I got off the train. I went in digs for a month or so before I got married on March 2. I'd scored on my debut against Spurs but missed the game after to get married; John Harris had me in his office for an hour saying 'we'll get you a fast car, get the wedding over with and get to Leicester ...' I said I couldn't, and we went down at the end of the season. So I experienced three divisions in about three months!

I never once had any reservations about coming up to Sheffield. Things were moving fast, I was an England youth international but I never thought I'd 'made it'. Len Badger and the like were great, they looked after me like a little family and I'm close to quite a few of them. We're like brothers. I had over eight years with Alan Woodward which was great – we had such a telepathy, especially when I went back into midfield when the goals dried up – and we had a good team, with internationals like myself, Gil Reece, Eddie Colquhoun, Dave Powell and Trevor Hockey. If we could have just added another couple of class players we could have done something, but there you go.

I also had the distinction of being one of the first, if not the first, player to be yellow-carded for being substituted! I was taken off at Swindon by Ken Furphy and Roger Kirkpatrick, who we used to call Mr Pickwick, booked me for leaving the field without his permission. But one of my biggest regrets is not getting more caps for England – in fact, I think if Sir Alf Ramsey hadn't got sacked, I could have been England captain.

There weren't many more skilful players than me at that time and I played about six in a row for Alf, then he left and everything started again. I missed the six months of Joe Mercer when he was blooding all the skilful youngsters and then Don Revie came in. I got one cap in three years, and the press got me that. I probably missed out on 20 or 30 caps with Alf and the same with Revie. Of course we didn't qualify for the 1974 and 1978 World Cups as well but look at the likes of Rodney Marsh who only got a few caps, Frank Worthington only got eight, Charlie George only got one ... and I got 17 on my own, so I suppose I should be grateful for that. But Revie put England back ten years.

Then when I retired, I was living at home with my mum and had nothing, although I didn't take the dole, when United offered me a testimonial. So I came up and they offered me a job in the community, which was a lifesaver. I got a house in Dronfield and I'm so proud of the work I did. We put so many bums on seats at Bramall Lane and a few players came through my Soccer Schools as well; Billy Sharp and George Long are just two. Harry Bassett signed on a month before I came back as community officer and I knew all the players personally, and obviously Chris Wilder was a part of that so I had a good relationship with him. I think he's taken a few things from Harry ... he plays a different way, but his man management style is great. I love the way they play.

Of course, I have a moan now and again when we miss a bleeding sitter but in the promotion season, the three midfielders we had were the best outside the Premier League. Coutts, Fleck and Duffy are phenomenal players but if you take one out, they're not as powerful. It's a bit like Iniesta, Xavi and Messi at Barcelona a few years ago! They're a joy to watch. I haven't ever seen a United team play possession football like that.

And now, they play it in front of the Tony Currie Stand at Bramall Lane after the South Stand was named in my honour, just to cap a fantastic year. My playing days were such a long time ago that children need to ask their great-grandparents about me rather than their father, but I have so many special memories because of the Blades and to have a stand named after me just fills me with genuine pride and happiness.

I was in a garden centre in Barlborough when Kevin called me to tell me the news. I was absolutely shocked and choked. I couldn't speak for a short while and I later 'unveiled' the stand before our friendly with Inter Milan. That's when it sunk in and became 'real'.

When I left as a player I never expected to come 'home'. I'd just like to thank everyone that I've met and worked with throughout my time associated with this club.

It is the best club in the world in my eyes and our supporters, I'm sure, will say exactly the same.

Now, as I'm getting older, I want to see us in the Premier League before long. The way Chris has got the team playing is phenomenal. They're not invincible, by any stretch, but we're a bloody good team and Chris has been a breath of fresh air. He's had nothing but success and I am really proud of him. He's one of our own, as they say.

October 2017 – The climb to the top
By Max Hill, Bramall Lane Upper

After an unrelenting start to the season, the beginning of October gave United a chance to draw breath and reflect on an incredible start to the season in a novelty of life back in the Championship – the international break! Trips to the Lane were replaced with visits to IKEA and Meadowhall but it did, at least, give us a chance to take it all in.

What a start it had been. I can't think of many Blades who genuinely thought we'd be sat in third after nearly a quarter of the season, but there we were. Early defeats at Middlesbrough and Cardiff gave stark reminders of the perils of the big scary Championship but it was a very positive start – albeit with our feet kept firmly on the ground.

While the fixtures were less frenetic in October there were still some interesting match-ups. Ipswich are a club who seemed to have specialised in just 'being' in the Championship for ages, without really doing anything. Some would call that being 'established' whereas I think the Ipswich support just found it boring – and under the firm but dour hand of Mick McCarthy, you can perhaps understand why. Either way they had enough Championship experience to be tough opposition – and a good example of how life at this level would be.

Chances for Waghorn and McGoldrick were a reminder of how easily you can be punished if you lose concentration even for a second, and the injury to Kieron Freeman looked bad at the time. It definitely felt like a serious blow losing him as he'd been fantastic the year before … even more galling that a clash with Cameron Carter-Vickers caused it. Glimpses of George Baldock suggested we had a very decent back-up in that position, though. Once we took the lead we never looked like losing and Chris Basham's effort was rewarded with a rare goal, which is always good to see.

On the face of it, Reading at home should have been a really tough game – a chance to pit ourselves against the side that finished third in the league the previous season, and were a penalty kick away from the Premier League. This was exactly the kind of game I'd looked forward to when we got promoted – a real test of how far we'd come. As it happened, Reading were suffering a massive hangover from the previous season and came to the Lane having only won three of their opening 11 games, sitting fourth bottom. At half time you could see why. We barely gave them a kick for 45 minutes and a two-goal lead could easily have been more. And Paul Coutts scored an absolute screamer, begging the question … why doesn't he shoot more often?

In the second half Reading woke up sufficiently to put us under real pressure – especially for the last five minutes after they pulled one back. A good win left me feeling a bit frustrated that we didn't really capitalise on the excellent first half performance and could have easily ended up drawing. After the game Chris Wilder was really pleased with the performance which annoyed me a bit at the time – I thought we were poor second half – but again another three points against one of the fancied sides ahead of our trip up the M1.

That Friday night under the lights at Elland Road, in front of the Sky cameras, gave us the chance to go top of the 'Big Scary Championship'. A real chance to put a marker down, show the rest of the league what we were about. What could possibly go wrong? Well, strangely for Sheffield United, not a lot. Leeds were fourth and the atmosphere was superb before the game, but the result at Hillsborough seemed to have emboldened players and fans. There was no fear.

But there were definite parallels with that win over Wednesday. Again we scored early, again we dominated the first half and again we conceded to pretty much the first half-chance the opposition created. This was a hugely impressive display, though, and but for a couple of top-class saves from their goalkeeper, and some profligate finishing from us, we could easily have been three or four up at the break. When Saiz slammed one into the post you started to feel like it might be our night and if David Brooks announced himself onto the scene with *that* nutmeg on Jack Hunt, he was about to go to another level when he slotted into the far corner with a calmness beyond his years. This was a special goal, and wonderful to see the shy young lad from the Town Hall steps last year deliver in such a big game.

What a time to score your first league goal and the chant of 'Brooks will tear you apart' sounded brilliant, as we moved top of the league. Fantastic. Six years in League One had left memories of some pretty low times. And if someone had told me at the Southend game the year before, 3-0 down inside the opening 15 minutes, that we'd be sat top of the Championship 14 months later ... well, let's just say I'd have struggled to believe it!

At that Southend game, I distinctly remember one guy shouting that our frustrated manager was 'out of his depth' and I thought 'crikey, you've got your work cut out'. So this really was a moment to savour and you could have forgiven Wilder for a triumphal tone in his post-match interview. Yet for the second game running he went the opposite to me – I thought we'd been superb, and while happy with the result, Wilder said that we'd been way below standard and it was a poor performance!

Top of the league, United completed their month at QPR's Loftus Road – the ground with potentially the least legroom in English football. After a particularly boring Blackwell-era goalless draw there I spent a good ten minutes after the game apologising to the poor lady in front of me for smashing her in the head and back with my knees every time I moved. As the Blades headed south I flew off with my family to Fuerteventura for some late autumn sunshine – proving the lengths some of us will go to in order to avoid trick-or-treaters – and although following a game slyly via *Twitter* is never easy, all I missed here was a Halloween horror-show. We came back down to earth with a bump – literally in Jamal Blackman's case – and for the second time in three games, Carter-Vickers inadvertently injured one of his own players. United never really recovered from the subsequent gift-wrapped goal.

It was a reminder that while we'd got to the top of the league, we couldn't afford to be complacent and we were there to be knocked off our perch. Once again, I wished we would sign Luke Freeman – who always impressed me whenever I saw him play. With Cardiff and Wolves both winning we ended the month outside the automatic promotion places, but there was definitely optimism that we could have a really good go at this now. And that instead of looking over our shoulders, we could think about trying to get out of the division the right way.

12

Fulham fireworks in bonfire month
November 2017

The afternoon of November 4 threatened to be one of disappointment and frustration but turned out to be a memorable and historic one, as United came from behind to beat Yorkshire rivals Hull City 4-1 at Bramall Lane. But the scoreline did not come close to telling the whole story as Leon Clarke, the nomadic striker with 17 clubs on his CV, scored all four goals to double his tally for the season in a single afternoon in front of 27,466 supporters in South Yorkshire. Hull had led 1-0 at half-time through Polish international Kamil Grosicki's well-struck effort from 25 yards but in the second period, Clarke ran amok to claim only the second hat-trick of his professional career.

Incredibly, he could actually have ended up with six goals but Hull goalkeeper Allan McGregor made two superb saves to deny the striker. "I didn't think it was going to be my day," Clarke admitted afterwards. "I should have done better with the header in the first half that he saved, but the one early in the second half was a bit more difficult for him. I did think, 'This is not going to be my day' but to come away with four goals was fantastic, and a real career highlight."

It wrote his name in the Bramall Lane history books, too, as the first Blade to score four at home since Keith Edwards on the opening day of the 1983/84 season, in the old Division Three. United went on to win promotion that season and, in his role as an expert summariser with BBC Radio Sheffield, Edwards was on hand to congratulate Clarke at the final whistle.

"The variety of the goals Leon scored were exceptional," Edwards later said. "And for that, I think they were better than my own. The technical strength he showed to put the first three away was superb and, if there was ever any doubt, he's just proved out there what a fine player he is. I can speak from experience when I say Leon will never forget that moment. When you get a hat-trick, it's something. When you get four, it just makes it that little bit more special. I've never seen him play as well as this and I've seen him at quite a few clubs in his career.

"Logically, great credit for that has got to go to Chris Wilder and Alan Knill. Getting the best out of your players, putting them in the right situations to perform, is all part of good management and they are certainly doing that. The consistency Leon is showing is the key to that. Clearly, he is being given the platform to perform and do what he's good at."

After netting his fourth and final goal in the 88th minute, Clarke was taken off in injury time to soak up the deserved applause and Wilder, who had instructed his striker to savour every moment by taking as long as possible, admits he can't remember a reception quite like it in his entire football career. While the remarkable events of that day sank in, and the majority of United's squad rested up over the international break, David Brooks instead earned his first caps for his adopted Wales after pledging allegiance to the country of his mother Cathryn's birth.

The first came in the grand surroundings of the Stade de France against Didier Deschamps' future World Cup winners and after replacing Leicester's Andy King in the 64th minute of a 2-0 defeat, the sight of 20-year-old Brooks tormenting Layvin Kurzawa, the Paris St Germain left-back, raised more than a few smiles amongst those watching on television back in South Yorkshire.

Players who shared a pitch with Brooks that evening included Real Madrid's Raphaël Varane, Kingsley Coman of Bayern Munich and 19-year-old Kylian Mbappé, who scored in the final victory over Croatia in Russia the following summer. And after Brooks managed to get his hands on the shirt of Antoine Griezmann, his first Wales start came against Panama four days later, at the Cardiff City Stadium. The opponents weren't quite in the same stratosphere but the occasion was no less memorable, and Brooks was named man of the match in a 1-1 draw before being replaced, to a standing ovation, in the 71st minute.

"For club and country, 2017 was a really good year for me," Brooks said. "It was filled with a lot of special memories for me and my family and hopefully I'll get more years like that. "On a personal level, to play for your country on a stage like that in France, and with my mum, my dad, my family all from Wales all coming down supporting in Paris, is probably the most special memory I've got."

Less than 24 hours later, Brooks was back at United's Shirecliffe training complex and although those close to him insist he will remain level-headed despite his success, his Blades teammates were not about to risk letting him get too carried away – and chose to graffiti his choice of clothing for the day, a pink Nike hoodie. Each of his teammates then signed it with messages of congratulations and the hoodie was later auctioned on *eBay* to raise money for Breast Cancer Care – but not before manager Wilder squeezed into it, interrupted a game of head-tennis at training and pulled off a slightly technically imperfect 'Klinsmann Dive' on the turf. Complete with mud stains on the front, and a little stretched, it nevertheless raised £640 and sits proudly in the collection of Gary Sinclair, United's matchday announcer.

It was a typical stunt from Wilder, who occasionally joins in the head-tennis group at United's training ground and is a big believer in squad harmony after playing in a similarly tight-knit group at Bramall Lane under Dave Bassett, frequently insisting that training should "not be like a holiday camp, but not a concentration camp either". United, in good spirits and even better form, had adjusted to life in the Championship better than most observers had expected and knew victory over Burton Albion on November 17 would send them top of the league.

"We'd talked about it at the start of the season, but no-one really wanted to listen," said Brooks. "It wasn't so much the league position that made us believe we could push for promotion, but more the way we were playing. Like when we played Wednesday, and Wolves … we were playing some really good stuff and were generally the better team against most sides. It wasn't a case of us scrounging wins. We played attractive football and that's what made us think we might have a chance."

United did beat Burton, and did climb to the summit of the division, but the mood afterwards was sombre rather than celebratory; the result of a devastating injury to their midfield talisman, Paul Coutts. United led 2-1 at the Pirelli and looked comfortable when Coutts ventured forward and attempted a volley on goal after the ball was cleared. Coutts got to it moments before Burton's Marvin Sordell and his effort was blocked, but a photograph of the incident told the sorry story; Coutts, eyes on the ball and technique solid, Sordell lazily hanging a leg with eyes closed, turning away. Then, the contact; Sordell's boot on Coutts' shin, bending at an unnatural angle.

At full speed it seemed innocent enough but the reaction of those around Coutts suggested it was serious; Billy Sharp, the United skipper, and a couple of Burton defenders called immediately for medical assistance and the Scot received gas and air on the pitch before leaving it on a stretcher. Clarke's header 12 minutes from time was cheered in a rather subdued fashion and as Blades fans filed out of the away end of the stadium, their side top of the Championship, the almost eerie silence in the Friday night air spoke volumes of their despair.

"We'd gone top of the league but that was almost not in anyone's minds in the ground," Wilder remembers. "It was all about Paul which, I guess in some ways, shows what this club is all about and how tight the group is." Incredibly, the man perhaps most upbeat than anyone else that night was Coutts himself, in the treatment room deep in the bowels of the Pirelli Stadium. By then, his initial fears had been confirmed, via a picture of the incident on social media that he ordered a member of United's medical team to show him, and a broken tibia meant his season was over.

"Couttsy is such a lynchpin of our team," defender Richard Stearman said. "I don't know what he was doing that far forward in the first place, but we'd have gladly sacrificed three points that night to make sure he was fit for the season. It was a real blow for us, and who knows what we could have done with him available for the full season? It felt like a defeat for us, certainly, even though the game was pretty comfortable in terms of the scoreline. We knew soon enough that it was season over for Couttsy and at the time he was one of our best performers, so it was devastating for us all. We didn't know where it'd go from there but we tried to continue without him, and hopefully he can come back with a new leg and pick up where he left off.

"Losing him just meant others had to step up, though. John Fleck had a great season and it pushed him to the fore a little bit. He's another of our players who hadn't played at this level before, but like a few others he's proved he is more than capable. He was one of the shining lights of our season. He went under the radar a little bit for many teams or fans of other sides in this division who won't have known much about him. But they will now."

Whilst understandably downbeat, Wilder was keen to ensure that Coutts' injury would not define United's season and going top of the Championship table offered at least a crumb of comfort. "We've obviously progressed as a football club, but how do we measure it?" asked James Beighton, who sits on the Kop with pal Lee Woodhouse and Lee's son, Reece. "The answer is, through the eyes of a six-year-old Blade. The three of us go to every home game; two of us wise and seasoned enough to know better than getting too carried away, and the other, my best mate's son. His first season ticket was in the promotion winning campaign.

"He saw a season where we just seemed to turn up and take three points. A few reality-check words from his dad at the start of this season were along the lines of: 'Don't expect the same again, it'll be a hard season and we won't be winning every week.' Fast forward to the victory away at Burton and United were top of the Championship. Six-year-old Reece turned and said: 'I thought you said this season would be hard, dad?'"

Of course, in one of the most competitive leagues in European football, tougher tasks lay ahead and Wilder's men began the post-Coutts era in the most memorable way, a remarkable 5-4 defeat at home to Fulham. Slavisa Jokanovic's impressive side languished in the bottom half of the table as they made the long trip north and it seemed ominous for them when Clarke put United ahead after just six minutes. But Cameron Carter-Vickers gift-wrapped an equaliser for Liverpool loanee Sheyi Ojo and Ryan Sessegnon, the 17-year-old top-flight target who Fulham valued at an incredible £50million, put the visitors ahead with a superb strike on his weaker right foot from 25 yards.

Clarke restored parity with a good run and finish through David Button's legs but Fulham went into half-time leading 3-2, Sessegnon again on target after being left unmarked at the back post. Ojo's second of the game, and Sessegnon's third, saw Fulham romp into a 5-2 lead – with United playing almost two at the back at this point in an attempt to get back into the game – before Samir Carruthers and Clarke's third gave United hope.

James Hanson, making a rare appearance off the bench, saw a header cleared off the line but United couldn't find a dramatic equaliser and as referee James Linington blew his whistle, six or seven Fulham players dropped to the Bramall Lane turf, exhausted. United, though, were beaten but unbowed after more than playing their part in one of the best games in S2 in recent memory and after scoring one hat-trick in his first 430 games as a professional footballer, Clarke now had two in his last three.

"There's a lot of things happening with Leon," said Wilder. "He really enjoys working for us, he enjoys being in our dressing room and being a main player for us. The respect between the supporters and himself goes two ways, they see what he does and he appreciates the support he gets. I've always said that the goals don't move and sometimes players become better through experience as they get older. Leon is at the top of his game and playing arguably the best football of his career."

Clarke ended October with nine goals in four games, scoring another in the final game of the month at home to relegation-threatened Birmingham City at Bramall Lane. But it was only enough to earn a solitary point on a frustrating afternoon, after United had conceded from yet another superb strike from long range – this time, Chelsea loanee Jeremie Boga taking the plaudits after beating fellow Stamford Bridge youngster Jamal Blackman from 25 yards out. Birmingham, who had scored only nine league goals all season before kick-off, frustrated United after matching them up formation-wise, but Clarke fashioned himself just enough space to beat David Stockdale at his near post – though United, despite having 69 percent of the ball, couldn't find a winner.

Remarkably, the result was United's first draw since March and the irony of the Blues, who spent £20m on new players in the summer, tweaking their formation to cope with United wasn't lost on Wilder as they continued to impress in their first season back in the Championship. "I was delighted with the way we were playing," he said. "We knew we'd take small steps backwards but the quality and level of consistency of performances in a new division, for me, was first class. I think we were showing that we're a really decent side."

My luck over my broken leg
By Paul Coutts, midfielder

It always seems a little strange to say that I feel lucky when I talk about breaking my leg, but it could have been far worse. When it happened, I thought straightaway 'I've broken my leg there' but then as the adrenaline kicked in, and the gas and air hit me, I remember thinking that it might not have been so bad after all. I didn't want to go off on a stretcher and then train on the Monday ... the gaffer would have been looking at me thinking, what's going on there?! But by the time we got to Burton's treatment room, the picture of the tackle was circulating on social media and one of the staff was wincing at it. I told him to let me see it and my initial thoughts were confirmed. I'd broken my leg.

In a way, the picture helped; it was pretty clear what had happened so it was fairly routine in terms of giving me morphine, calling an ambulance and everything else, but then the real luck came. Our club doctor, Subhashis Basu, was on the train home from London where he'd been watching the tennis. He'd seen that I had come off with an injury after a long stoppage, so got off the train early at Derby and got a taxi straight to the hospital to meet me. I'm so glad he did.

The doctors there wanted to put me in a cast below my knee

only, and Dr Baz, as we know him, fell out with them until they agreed to put me in a full leg cast. When I got to Sheffield to see the specialist, he said: 'thank God it was a full leg cast or it would have moved further' because it wouldn't have been stable. In the end, the bone was only 10 percent unaligned and would have been much worse if Dr Baz hadn't got off that train. He saved me an operation, and probably a couple more months in the gym, so I'm really grateful for that.

I remember waiting for the ball to come down out of the air, but it seemed to take ages. I had one eye on the ball and the other on Marvin Sordell, waiting for him to make his move so I could chest the ball around him. But he didn't, so I thought I could hit it first time. I don't know what I was doing that far forward but I caught the ball really sweetly, and then he's lunged over late and I've caught the sole of his boot with my shin. Then I heard the crack. Jake Buxton, who I know from Derby and who's quite a hard man, was slapping me on the back, asking if I was alright. I'd been better!

I initially thought I'd broken my tibia and fibula but somehow the thinner bone held on, which again was quite fortunate. The ambulance took ages to come and arrived just as the game was finishing, so fans were banging on the windows and singing my song. I was on morphine by then so had a chuckle about it, talking to people on *FaceTime* and generally buzzing that we'd gone top of the league. It was only when I spoke to people the next day that I realised how down people were about it. I was thinking 'we're top of the league ... what are you on about?'

They were obviously feeling sympathy for me, but I was just concerned about the group. We were set in our team selection and shape at that point, and everyone knew how the pattern of the game would go pretty quickly after kick-off, because we just asserted ourselves. If we'd lost any one of the other players, it'd have a similar effect. That's how I see it, anyway. The most painful part actually came when I went to see the specialist, and the cast was so bad that I couldn't sit on the toilet or anything like that. So they agreed to cut it just to the knee, but I couldn't move my toes into the right position. So the specialist grabbed my foot and moved it into place himself. That was more sore than the tackle itself ... it was unbelievable.

I've also realised that I'm a terrible watcher of games, too. It's weird, really; when I'm playing and people say afterwards 'why didn't you do this or that?' it looks completely different down on the pitch. It's so much harder. Then I go into the stand with my leg in a cast and start saying 'ah, why has he done this or not done that?' It looks so much easier from the stands! I know it's not but I can't convince myself. It was horrible to watch the boys, knowing I couldn't do anything to help them. But I've no concerns about getting back to full fitness. The bone will be stronger, I know my body now more than when I was younger and also my role in the team – and I have a manager who trusts me, too, which helps.

Chris is by far the best man-manager I've had in my career. I was brought down from Scotland by Darren Ferguson at Peterborough after playing non-league north of the border, and in my first game on trial we played Manchester United – I was pitched against Scotland captain at the time, Darren Fletcher, which was a real eye opener! They had won the Champions League the season before and had some big guns playing that day, like Rio Ferdinand and Carlos Tevez, but I did well in my 45 minutes and earned a move down.

Darren then took me to Preston where he got the sack and was replaced by Graham Westley, who used to text us in the early hours of the morning before a game asking us who should captain the team, and then talk about us being professional! When I was Westley's captain, he used to have us running at 5pm the day before a game and then pull me in and ask why we weren't getting results. I said it was because the lads were knackered!

I then had a good time at Derby before suffering a knee injury and falling down the pecking order, so when Nigel Clough called me to bring me to Bramall Lane I couldn't say no. Nigel can be quite persuasive when he wants to be, but it wasn't needed that time! I signed just before the second leg of the League Cup semi-final against Spurs at Bramall Lane and the place was rocking.

I remember thinking, this is a proper club and imagined what could happen here if everyone pulled in the right direction. Unfortunately, Nigel couldn't get us promoted and paid the price with his job and after a tough year in between, Chris stepped in and took us up.

There was a complete change in everything when Chris came in. Training standards, playing style, fitness levels, connection with supporters, calibre of player he brought in ... everything went up. He placed demands on us as players and galvanised everything, and did it quickly. He built a spirit and a camaraderie which saw us going into games expecting to win, rather than hoping. It was a great feeling. Not so much when he put me on the transfer list! I had a year left on my contract and when he called me, he was great about it; he just said he was going in a different direction and changing certain things, but that didn't mean I wouldn't have chance to train with the first team or change his mind. And he was true to his word.

At other clubs a lot of players are binned off to train with the kids when they're on the transfer list, but that never happened to me and I applaud him for that. It was an interesting time because my partner had given birth to twins on the day pre-season started and we'd just moved to Sheffield. I was close to going but I said 'I can't now while my partner's in hospital, let me do pre-season and take it from there'. I ended up doing okay in pre-season, the gaffer said he wasn't in a rush to get me out and it ended up working perfectly.

The change in formation did help my game, I guess, but it wasn't all part of some grand plan; it almost happened by accident. Jake Wright and I were both in the reserves at the start of the season, and he didn't want to be stepping into midfield and playing the ball so I'd literally go and get it off his toes and use it. Then, we both ended up in the first team so carried on doing just that! It also meant I could get a bit of a partnership going with John Fleck. Flecky used to come with us on Scotland U21 camps when he was like 17 or something, but he couldn't get a game as we had a strong midfield – myself, Kevin McDonald, Barry Bannan and Scott Arfield. But I got to know him quite well through the camps and when he signed, I remember thinking we'd done well to get him on a free – I couldn't get my head around it. I thought there must be something he doesn't do or isn't good at, but as the season went on, I realised I would love to play with him. He's so good on the ball and so comfortable. Why he isn't a mainstay in the Scotland team is beyond me, to be honest.

I'm often asked about the story of going from transfer list to winning the league and playing nearly 50 games and when I look back now, it is amazing and something I never thought would happen. But from the outside it maybe looked like the door was more shut on me than it actually was, which is another of the manager's strengths. He worked us hard but made sure we enjoyed it, too – a lot of people talk about going to Las Vegas for four days at the end of the title-winning season, but the constant awards nights in Sheffield were probably harder – and the team spirit was brilliant from the first pre-season in Marbella, when he let us have a night out.

It probably helps that a lot of the squad have experienced rejection in their careers – I worked for an oil company while playing non-league for Cove Rangers after being released by Aberdeen, and getting up at 7am to work for nine hours and then go to training helps you appreciate the life of a footballer, and how close it was to slipping away.

I've even got a song, which gives me a little chuckle every time I hear it from the terraces. People talk about turning the fans around after being criticised under the previous manager, but that's been far outweighed by the support the fans have given me, especially after the injury. The amount of letters I've had from people wishing me well has been incredible and a lot of that is down to Chris, I think, who has helped my relationship with the fans. How can I sum him up? He's never satisfied.

We won the league with four games to spare and then he set us the target of 100 points, and in the dressing room it was honestly like we were fighting for our lives. Nothing other than a win was acceptable and looking back at it, it's quite weird – but everyone bought into it at the time. I'm totally at ease in the manager's presence, playing pool or whatever, but there's still a line because everyone has the utmost respect for him. That's the perfect blend of both, really.

November 2017 – 'He never gives the ball away'
By Jonathan Bradley, Kop

"Coutts is injured mate, it looked an absolute shocker," chirped my mate Rich as I emerged from the bar under the stand at Burton Albion's Pirelli Stadium. *"Shut up!"* I jokingly replied. Minutes earlier we had been waxing lyrical about how we were playing, and Paul Coutts in particular. His sheer elegance on the pitch. "No mate, I'm being serious," said Rich. Oh dear. Among the usual 'oreights' and 'ey-ups' at half-time, I didn't have time to think about the injury. But as I sipped my Fosters, gripped tight in my frozen fingers, I foolishly checked my *Twitter* feed. There the photo was, for all to see; the foot of Marvin Sordell wedged into Coutts' leg. It simply had to be broken.

For me, our very able United team would simply not be quite the same again from that point and the second half proved a rather unpleasant experience. And I wasn't alone in feeling that. The away terrace at Burton is hardly renowned for comfort and despite the Friday evening beer that had been flowing, the atmosphere was flat and subdued. Not too dissimilar to the waiting room at the doctor's – the only difference that we had all seen what had gone wrong. We knew it was bad. It was a case of – how bad? United won the game and went top of the Championship, but the sombre mood continued on the way home and I couldn't help but think, for God's sake. And that's the PG version.

November on paper looked set to be a fantastic month for United. We had all slightly started to calm down from *that* Sunday in September and just about got over the elation of the outstanding victory away at Leeds, for me United's best performance under Wilder. Despite a disappointing loss at QPR (although I can't recommend a pub crawl round Belgravia enough), we kept creating lots of chances and when the fixture list presented us with four bottom-half teams in November, we had a real platform to kick on. Hull were truly dreadful but Leon Clarke looked unplayable; personally giving me a real sense of smugness due to the nonsense comments from our friends across the city, about how terrible he was.

Then, an international break which were becoming all-too frequent. I have many good friends who assure me England games are a fantastic experience, yet I often spend the weekends in particular lamenting what I would much rather be doing than watching England. This time, though, I had more than one eye on what was going off as David Brooks made his international debut against France in Paris. Brooks is a tremendously talented footballer; with the ability to get you up off your seat when he gets on the ball. When he had performed so well in our two biggest games, away at S6 and up the road in Leeds, the talk was not of how good he was, but rather when he would inevitably leave. We really are a cynical bunch, but it really should not detract from the very talented and potentially massive player he is. He has the footballing world at his feet.

Then came Fulham. I sat in the Sheaf View as the team rumbled in across social media, and the question was raised: how on earth are Fulham so far down the league with that side? It proved a fair one. But how do you score four goals at home and not win? Who knows. Fulham's midfield duo of Tom Cairney and Kevin McDonald certainly helped matters, as did the amazing Ryan Sessegnon. Cameron Carter-Vickers gave Fulham a leg up, too. But personally, I felt like the game proved a further turning point in our season. Unable to rely on the ability to compete in the midfield a player like Coutts gives you, United squandered too much possession which meant that we needed to overcompensate in attack. Wilder duly did what every fan would have done and pleads to be done in such circumstances ... he went for it. Unfortunately we got our fingers burned in the process.

Did it have a serious long-term effect on Chris Wilder and his willingness to make such radical changes going forward? Rightly or wrongly, a more conservative approach from the bench in the second half of the season was the result of losing a game 5-4 we desperately wanted, and needed, to win. The draw at home to Birmingham – United's first in 26 games – was quite telling, considering the post-Fulham reflections mentioned previously. The events of the previous Tuesday seemed to have tired the players out, in front of the Sky cameras. Whoever thought anybody would want to watch United and Birmingham on a Saturday evening must have a screw loose; the viewing figures of a very drab affair probably resulted in a very difficult conversation in the office on Monday morning!

So that was November 2017. A strange month all in all. Leon scored two hat tricks and nine goals across four games while Brooks tested his skills against one of Europe's great footballing nations. United lost a game where we scored four. But above all there was the injury to Coutts, who wasn't instantly warmed to by United fans. Between his deep and sharp draws of breath, Nigel Clough told us how great he would be when he was fit. Nigel Adkins said Coutts was a very good passer of a football, a refreshing comment from someone whose own signings didn't seem to have that ability. Maybe a few bottles of Peroni did the trick? Coutts became an integral part in a hugely effective system and was duly missed for the remainder of the season.

I don't regret going early to get a half-time pint at Burton. If anything it was a blessing in disguise. But I certainly didn't like what happened to Coutts. And to make it even worse, they were only selling Fosters. It could have at least been Peroni.

13

No Christmas gifts for the Blades
December 2017

As the curtain closed on the 2016/17 League One season, Sheffield United finished a massive 27 points ahead of Millwall in the table but after their play-off final victory over Bradford City, marred by pitch invasions and fan trouble at Wembley, the Blades and Lions began the Championship season as equals once more. As the smell of marijuana once again drifted across the press box at The Den, it was somewhat comforting to know that, in a season of such change, some things do not. Still, only four players that started that fateful defeat at Millwall back in August 2016 lined up for United this time around but it was a similar story as they went behind again, when Sheffield-born ex-Blades youngster Lee Gregory fired Millwall ahead in the 14th minute.

David Brooks dragged United back on level terms with a volleyed finish from Mark Duffy's clever clipped ball, although the youngster later admitted it may have been something of a miscued effort, but goals from Mahlon Romeo and Jake Cooper condemned United to defeat in South East London for the second successive season. From their vantage point in the main stand at The Den, journalists must snake through the inner sanctum of the stadium and through the tunnel area to reach the pitch and conduct their post-match interviews, and in doing so they passed each United substitute and various members of coaching staff in the tunnel, sheepishly staring at the floor. The reason quickly became apparent when, through the dressing room walls, Wilder could be heard letting his players know, in no uncertain terms, what he thought of their performance.

When he eventually emerged, almost an hour after the final whistle, he was calmer; but only just. "I've got my ideas about what happened but I'll keep those to myself," he promised, before doing anything but. "I told the players what to expect when we came here and, possibly, they had their headphones on when I was speaking. I think we've got ahead of ourselves a little bit, but I haven't. I know how tough this division is. But sometimes players get a little bit ahead of themselves. How many big headers, how many big tackles did we make? When we play positive football, we don't get out-muscled or out-fought. And, I thought that did happen to us today."

Defeat at The Den also marked Clarke's first as United skipper, with regular captain Billy Sharp on the bench and Paul Coutts, who had previously taken the armband, injured. "He seemed a natural choice for us as skipper and we thought he'd enjoy the responsibility as a senior player," Wilder later reflected. "Couttsy would have pushed him close if he was fit, but after his injury it was an opportunity for Leon to take a bit more responsibility. And he did.

"He's a big figure down in the changing room, although he's not a shouter and bawler and goes about things in his own way. But he's had a long career and he's an experienced boy. We'd spoken to a couple of people who had managed him in the past, but we go with our gut feeling. He's part of a team and can't step over the line, but mostly we just let Leon be Leon and let him get on with it. He's comfortable here and in the changing room; that's what we try and do. Treat players as people, and how we would like to be treated ourselves."

After beers on the bus the last time United were beaten in Bermondsey, this time it seemed that tough love was very much Wilder's method of choice to provoke a reaction as United slipped to fourth. It certainly helped spark United into life in their next outing, against fellow promotion-chasers Bristol City in front of the Sky cameras at Bramall Lane as the Blades hit the woodwork three times in the first half, before falling behind to a decent strike from Jamie Paterson. That man Clarke helped the hosts back into the game with an equaliser and Duffy hit the post once more before the game's turning point, when John Fleck saw red for a tackle on City's Korey Smith. Even with ten men, Wilder sensed United were in control of the game and took off centre-half Chris Basham for attacking midfielder Samir Carruthers in an attempt to win it. Instead, they ended up with nothing when Aden Flint swept home City's winner in the first minute of added time.

"Between myself and the staff, we've spoken a lot about the approach," Wilder said as he reflected on the season. "We were in the ascendancy and had attacked every game up to that point … we beat Wednesday, beat Wolves, were outstanding against Forest and hit the woodwork four times against Bristol. For the goal, the ball ricocheted off George Baldock, their lad's had a tackle against Samir and it falls perfectly for the lad Flint. That's nothing to do with pressure, because there wasn't any when we made the change.

"We'd done it before at Hillsborough when we took off Jake Wright for Duffy and that was the approach. We're always looking at things and now, head to head against sides who will be up there, we might have said 'let's take a point'. But it's a learning curve. At the time we were playing very well, and unfortunately it went against us. We look at that game and the home one against Villa, when Sam Johnstone kept them in the game and then Snodgrass won it and they ended up in the play-off final. It's about being better in both boxes. We look at ourselves, first and foremost, and see where we can learn. I'm sure we will."

As he faced the media afterwards, Wilder only had complaints about his side's luck and the performance of the referee – "The game has gone if you can't tackle like that now – that was just a proper tackle and I don't think it deserves a red card," he said – but was doubly determined to arrest his side's mini-slump which had seen them fall from top of the table, to fourth. But the fickle hand of fortune had its say again on the eve of their next game, away at Preston North End, when Duffy and Brooks both fell ill, meaning that the successful midfield triumvirate of Coutts, Fleck and Duffy that had served them so well was missing, through a combination of injury, illness and suspension. With a makeshift midfield three of John Lundstram, Basham and Carruthers, United were below par throughout and it was no real surprise when Jordan Hugill scored Preston's winner, to extend United's winless run to five matches for the first time in Wilder's reign.

Less than a month after going top of the Championship table, United were now 14 points behind leaders Wolves and had dropped to sixth, just two points clear of ninth-placed Preston. And as the rain fell around Deepdale, Wilder was once again in belligerent mood. "I think some of the players may have taken their eyes off the ball a little bit and if that's the case, then they had better get ready for the consequences of that," he warned. "I don't like the spike that's appeared in the team over the last few weeks. I don't enjoy it. I am one for a consistent approach and performances and we are not getting it. There have been a lot of plaudits gone to the club and to the players and the staff, so we have to find an answer. Whether that's personnel or my attitude towards them, we have to find a way."

Wilder forgave himself a wry smile in the week after when discussing the game facing them next; the straightforward task of facing Aston Villa, fresh out of the Premier League, at Villa Park. Wilder played under Villa boss Steve Bruce when the latter cut his managerial teeth at Bramall Lane some years earlier, in somewhat more trying circumstances, but was now tasked with returning Villa to the Premier League – with a substantial budget to achieve that aim. Former England captain and Champions League winner John Terry signed on for a tilt at promotion, with a reported £70,000 a week contract thrown in to sweeten the deal somewhat, and Jonathan Kodjia and Scott Hogan, who was playing for Stocksbridge Park Steels six years earlier, arrived for a combined fee of almost £30m. Little wonder then that Wilder, whose most extravagant purchase so far was Lundstram at around £700,000, moved to play down his side's chances.

"Villa is a powerful, historic, fantastic football club," he said, "and everybody wrote us off. I understand that; it is football. There are standout fixtures in the calendar, and this was one for us. It was up to us to put in a performance and get a result which upset the odds. Our players should have been rubbing their hands together and saying 'come on, let's get ourselves back on track, we have not done ourselves justice in the last three or four games in terms of results'. That's the attitude we had."

At 2-0 down inside nine minutes, it hadn't gone to plan. Backed by a vociferous Villa Park crowd, the home side swarmed all over United almost from kick off and after Richard Stearman was harshly adjudged to have fouled Villa's Keinan Davis, Albert Adomah dispatched the resulting penalty. It got worse for Wilder's men when Mile Jedinak powered home a header, but it was former Birmingham striker Clayton Donaldson, who cost £50,000 on deadline day, who got them back into it on his return to the second city, chipping coolly home after Lundstram's exquisite through-ball.

And in the 26th minute of an absorbing contest, again played out in front of the Sky Sports cameras, it was 2-2 when Jedinak let in Donaldson and he fired through Johnstone's legs to earn what was a fully deserved point. It wasn't enough to stop them falling out of the play-offs, and nine points off automatic promotion, but after staring down the barrel of their fourth successive defeat, the Blades had stopped the rot. "It may not have been the biggest result of the day in England but, in our dressing room, it felt like a win," Wilder remembers. "We thought it could be a turning point for us. It had to start somewhere."

The United manager also reserved a few barbed comments for youngster Brooks, who had missed the games against Preston and Villa with illness and posted a picture on *Instagram*, showing him in hospital on the eve of the trip to Villa Park. Wilder, who is about as likely to be seen in a Sheffield Wednesday shirt as he is on *Facebook* or *Twitter*, is not a fan of social media – although his players are not prevented from using the platforms – and reminded Brooks of his responsibilities after he risked alerting Bruce and Villa to his unavailability before the game. Brooks was initially suspected to be suffering from tonsillitis but was then diagnosed with glandular fever and missed a key chunk of United's season, just as he was beginning to establish himself with both club and country.

The youngster later apologised profoundly for what he admitted was a "stupid mistake on my behalf" but revealed some of the thinking behind the decision. "I had people on *Twitter* saying 'it's only a throat infection, why isn't he playing?' and a lot of people thought I was chucking it in and just trying to get through to January, things like that. So that was annoying to see and listen to, especially when you're feeling like I was and all you want to do is get back out there and play football, but you're not physically able to. It was almost like I was trying to prove a point that I *was* ill, but it was a stupid mistake from me and I was a bit naive with it. It wasn't the right time or way to do that, I slipped up with that and I apologised, at the time and again now, for doing that."

United then completed a first double of the season with a 3-0 Boxing Day victory over sorry Sunderland and Wilder thought the win saw United regain some of their early-season 'swagger' as Lundstram, Stearman and Baldock got their names on the scoresheet. The result saw them back in the play-offs, but they were to end the year on a bitterly disappointing note with a shock home defeat to fellow promoted team Bolton, who travelled across the Pennines in the bottom three while United targeted a victory that would have set a new club record for the number of points won in a calendar year.

Ironically, it was former Sheffield Wednesday striker Gary Madine who scored the only goal of the game, somehow making himself an even more unpopular figure around Bramall Lane after his visit the season previous, when he took his time getting off the coach outside the players' entrance, was absent from the Bolton teamsheet and promptly returned home in a taxi before kick-off. Officially, Madine's absence was explained as illness but in the build-up to the game, a video had emerged on social media of him calling United skipper Billy Sharp 'a fat pig'. Sharp scored twice in that game, celebrating in front of the Bolton fans with his finger on his lips and his other hand rubbing his stomach, but it was Madine – described as "outstanding" by Wilder afterwards – who had the last laugh this time.

Keeping the faith through the bad run
By Richard Stearman, defender

December was a difficult period for us but throughout it, there was never a drop in confidence. We played really well against Bristol City and we knew that the performances were there. As professionals, we know when we've played badly and don't deserve anything, but that wasn't the case throughout that run in December. We knew that it'd turn if we carried on playing how we were, and it eventually did.

The trip to Millwall was my first game back after damaging my hamstring early in the season at Cardiff, and it was a relief more than anything. I'd got myself fit but the lads were on a great run, so I had to bide my time for another chance and make sure I was ready when it came. In the first third of the season we were flying, played really well and picked up a lot of points, and in the second third there were a couple of performances that really weren't like us, but also a couple that warranted more points than we picked up. Maybe we owed a lot to our good start to still be in touch with the play-offs after that difficult period.

A spell like that always helps you find out more about the characters in your dressing room. Winning can paper over the cracks a little and when it's not going so well and you have to fight your way off the canvas, it's difficult sometimes. So for us to maintain that belief, means the players and staff deserve a lot of credit. The manager was new in the division and we have a unique style of play, so it would have been very easy for him to revert to something a bit more standard or recognised to try and get the results. But he stuck to the strengths of the group, and we turned a corner from that. He makes us play without any fear.

Then, on Boxing Day, I managed to get off the mark with my first United goal, in front of the Kop as well. It was a relief because although my primary job is to keep the ball out of our net, defenders always like to chip in and help the team with a goal or two when they can. All my family were there, so that was a great feeling.

I actually had the chance to join United when I left Leicester in

2008, when Kevin Blackwell was in charge, but I went to Wolves instead as they are my hometown club and I ended up winning the Championship title and playing in the Premier League, which is a really special feeling – and something the gaffer here has experienced with 'his' club, too. When it came up that there was interest from United this time around, he didn't need to sell the club to me at all. I'd obviously played against United before and had always been impressed with the stadium, the stature and the fans. I doubt it would ever need 'selling' to a player interested in coming here.

As you get older as a player, I think you're less blasé about football and I'd kept tabs on what United had done the previous season in winning the league, and also because I'd played with Leon Clarke at Wolves and was keen to see how he was getting on. They were obviously on a massive high, and I just asked where I should sign. The gaffer isn't happy settling for mediocrity and wants the best for himself, the players and the club, and he was brilliant. From the outside in, I guess a lot of people would have thought we'd be happy with just staying in the Championship, but that was never our main target. We wanted to get safe as soon as possible, of course, but we were only looking up.

Apart from Leon, I didn't know too many of the boys and was mindful that they'd done so well the previous season, so went in with an open mind and just got stuck in. I signed just in time for the pre-season trip to Malaga so I had to do my initiation – although I'm keeping the song I chose to sing a closely-guarded secret – but the team spirit here is superb. It's not just a cliché, either ... I've been in dressing rooms where the team spirit is really good and I've been in dressing rooms where it's bad. If it's bad and you're not a together group, people can go missing and it's tough to turn it around. Sometimes there are little groups in corners and players are knifing each other, but that's not the case at all here. When we're up against so-called bigger teams and players, that can make all the difference.

That is why, I guess, the gaffer does his homework on the attitude of players as well as their ability. Just one or two bad players in the dressing room can become poisonous and damage it quite a bit and as senior players, we have a role to police against that too. It's almost an unwritten rule and the skipper is brilliant at that. I want to help the youngsters progress and help them on and off the pitch ... it's a role I certainly enjoy and it helps my game as well. Leon's someone I know well, too, and he also falls into that senior player bracket now.

When I played with him before, he showed glimpses of what he did in that first season back in the Championship but he'll probably admit himself that he didn't do it on a regular enough basis. He was 33 at the end of the season but still finished with 19 goals and worked so hard for the team, so it's an incredible achievement and I think the love he gets, from the staff, players and the fans, helps massively. He has a vitally important role around the club – the gaffer just lets Leon do what Leon does, and I think he responds better to that. It's another thing the gaffer must be congratulated for, that man management and the ability to work with players in different ways.

Leon isn't an average player, people need different things to be successful and he's recognised that, and you can see the benefits on the field. In Couttsy's absence he even became our vice-captain and I think he's thrived on that, as well as the love he gets from everyone around the club. The boys all love him and respect him, the fans love what he does and it's culminated in a fantastic season for Leon. He's not one for big speeches, at all, but different captains do the job in different ways; some are very vocal and some inspire through their performance, and Leon's work rate and aggression on the pitch is an inspiration to the other lads. He does speak very well, don't get me wrong, but that's not his main attribute as a skipper. He leads more through performances than words, and long may that continue.

December 2017 – A year to remember
By David Beeden, South Stand

After the blow of losing Paul Coutts for the season, and then gaining only a single point from home games against Birmingham and Fulham at Bramall Lane, United travelled to Millwall looking both to avenge last season's defeat and give their current campaign a much-needed kickstart. But they did neither. David Brooks' equaliser, guided into the top corner as he came across the ball, was a tremendous finish but that was as good as it got, in a performance as poor as the fans had witnessed for some time.

One thing was clear; we missed Coutts, badly. We were maybe too kamikaze at times and John Lundstram in midfield was still not convincing. Enda Stevens' form had dropped off after an impressive start to life at the Lane and he didn't seem the same player. Mark Duffy was still the main creator but we were still making too many defensive mistakes. Jamal Blackman was still getting criticism, but I'm not sure why? Fans still seemed to want Simon Moore in the side.

But then, Lundstram showed signs he was getting better in the defeat to Bristol City. John Fleck was stupid in his tackle, and cost us any chance we had of winning the game. We were in control at that point. In this game, we *were* too kamikaze, bringing on an attacker and going for all three points and ending up with none. Wonder goals kept going in. Moore was back, but was beaten with a long range shot. Brooks did not make any real impact when he came on.

Fans were split: should we have just settled for a point with 10 men or do we keep the same approach? This was the sort of game a month earlier we would have won, but in both boxes we were not ruthless enough. We had enough chances to win three games and to hit the woodwork four times was very unlucky. But we had to stop conceding as many as we were.

Again, at Preston, we missed Coutts. We are a different team without our midfield trio, of him, Fleck, and Duffy. If Leon Clarke played badly we did not look like scoring and at Deepdale, we missed the zest and hunger we had all season. Yes, we missed key players and yes we had some bad breaks with injuries, illness and suspension. But we looked punchless. We lacked that bite and did not create any clear chances. We looked a tired side. One thing that is for sure, though, is that the spirit was still there. We showed that at Villa – going two behind so early on, while on such a poor run, to fight back and win a point. Villa looked nothing to be scared of and made a lot of mistakes. We showed again we were not far off. A really good point that stopped the rot.

We needed a rubbish opposition and got it on Boxing Day, against Sunderland. George Baldock scored the third, and looked the real deal – up and down, a proper header that was reminiscent of a striker. Superb play from him all game. Lundstram also played well. We had a lot of good performances against a shocking side. Sunderland had one shot that went out for a throw in. Their fans looked disgusted. They were beaten easily. If United wanted more goals they could have had them.

No such luck at home to Bolton; a shock home defeat to end a really poor month. Former Wednesday man Gary Madine missed the last game between the sides in League One after being filmed abusing Billy Sharp on camera; this time, he played and scored the winner. Really irritating but he played really well. He plays the pantomime villain but he is big, strong and powerful – it's easy to see why Neil Warnock eventually took him to Cardiff. He even gave the powerful Jack O'Connell a tough ride and was the difference between the sides. We passed it too much and too slow. We looked a bit tired. We needed some fresh faces. We needed to build on Sunderland but could not, and put in a really flat performance. It was like that for a month or so.

Too many who played okay a few days previous were not at it with likes of Lundstram and Stevens particularly poor. The latter probably needed a rest; the former is maddeningly inconsistent. Bolton fought and harried and like Preston and Millwall, we did not match them. When we had the ball it was too pedestrian and we looked a bit short. Clarke's drop off sadly continued. The momentum had stalled. United went into 2018 knowing they were still firmly in a play-off place, but now any thoughts of a second promotion in a row were dimming.

Fans were split on the goalkeeper debate; both Moore and Blackman had a go but neither convinced. Maybe it is not totally down to the 'keeper! Perhaps we were just having no luck. Overall, a really down month with need for United to regain the hunger, sharpness and thrust they had shown most of the season. Personnel had been affected but there had been a drop off and some very winnable games spurned.

Still, as the New Year celebrations loomed, United could point to an incredible calendar year. They had won the League One title with 100 points, enjoyed a great start to the Championship and had been top for a period, winning at local rivals Wednesday and Leeds. They still sat right in the heart of the play-off places and had a lot to be proud of as they entered 2018.

14

Happy New Year?
January 2018

As the clock struck midnight on January 1, 2018, the transfer window officially opened for business once again and the month of madness began. United, widely expected to resume their pursuit of Southend's Ryan Leonard, were also crying out for a replacement in the mould of Paul Coutts, their talismanic 'quarterback'-style player whose broken leg in November had coincided with an alarming set of results, which saw United slip from top of the table to sixth. John Lundstram, a summer signing from Oxford United, had shown glimpses of his ability when handed the unenviable task of replacing Coutts but, through no fault of his own, was not able to do so seamlessly. The Scot had turned his career full-circle, from the transfer list to an accomplished Championship operator, by making the game look almost easy; picking the ball up from United's centre-halves and making the team tick. But without him, their style was noticeably different. Blades fans may be divided on the issue of their side's *best* player but when it came to who was the most *important,* there was little argument.

Chris Wilder's men began what they hoped would be a memorable 2018 with a short trip to one of Coutts' former clubs, Derby County. Traditionally one of what Wilder would term 'the big hitters' in the Championship, Derby were second in the table at the time and managed by Gary Rowett, a friend of Wilder's from their non-league days and one of two managers – Burnley's Sean Dyche the other – that the Blades boss remembers calling for advice after promotion from League One was secured. Rowett started out at Burton Albion before being harshly sacked by

Birmingham when they were seventh in the Championship, but was now working in a vastly different market; rudimentary maths before kick-off suggested the Derby squad on the day had cost north of £30m. The United 18? Around a tenth of that.

On the day, though, they couldn't be separated with the league's leading scorers, £8m Matěj Vydra and £150,000 Leon Clarke, both on target. But a dominant United performance saw Rowett concede afterwards that his side didn't deserve a point, and Curtis Davies admit that "United were by far the better side". Derby tried a combination of Vydra, David Nugent, Sheffield Wednesday loanee Sam Winnall and Chris Martin in an effort to overwhelm United, but United defender Richard Stearman spoke volumes as he faced the press afterwards and described United's work against the Rams' impressive offensive quartet as "pretty easy". This, as the local media's headlines screamed the following day, was yet another Wilder triumph of cohesion over cash.

The draw for the third round of the FA Cup then sent United all the way to Ipswich, but the groans of disappointment were drowned out on the eve of the long trip to Suffolk with media reports that United's pursuit of Leonard – whose contract at Roots Hall expired in the summer – had finally paid off. Wilder all but confirmed as such after watching Nathan Thomas' stunning strike seal a fourth-round berth for his side, but it was a second-half tackle by academy graduate Regan Slater that arguably pleased the manager the most. "He's absolutely cemented their lad," said Wilder, inventing a new verb through his beaming smile. Even the recipient, Manchester City loanee Bersant Celina, expressed his own admiration afterwards and at the final whistle, Wilder almost knocked Slater off his feet as he pushed the midfielder towards the United fans to celebrate. The applause, for two of their own, was probably the loudest it had been all afternoon.

Ironically, though, Slater was to move further down the pecking order of Bramall Lane midfielders when Leonard was officially unveiled as a Blade, after nine months, countless bids and counter-bids and a great deal of patience from Wilder and his staff. Even then, and perhaps fittingly for one of the longest-running sagas in recent United memory, his signing wasn't straightforward; the

25-year-old arrived at Bramall Lane too late to complete a routine heart scan as part of his medical, and his signing was delayed as a result. But eventually he was in the Lane tunnel, shirt aloft, admitting it was "an honour" to be a Blade. His last outing for Southend was a 2-0 defeat to AFC Wimbledon at Kingsmeadow and after completing the formalities, he was in line for his Blades debut three days later. The opponents? Sheffield Wednesday.

As the whole of the Steel City began to look nervously towards the second derby of the season, moved to a Friday evening to accommodate Sky Sports, Wilder preoccupied himself with more transfer work, confirming the captures of Manchester United's James Wilson, on loan, and Welsh international Lee Evans from Wolves for around £750,000. Evans, who worked with David Brooks following the Blades wonderkid's call-up to the Welsh senior squad, recalls a conversation with Wilder in which the United manager tried to sell United to him: "But I told him there was no need. He didn't have to try and sell it, because Sheffield United speaks for itself. It's a massive club, with a great stature, history and pedigree, and one that's moving in the right direction. In short, everything you could want as a footballer."

Wilson, who made 19 appearances for arguably the biggest club on the planet after being handed a debut by Ryan Giggs, told the media he wouldn't be fazed by facing Wednesday after travelling with his parent club to places like Anfield and Arsenal, but all three players were left in no doubt what this game means in this corner of the footballing world. Exactly 111 days on from the last meeting, which saw Wilder's men prevail 4-2 and Brooks, Mark Duffy and Clarke write their names into Bramall Lane folklore, the teams met again, at Bramall Lane for the first time since October 2011. Unusually, for a game of this type, large sections of both fanbases thought the result was almost inevitable; Wednesday, languishing in 16th before kick-off, had underperformed all season and parted company with Carlos Carvalhal on Christmas Eve, unknown Dutchman Jos Luhukay succeeding him. United, meanwhile, were chasing the play-offs with memories of that day in September still fresh in their mind.

Despite the 12-point and nine-places gap between the sides

in the Championship table, though, both actually went into the game in pretty poor form – United with one win in their last nine, Wednesday with just two – and with Luhukay setting up the visitors not to lose, rather than trying to win, the end result was a frustrating and unspectacular goalless draw. The closest United got to a winner was a Clayton Donaldson header that Joe Wildsmith did well to parry over and after skipper Glenn Loovens was sent off for two fouls on Donaldson, Wednesday came close to snatching all three points late on when Adam Reach volleyed towards the top corner. Simon Moore, the United goalkeeper, had been almost down on his haunches seconds earlier after hurting his ribs in a collision with Stearman but as Reach let fly from outside the box, Moore sprung from almost on the turf to superbly turn the volley behind.

One man left feeling underwhelmed by the game was Josh Pinder, a Blades fan who made the 36-hour journey from his home in Australia to be at Bramall Lane. "I came out here 15 months ago after getting a job with Diabetes Australia, but as a result I missed the 100-point League One title win," said Josh, "and the best year as a Blade in my lifetime! I was missing the games big time and thought this was the perfect occasion to come back. You can't beat a sell-out under the lights on a Friday night at the Lane."

Despite the disappointment, United's supporters did take great delight in the reaction of Wednesday's supporters to the goalless draw, at the home of their neighbours fresh out of what they labelled as 'the pub league'. Wednesday's players threw their shirts into the joyous crowd in the away end and, at the Rawson Spring pub near Hillsborough, one fan recalled his embarrassment at seeing fellow Owls supporters celebrating on tables after avoiding what they felt was an inevitable thumping at the home of their biggest rivals. "That was a terrible result for us and really put a dent in our promotion push!" Wilder remembers, with more than a hint of sarcasm and schadenfreude.

"I think that showed how far we had come. They definitely came to frustrate us and they ran around, because they had to, but my boys had done that for a season and a half. I was disappointed because I don't think we played – we got into a bit of a row with them and wanted to show how strong and physical we were. They bashed it that night, but we didn't play as well as we should have done.

"So we were a bit disappointed to not have done the double, but four points out of six is still a decent collection and they were chucking shirts into the crowd, when they were 15th in the Championship. If ever there was a moment to look back and ask if we have closed the gap … I think that was it. They might still think the gap is still there, but if you ask me I think we might have closed it. At least a little bit."

One neutral, for the time being at least, watching the game was Ricky Holmes, the Charlton midfielder who had hoped that his move to United would be completed in time to allow him to play in the derby. It wasn't, but went through the following week and Holmes was a Blade. Wilder, who worked with Holmes in their title-winning campaign at Northampton and attempted to sign him from Charlton in the summer, was frustrated in his efforts when Holmes elected to sign a new contract at The Valley. His arrival, on January 15, signalled the end of United's business for the month – a marked departure from the attitude of Wilder's predecessors, who were criticised by fans for leaving their moves until the last hours of the window – and three of the four new recruits made their United debuts the following Saturday, when Wilder's men avenged that infamous defeat at home to Norwich earlier in the season.

Wilder admitted to having a slight smile on his face in the build-up to the game when the Canaries took Premier League champions Chelsea to penalties in their FA Cup replay in midweek, and was in similarly good form during his pre-match press conference as he was reminded about his comments about Norwich turning up late to Bramall Lane and then wasting time at almost every opportunity. "I can't be late," the manager smiled. "We'll be setting off from the hotel at 9am. The players have been told 'get yourselves up and get ready.' Breakfast is at 6.30 in the morning. Everybody has got to be packed by then."

Wilder may have been joking about the wake-up call but

his players still made a remarkably early start to the game at Carrow Road, going ahead in just the sixth minute through Wilson's full debut goal and dominating proceedings for almost the entire first half. With James Maddison, a particular target of United supporters' ire for his theatrics, growing more and more frustrated, Donaldson pounced on a weak back-pass to put United 2-0 ahead in the second half before City's Josh Murphy drew one of the biggest cheers of the afternoon when, without a hint of irony, he pointed to his watch and accused the visitors of timewasting. Ivo Pinto gave the hosts hope with a 70th minute header but United held firm to register a first win since Boxing Day, and spark a witty chant poking fun at Norwich's antics: 'Take your time, take your time, Sheff United … playing football the Norwich way'.

Wilder inadvertently ensured that this mini-rivalry between the Blades and Canaries would continue in seasons to come with his post-match celebrations, which saw him punch the air in jubilation in front of United's excellent travelling support and also point to his watch, mocking Murphy's protestations to the referee. Home fans behind the goal responded with far from complimentary chants of their own, and some even stayed behind to bizarrely abuse United's unused substitutes; before a steward intervened and advised them to continue their warm-down elsewhere on the Carrow Road pitch. Billy Sharp incensed the home fans further by pulling off a celebratory 'Klinsmann Dive' to retrieve a cone and as Duffy smiled afterwards: "They were all kicking off. They can give it, but can't take a bit back."

When the adrenaline wore off, Wilder made a point of explaining his 'emotional' reaction. "The win meant a lot to me because a few things happened over the week," he revealed. "My father-in-law wasn't very well back in Sheffield and he's a big fan of me and of the team, so there was a bit of emotion at the end. It wasn't anything directed at the opposition or anything like that." In the cold light of day, Wilder would concede that it was, a little bit, but "the revenge aspect of the win wasn't spoken about the whole week.

"The focus was on a big performance, and we were due a big

result. We had to go there and win and it felt like a big result, because they're a good side. But a lot of people go on about my reaction afterwards and I think it was quite arrogant of Norwich City, and their reporters and few other people to think it was aimed at them. Okay, maybe it was a little bit, when I tapped my watch because I was frustrated at the way they went about things at Bramall Lane, but not as much as they might think."

Another break for the FA Cup saw United reach the fifth round courtesy of a 1-0 victory over play-off rivals Preston, Sharp's penalty the difference between the two sides in a wholly forgettable contest at Bramall Lane, but there was another harsh reminder of the relentless nature of the Championship to come when Aston Villa journeyed north to Sheffield on Tuesday, January 30. Wilder, who paid tribute to his former Blades teammate Steve Bruce in the build-up and joked that taking charge during a turbulent chapter of United history would have been some baptism of fire for the former Manchester United legend, saw his side dominate the big-spending visitors, who were indebted to goalkeeper Sam Johnstone's four superb saves after Jack O'Connell hit the bar with a header early on. But the suckerpunch came in stoppage time when Enda Stevens allowed Robert Snodgrass to cut onto his left foot, and the Scottish international curled home a stunning effort to break Blades hearts.

He's one of our own ... and so am I!
By Regan Slater, midfielder

I first suspected I'd be involved at Ipswich when I got told to bring my stuff to travel with the team, but I still didn't know for sure until I saw my shirt hanging up in the dressing room. Even then, I had to ask to make sure I was on the bench! It was a great feeling and even more so to come on at half-time for Nathan Thomas. I just wanted to show what I'm all about and I think I did that, especially with the tackle on Bersant Celina. It was nice to show that tackling hasn't gone completely from the game and there's still a place for it, if you get it right. Luckily I did. Afterwards, it was all over social media and even Celina wrote about it on

Twitter. It was good that he took it so well, but I do think tackling is going out of the game a little and referees don't really help nowadays. Everyone's just a bit soft now, aren't they?

The gaffer described that tackle as his personal highlight of the game and made a bit of a fuss of me afterwards with the fans, which was nice. Although I didn't realise he was coming up behind me and I was lucky not to land on my face when he shoved me towards them! But it was great to be appreciated by the fans and share that moment with them, obviously with being a Blade myself. I know how much the club means to them, and to Chris. It's no surprise he's so passionate because it's his club, although that does bring some added pressure. When I play for United, I don't want to let the fans down; if I was still sat on the Kop and someone's giving the ball away, I'd be jumping on them too!

But I see them chanting the gaffer's name, about him being one of their own, and I want a bit of that as well. That's a dream of mine. Obviously as a footballer you have your main targets for your career but there's little side-goals as well, and that's one of mine. To be a Blade and have United fans chanting your name must be very special, and hopefully I get to experience that in the future. It's a big part of my game and the way I play, that I love football and Sheffield United. I've supported the club all my life and to play for them just means that little bit more. It's not just a game, especially when you've got that badge on your chest.

I used to come to games at Bramall Lane with my dad and I've sat all over the ground, although when I had a season ticket with my mates it was on the Kop. I've got a lot of good memories and a fair few bad ones, too, like most Blades. Stand out ones are defeats at Wembley but one of my favourite ones was actually beating Wednesday 4-2 at Hillsborough. Every United fan loves to see that! The first players I really remember were the likes of Chris Morgan and Michael Tonge, and the year in the Premier League under Neil Warnock was great. I remember collecting the Match Attax cards from that season! There's been a few down years since then but we're moving in the right direction now.

As a youngster I always used to look up to Steven Gerrard and, more recently, Jack Wilshere. He has that little drive from midfield that not many have; that's something I need to keep in my game and get better at. Nothing against Nick Montgomery, I think he was a great player, but I like to think I have a little bit more excitement in my game! I started at Handsworth Boys at five or six years old and got scouted by United then, although I had to wait until U8s to join them properly. There were always better players than me in the age groups, which helped push me on, although they perhaps didn't make it because their attitude wasn't right. I've always played above my age group and even at 18, I captained a very young United U23 side.

Chris came to the club when I was on my scholarship so I hadn't really been involved with a first-team setup before, but in pre-season we were training on the pitch next to them when a player picked up an injury and I was called up to cover. That was when my heart started racing! Obviously as a player you never want to see a teammate get injured but it gave me a little chance, and I like to think I took it. My debut then came in the Checkatrade Trophy away at Grimsby, which was a very special moment – especially when I scored. I remember the ball breaking to me and I just thought 'hit it'. When it went in, I didn't know what to do ... I'd been dreaming about that moment all my life. It was my first goal of the season, at any level, and a perfect time to get it.

All the lads were great with me and knew what it meant, especially the younger lads who maybe knew me better. But I never thought I'd 'made it' or anything like that. I actually went straight back to the U18s afterwards. But it made me want it even more, having got a taste of first-team action. I knew I wanted to be back there, so gave everything to make it happen. I absolutely love being captain, too; I had always been jealous of players who had the armband before I got it, because I always thought I'd be a good skipper. It shows you have the respect and trust of the coaches and your teammates, and you have to have it inside you I think. In football, you won't always be 5-0 up on a sunny day and you find out a lot about people when things are going against you. That's when the team spirit can come into play, and it's great here which is big. It helped Leicester win the Premier League and it helps us get the best out of each other here.

I moved up to train with the first-team around Christmas which helped me get used to the intensity, and seeing how midfielders like John Fleck perform in certain situations is great for a young player. After getting my initiation out of the way down at Millwall – I sang 'Build Me Up, Buttercup' because it's the only song I know the words to off the top of my head – I made my league debut at Preston, which I'll always be proud of even if the day could have gone better for the team. A lot of people helped make it happen – they know who they are – but mainly all my coaches and my family, who took me to games and training when I was younger and played a huge part. As for me, I joined Carlisle on loan in July 2018 but first and foremost, my aim is to play for Sheffield United; and I'll do whatever I have to do to make that happen.

From Sunday League to Sheffield United
By Ricky Holmes, forward

I don't think it's an exaggeration to say that Chris Wilder resurrected my career. I was down at Portsmouth and it was hit and miss, to be honest; I wasn't consistent and I fell out with the manager, so I wasn't playing. Chris took me to Northampton and we really hit it off straightaway. They were struggling at the time and in 18 months we managed to consolidate towards mid-table and then the next season, we took the league by storm. I had the opportunity to join United in the summer but I didn't worry that the chance wouldn't come around again and I was grateful to Charlton for letting me go, and giving me my chance in the Championship at the tender age of 30.

To know that Chris obviously kept an eye on me and came back in for me in January is a big thing for me. He's a manager I've worked closely with before, we had success and sometimes when you go to a new club it can take six months or so to earn the trust of the manager and the staff. I've already earned that under Chris and I was desperate to play under him again. I narrowly missed signing in time to be involved in the derby against Wednesday but I was at the game, and the atmosphere made the hairs on the back of my neck stand up. It was unbelievable. I didn't need selling on the move because of Chris and the size of the club but that alone would have sold it to me.

The crowds were brilliant at Portsmouth and it was good when it got going at Charlton, but this was a 30,000-plus sell-out and you don't get that at many clubs. They're football crazy and get right behind the players, which is a big thing for us. There's a good unity which is what Chris always talks about. I was up here with my agent and a few others and I turned to them and said 'this is a proper place to play football, let's get this deal done'. From there, it was about making up for lost time. I've come from Sunday League football, playing for a team called White Ensign on parks pitches in Southend, and I used to pay to play football with my mates. I went to college and university and it was slow progress but then I was dibbing around in League Two, before Chris got hold of me and got me going. He'll probably say it's all down to him! But there was a lot of hard work, too. If you have success in League Two, that's sometimes the only way to get a move higher up and luckily, it's been good progress since then.

All the boys are brilliant and welcomed me with open arms. It probably makes it easier that a lot of them have taken a similar path here, from the lower leagues. If I went into a changing room full of Premier League superstars dropping down, they probably wouldn't even know my name. But I've played against a lot of these boys, they've seen what I can do and I know what they're capable of, so it was a great changing room to come into. But it's that grounding that helps me appreciate where I am and how far I've come. We get a lot of things done for us which I used to have to do for myself, like washing the kit. I have worked hard for it, it doesn't just come out of the blue, but if I have any advice for a young lad, it would be never to give up hope ... because I am proof, I guess, that it can happen.

January 2018 – The New Year blues
By Matthew Bell, Kop

Up until the middle of November 2017, when the question was asked about who Sheffield United should sign in the January transfer window, the answer was usually another question: "Who do we need to replace?" The team was settled, with Paul Coutts, John Fleck and Mark Duffy outstanding in midfield. But that all changed one Friday night at Burton Albion, when Coutts broke his right leg. A few weeks later Fleck was sent off, picking up a three-match ban. Next, Duffy and David Brooks fell ill, missing the away game at Preston, where United played poorly and lost. Not surprising to many, considering that John Lundstram – a summer signing from Oxford United – was now the midfield mainstay, having never played at Championship level before. Lundstram was improving with each appearance but he couldn't do it on his own, especially as Samir Carruthers once again failed to take his opportunity at Preston. Reinforcements were needed.

Fortunately, or more likely due to meticulous planning, Chris Wilder had pinpointed his chief targets many months before. In fact their identities were public knowledge thanks to somewhat less-than-confidential negotiations the previous summer. Back then, though, their clubs Southend United and Charlton Athletic refused to budge on their asking price and United refused to increase their offers for Ryan Leonard and Ricky Holmes. But half a season can make a big difference. The two players were that much nearer the expiry of their contracts – a circumstance that tends to reduce value – and United, emboldened by a stirring return to the Championship, now had more bargaining power.

Blades fans had already seen first-hand what Leonard and Holmes could do. In the 2015/16 season Leonard volleyed in off the post from 25 yards in Southend's 2-2 draw at Bramall Lane; a year later Holmes skilfully bent a free-kick past Simon Moore for Charlton and was impressive throughout. Leonard possessed another characteristic of which we were not necessarily aware; speed, which has never been known to impair a team. Less was known of Wilder's third midfield signing, though he was actually the one with the most experience in the Championship – albeit still not a great deal, having played most of his football in League One for Wolves, Bradford City and Wigan Athletic. Lee Evans was signed to be an almost like-for-like replacement for Coutts.

Leonard and Evans cost what might be considered by many Championship clubs as piffling sums, in the region of £700,000 each. When United signed Clayton Donaldson in August for £50,000, Wilder likened it to shopping at Aldi. In January United had moved on to the Co-op, but the problem is that in football, those who purchase their wares at Fortnum and Mason generally rise to the top – exemplified by Robert Snodgrass' winning goal for Aston Villa. Transferred for over £20million throughout his career and reputed to be earning around £50,000 a week, his extra class told. United's players who won promotion and most of those signed later were, of course, among the best League One had to offer, but such quality can only take a team so far.

But such a drop off in performance was always likely to happen; it is rare for a team to rush straight through from the third level to the first. United did it under Dave Bassett and Southampton when Nigel Adkins was their manager, but in those days the Championship was not populated by so many clubs desperate to gain or regain Premier League status and who were willing to gamble fortunes to do so. In November 2017, *The Star* asked correspondents from other local media what they thought of United who, at the time, were vying with Wolves and Cardiff City for the top three places. Two particular comments stood out. Paul Taylor of the *Nottingham Post* said: "United are one of the best sides to have visited the City Ground this season ... some of the football the Blades played was superb. They will be up there by the end of the campaign, still." On the other hand, Tom Marshall-Bailey of *Leeds Live* said: "I expect Sheffield United to eventually fizzle away."

At the time of that article everything was going well and, unusually for Blades fans, optimism was unbounded. The following week United won 3-1 at Burton and went top for 24 hours. But that was the night Coutts broke his leg. From that game onwards United's record was more bottom than top, despite the fact that they played well in most matches. Misfortune also played a part: hitting the woodwork four times against Bristol City, mistakes such as the one by Cameron Carter-Vickers against Fulham, great displays by opposition goalkeepers, Leon Clarke's loss of potency and wonder-goals scored by City, Aston Villa and Wolves. All that cannot be put down to Coutts' absence.

There were other matches in January in which United did not play so well, the Steel City derby being a case in point. Leading up to the match United's and Wednesday's records over the previous nine league matches were exactly the same (one win, three draws, five defeats) but the moods of the two clubs could hardly have been more different. United should have won five of the games they did not, whereas Wednesday had been pretty dismal most weeks and parted company with Carlos Carvalhal on Christmas Eve.

Jos Luhukay got them organised quickly, a feat that seemed beyond his predecessor, and the Wednesday fans celebrated the goalless draw as though they had just won promotion. Although United fans were frustrated by the result, they lapped up this over-the-top response. Dubbed in pre-season as a team from the 'pub league', United had turned the sneer on its head and Blades fans now mocked their counterparts' reaction to a point gained away to the 'Dog and Duck'. But the derby night draw had become symptomatic of United's performances; sometimes good, often not bad, occasionally poor, but even the good did not carry the zest and panache of what we had seen in the autumn. It was still early days, but there was a general impression that the three January signings had improved the depth of the squad but not its quality.

15

Mauled by Wolves ... and the Tigers
February, 2018

As the January transfer window slammed, as Chris Wilder had promised, shut without any further incomings at Bramall Lane, the irony was not lost upon many who followed Sheffield United that their first commitment of February 2018 was a trip to Molineux, the home of the big-spending league leaders Wolverhampton Wanderers. Even by Championship standards, where more and more clubs seem willing to gamble with their financial futures by the season in pursuit of Premier League riches, Wolves' outlay was enormous and they had, with a nod to Reading in 2005/06 and Newcastle four seasons later, assembled what is considered by many to be the best second-tier side in recent memory.

Wilder described Wolves as the "Manchester City of the Championship" during his media briefing before making the trip to the Black Country, but reiterated that United would not be fazed or fearful of the proposition. "Other things than money can win games and that is the beauty of football," he said. "It is not always decided on bank balances and the financial aspect. We have always tried to put a dent in that this year, and the majority of times we have." But the task of doing so again at Molineux proved beyond them as, after £15m man Rúben Neves found the top corner with an unstoppable effort in just the fifth minute, Diogo Jota and the impressive Ivan Cavaleiro capped a dominant 3-0 victory. United's misery was complete when goalkeeper Simon Moore was sent off after racing off his line and poleaxing

Jota, Cavaleiro's resulting free-kick deflecting off the United wall and wrong-footing young sub stopper Jake Eastwood.

United were well-beaten but, with Wilder leading from the front, they were unbowed. "The gaffer got us in the dressing room afterwards and his head was held really high," George Baldock, one of the few United players to emerge with any credit on a difficult evening, said. "It was February 3 and it's the first time we've had to stand in front of the press, or anyone really, and admit we got battered. He was brilliant in there. He said: 'Listen, that's the first time we've been beaten by a better team.' So for that to happen, for the first time, at that stage of the season, I thought that was pretty good." United, who had led Wolves by a point both times they reached the summit of the Championship table, were now eighth and 22 points behind the runaway leaders – and, more realistically, five points off the play-offs.

Their mood was hardly assuaged a day later when news broke from Elland Road that Leeds, their Yorkshire rivals and next opponents, had sacked Thomas Christiansen after eight months in charge and a winless run of ten games. Wary of the inevitable 'bounce' that often seems to follow the appointment of a new manager, Wilder would have been forgiven for paying more attention than usual to United's next opposition and Leeds eventually unveiled Paul Heckingbottom, the former Barnsley boss, just three days after he had signed a new and improved contract at Oakwell. But Heckingbottom could only stand and admire as skipper Billy Sharp, restored to the United line-up for his first start of 2018, netted a sensational, acrobatic volley in just the second minute of the game – the 200th league goal of his career – and, after Pierre-Michel Lasogga's powerful header levelled the scores just after the restart, confidently sealed all three points from the penalty spot after John Fleck had been tripped in the Leeds area.

Remarkably, the goals were Sharp's sixth and seventh in six starts against former club Leeds, who he left to rejoin United in 2015, and another triumph for his dad, Steve, who revels in a 'statto' reputation and, according to his son, 'knows everything'.

"My dad texted me before the game, to say that I'd scored five in five against Leeds and that he believed I'd score again," Sharp smiled. "And to be honest, I felt the same. He's always doing stuff like that, reminding me about little bits and pieces, so it felt good when his prediction came true. To be honest, my dad kept me going in that spell when I'd not been playing. It was nice to get a text off him, it gives me confidence. If I have a good record, he texts me … he knows all about the stats. I have had spells like this before, when I've not been in the team. You just have to get on with it, especially now I'm captain, because I have to keep the boys going. The goals were for them … they are the ones who had been grafting but not getting the results."

Less than a week later, United's FA Cup run came to an end at the home of the former Premier League champions Leicester, but David Brooks did make a long-awaited and timely comeback after recovering from glandular fever. United, who ultimately lost 1-0 to a somewhat inevitable goal from Sheffield Wednesday supporter Jamie Vardy, gave a good account of themselves and Harry Maguire, the former Blades defender now in the England squad, was forced to fling himself at Enda Stevens' shot when the left-back could, and probably should, have opened the scoring. The atmosphere inside the King Power Stadium, artificially influenced by the provision of paper 'clappers', only cranked up when Riyad Mahrez was taken off – and received a standing ovation – on his return from a self-imposed strike following the collapse of his January move to Manchester City but, as Jake Wright opined afterwards, there were positives to take from the game. Not least in the press room, where members of the media were greeted with a choice of three curries, with all the trimmings, before the game and bottles of Thai beer, as well as cheese and biscuits, afterwards. One local journalist, who shall remain nameless, took full advantage and waddled out of the media suite with a bag stuffed full of Pepsi and enough pick 'n mix to last for the remainder of the season.

Back at Bramall Lane, Wilder's men breathed fresh life into their play-off push with a 2-1 victory over QPR, to move back within a point of sixth-placed Bristol City. Defender Richard

Stearman put the Blades ahead with only his second goal for the club and John Lundstram made it 2-0 in the second half, but the impressive Luke Freeman set up a nervy finish by pulling one back just after the hour mark. "We played a very good team," said QPR boss Ian Holloway after the game. "Their manager deserves all sorts of credit, their staff deserve all sorts of credit, the crowd deserves all sorts of credit for how far they've come." United had put themselves in a position, with a win on the road the following Friday, to go back into the play-offs. The opponents were troubled Hull City; managed by Nigel Adkins.

Adkins, the former Scunthorpe and Southampton boss, led United to an 11th-placed finish in League One in his only season in charge and paid the price with his job, which went to Wilder in May 2016. Few, if any, United supporters look back on the Adkins reign with much fondness but the man himself admitted, in a pre-match interview in the *Hull Daily Mail:* "It was a great experience. It was a shame it didn't work out because I met some really good people at Sheffield United ... and I still really enjoyed my time there. I learned invaluable lessons, which is maybe why I took a little bit longer to take a job back in football. Chris was a great appointment for United, having been there before under Dave Bassett. The way the supporters want their teams to play and what they demand of them, it's hard to play in that arena. Great credit to the United players because they're doing it."

They were, anyway, until kick-off at the KCOM Stadium. Home supporters planned protests before and during the game against their owners, the Allam family, and the game was stopped when sponge balls were thrown onto the field, but United barely got going at all throughout the evening and there was little surprise when Nouha Dicko netted for the hosts, ten minutes into the second half. Not even that could spur United into action and apart from one effort from Sharp, Hull goalkeeper Allan McGregor was comfortable throughout. The mood in the visiting dressing room was less so after the game and when Wilder eventually surfaced to face the media, he completely wrote off United's play-off chances in an extraordinary diatribe.

"We didn't deserve anything from the game … I'm wasting my time and energy thinking we're going to get in the top six because to produce a performance like that, with everything at stake, is not good enough," raged Wilder. "And it won't be good enough to get into the top six. I'm not trying to play spin, I know other managers do, but … I think the only two players that come out of it with any credit were the skipper [Sharp] and Leon Clarke at the top of the pitch. And I just said to them that I'd have been looking behind me with about 15 or 20 minutes to go and thinking 'why bother?' because everything else behind was way off. Every part of our performance was below the standards we've set and like I said, that's us now. Because we've clearly not shown the qualities that are needed to get into the play-offs.

"I think I've got the maximum out of them, I really do. They've had a go so far this season, and it's been a decent season but I'm possibly looking at it and going 'What do we need to do in the summer?' because this was a big night for us, and we've failed to turn up. I'm wasting my time talking to the players. How can we not drive this game forward? I said at half-time we were playing in second gear, and it's up to them how the players take it on board.

"Everyone knows what I want to do and they know exactly what I thought we could do, but I must have been away with the fairies and possibly in the nuthouse if I thought that we could … clearly tonight we've shown that we can't. I'll not waste my energy on them, I'll not motivate them from now on in and I'm looking to see what the players are about and see if we can have a strong finish to the season. But as far as I'm concerned, tonight has cemented where we are really, we're short and we haven't got enough to get in that top six.

"Regardless of what anyone says, I've had to turn this club around from a really poor position, to the position where we are but as anyone who knows me will tell you, it isn't enough. It isn't enough. I want to keep going forward, it's never enough, never enough, never enough. Whether we're overachieving or not, it's never enough. I want us to do as well as possible.

Sometimes I have to take a step out of it but my drive and my desire to take this club as high as possible, regardless of budgets or this, that and the other, requires my players to be on the same page as me, and maybe some of them are and some of them aren't. Tonight has hurt me ... I'm not being like a spoilt kid, I just thought we were better than that. It's the biggest game of the season by a million miles and we've not turned up. Not one of those players can come to me and say I think you're out of order. Not one.

"I had to work overtime at half time to motivate the players and it doesn't always have to come from me. I'm at it 100 percent with this club, 24/7, and everyone knows what we've had to do to get it moving forward but it's never enough for me. I've got the maximum out of the budget I was given in January and I'll come in and be professional on Sunday, set up a team to go on Tuesday, and it's over to them now. It really is over to them. You don't become bad players and characters overnight, but I'm deeply disappointed and it's possibly given me an insight into one or two characters. Maybe it's just caught up with us tonight ... but it's a big reality check to see where we are."

It was an extraordinary and emotional stream of consciousness from Wilder, delivered inside a small cupboard-sized room just off the tunnel of Hull's stadium, and a sentiment that was repeated – albeit in a slightly more considered fashion – once he had marched through the maze of corridors to the media suite to face the national press. The look on the faces of United's players as they scurried onto the waiting coach outside suggested the manner of delivery was not held back for their benefit in the away dressing room, either.

Months later, Wilder conceded that his outburst was part emotion, and part designed to elicit a response from his players. "I thought that night that we were really poor," he said, "but looking back at it, I've got to give the players a bit of leeway. The atmosphere in the ground was a really surreal one, and reminded us of Coventry and Charlton the season before. Players shouldn't have to go through that. Football was secondary that night, and should never be. The tempo was slow and we certainly didn't turn up, but there were other times we didn't either, before Christmas; for every Hull and Birmingham away, there's a Millwall away and a Preston away. These things happen through a season and I don't regret what I said ... I'm open, upfront and honest and to be fair to the players, their reaction at Reading showed what they're all about."

Four days later, on a snow-dusted pitch amidst freezing temperatures at the Madjeski Stadium, United ran out 3-1 winners with Sharp at the double, and Mark Duffy also netting a stunner from long range. But the game itself hinged on two second-half minutes when, after Omar Richards had reduced the deficit to 2-1, Moore saved Leandro Bacuna's penalty before Sharp put the game beyond doubt with his second just moments later. Wilder this time left post-match media duties to his No.2, Alan Knill, who insisted the manager was right to let his players know they had slipped well below their usual standards, adding: "That's what we're all about. The intensity was there and when we're full-on like that, we know we've got some very good players out there. No, the play-offs aren't over. But we've got to keep those levels now because every game is a big one."

'A job like any other ... at a club like no other'
By Alan Knill, assistant manager

There have been times when I've had to try and rein Chris in a little, but it's really hard to curb because that is him – what you see is what you get, and he's only saying what everyone is thinking anyway. I think that's part of what gives him such a special relationship with the Blades fans, because they would say the same if they had the chance. You hear a lot of managers these days talk and it's just 'manager speak', about a plan or a DNA or something ... I think 'just talk properly, tell us the truth'. If you're not happy then you're not happy. Just say it. And that's something Chris isn't shy of doing.

The players know what's happening anyway so he's very honest and at times brutal, but that's the job isn't it? Footballers are paid really well to perform and when we don't feel like they've run around, and have just gone through the motions, there's no excuse for not being competitive. In football there will be games when you don't have the quality of the other team but when he feels they haven't competed, that's usually when he lets them know. There have been some unbelievable times when I've seen him fly off the handle but again, it's a job. In any other industry, if you give someone all the tools and preparation they need to do a job and they don't do it, then they'll get a rollicking. Just because it's football, why should it be any different?

At previous clubs when we've not had many players, we've sometimes had to tread a little more carefully but we've not got that problem at United, so if you're not good enough or won't compete then you won't play. Of course there are times when Chris has to put an arm around someone and he's very good at that side, too, but the majority of the time he's just telling the truth. One thing I hate is the phrase 'modern-day footballer'. It's rubbish. It just reminds me of a pampered prima donna and we don't want that. We just want footballers who want to work hard and he translates that to the players pretty early.

If we have a good player, as a coach you look at him and think 'I can make him better' but if he doesn't want to be better, it doesn't matter how good a coach you are. So for us, it's attitude first and it has been pretty much since we first worked together in management, when he was my No.2 at Bury. We obviously grew up in Southampton's academy a few years apart but didn't speak much during our playing careers, but then got back in touch a little when I was at Rotherham United and he brought a team to play us in pre-season. Then after Halifax went bust, I told him to come and work with me at Bury and have a bit of a break, not from football but from the pressures of being a manager.

It was great for him, and he was great with the players, but I wasn't surprised six months later when he left for Oxford. He's just really good at managing and really lives for it whereas I had had enough of managing and prefer coaching, being out on the grass with the players. To be a good manager, you have to love that part of it and Steve McClaren said the same thing of Sir Alex Ferguson at Manchester United; he never touched the grass, but loved managing players. I'm not comparing Chris with Sir Alex, but they have the same traits.

Like Chris, I left Southampton without getting many chances but to be successful back then, you had to head it and kick it and that's what I did. As I got to 26 or 27, in training, I'd think 'that wasn't the best training session I've ever had' and would think I could do better. So I always thought I'd end up coaching. I did okay in my career, and was even a one-cap wonder for Wales – marking the great Marco van Basten! I was at Swansea in the fourth division and our manager, Terry Yorath, was also in charge of Wales and had a bit of an injury crisis, so I got the call to go on standby.

There were some big names in the Wales set-up then – Hughes, Rush, Saunders, Southall – and I never thought I'd play, but I ended up in a three at the back – which is quite ironic, given how we play at United these days, although it wasn't quite the same! Barry Horne marked Ruud Gullit and I had van Basten, man-to-man, months after he'd scored a hat-trick against England and won the Euros. On the Friday, I was marking Roy McDonough of Southend and the week after, I was up against van Basten in Holland. Everyone was saying how well I'd done and that I'd play for years ... the first-choice centre-halves came back and I never played again. It is what it is, I guess. And it's a decent story!

After retiring I had nothing, and then a youth coach job came up at Rotherham. I had no interest in playing football any longer because I couldn't get up for any game, and they all seemed the same to me. I couldn't wait to finish but if the Millers' job didn't come up, I guess I'd have had to play in non-league. That was really good. Eventually, I ended up in charge and the club was in all sorts of trouble. I remember doing a sponsored walk before one game and at Southend away, I had a bucket for donations from their supporters. When I see top-level players walking straight into management ... whatever you think being a manager is, it's so much more. It rules everything in your life and wherever you are, it's always football on the brain. My missus used to say 'you're in 4-4-2 world again' because she was speaking to me and I was thinking about the game. You have to love managing to do it; you have to throw everything into it, or you'll come up short.

I remember going to Torquay and they asked if I could keep them up, which I did. They put us in a hotel and found us a house right on the beach. It was lovely. The sunniest day ever, there were yachts in the sea. I said to my missus that we could maybe have a life alongside football down here, and I took the job permanently. About three months in, I never noticed the sea. I hated every minute of it. My missus said 'it could be Handsworth Road out there instead of the sea!' and I told her I'd rather it was. Chris phoned me to tell me he was going for the Portsmouth job and I said I'd ditch Torquay, because I'd had enough. He didn't get it and by the time he got the Northampton job, I'd left Torquay so we linked up again, with me as his No.2. It was ideal for me, really, as I could work with the players and I'm not bothered about roles or being a No.1 or a No.2 – if I'm allowed to do what I want to do then I'm happy, and there were no issues whatsoever with the role reversal.

In a way, it helped because I know what Chris is feeling. If we lose, it hurts me but it kills him. He lives and breathes it, and is really intense. We used to travel to Northampton on a Thursday and room together down there. The last question from him on Thursday night would be about the team, and as soon as I woke up on Friday morning he was talking about the team! It probably helps as well that our relationship is just a working one; we're not going out for meals or spending a lot of time together outside of football. Then he knows that when he asks my opinion, I'm not giving it because he's a mate – I'm doing it because it affects my life as well. We'll phone each other and talk about stuff quite often, but it's a working relationship. We're not best mates and have different personalities; Chris has a big circle of friends, but that'd never be me. I like to stay out of the limelight. We're good cop, bad cop I suppose. I'm always good cop, though!

I've lived in Sheffield for 20 years or so now so that, coupled with Chris' obvious connections, gave us a good insight when we took over at United in 2016. The players, led by the skipper, were good and wanted change and there were some that we knew would never work for us, and some we thought wouldn't but ended up working very well, like Couttsy and Kieron Freeman. It still had a big club mentality but in the reality of League One, so it needed bringing back down to earth a little. We just wanted players to run around, and make tackles and headers. Here, you get a bigger clap for a tackle than you do a pass. It's a working-class club so needed working-class players who would work. Expectation was still high, of course, but we wanted them to put a shift in.

Then as the season went on, I realised how much it means to people and how big the club is. We played Charlton away in November and I stayed down in London with the family, so we met their manager for an hour after the game and left The Valley when I thought it'd be quiet. The station was absolutely rammed with Blades fans. I got on the tube for one stop, got off and there were more there! We got the train home at 4pm the next day and there must have been 250 Blades still there! I went to watch Noel Gallagher recently in Manchester and was sat outside a bar when a group of United fans started singing. I've been all over and Blades have said hello to me and with respect to our previous clubs, I've never had that before. I've never been a supporter as such; never followed a team or stood on a terrace, and so never really understand what it means to people. That season really drove it home.

So what is Chris' secret, apart from good staff? In all seriousness, I think he is born to manage. He wanted to win as a player and carried that on as a manager. We all do, but he's just a little more extreme with it and it has worked. Between us, it works really well. He lets me get on with my bit, trusts me with it, we have a chat and then off we go. As I say, he's really driven and has a clear vision of how his team should play – and is never happy until he gets that. Then, he speaks the fans' language too and always has, no matter what club he's been at. He says what they're seeing – if the team plays well, he says it and isn't shy if they've played badly either. Between all the staff, we've found a formula that works. Now, the challenge is to get even better at it in the future.

February 2018 – No love lost in Valentine's month
By Peter Beeby, Kop

Having already exceeded most reasonable expectations, Chris Wilder's team stuck doggedly to the almost weekly challenge of competing against teams with much heftier wage budgets and bigger name stars and began February seventh in the Championship.

Having topped the table in mid-November, United struggled to adapt to the loss of their 'conductor' Paul Coutts, regarded by many as amongst the Championship's finest playmakers, but eventually rallied to collect eight points from the six games leading into February. Hardly promotion form but, on the back of an outstanding start, enough to keep them well in the hunt.

A daunting trip to the champions-elect Wolves at Molineux ended in a 3-0 reverse that was, in truth, a fair reflection and, for the first time all season, the Blades were comprehensively outplayed – as Wilder himself acknowledged in his post-match analysis.

Consecutive home league victories followed, against Leeds and QPR, interspersed with a 1-0 FA Cup defeat at Leicester, where, again, a gulf in class was apparent despite the modest margin of victory. But even in defeat, there was a consistency of performance from the Blades built on foundations of strong organisation, honesty and a fair dosage of ability.

The QPR victory preceded a run of winnable looking fixtures, with the potential to put the Blades comfortably back into the top six. The first of these was away at lowly Hull, struggling to escape the calamitous possibility of consecutive relegations and now under the tutelage of former Blades manager, Nigel Adkins. Adkins arrived at The Lane as a popular choice amongst supporters. By the time he left, less than 12 months later, he had confused players and supporters alike with his team selections, tactics and Adkinisms. Nigel was a perpetually-positive bloke but, especially when things aren't quite going your way, some things are sometimes best not said.

By the time of his inevitable end-of-season departure Adkins had led United to 11th in League One, their lowest finish since 1983, so the prospect of facing his Hull side held little fear for the Blades faithful. Nor, one would suspect, Wilder. The Tigers subsequently beating United 1-0 was far from the season's biggest upset, especially given Hull's plethora of big-name players and associated wage bill. What surprised those who watched from the terraces, and on TV, was the Blades' performance, which lacked tempo, verve, precision and all of the many qualities that have made Wilder's side such a joy to watch since he took over.

Wilder's description of the performance – "flat from start to finish" among other things – was succinct and accurate. Offended and dispirited by what he had witnessed, Wilder went on to dismiss his team's play-off prospects and questioned the character of some of his players – something he had notably avoided doing after previous defeats.

Some were taken aback by the venom and potency of Wilder's critique. In response to a question about the reaction he expected from his players following the defeat, his "I don't care" comment will not be remembered as his finest moment but for the most part his observations were calculated in their brutality. His suggestion that "maybe we've maxed out with this group" was all the more cutting because of its legitimacy. How many supporters would seriously argue against the suggestion that the Blades had outperformed their Championship capabilities at the time of Wilder's comment?

As a player, Wilder had good technique and a positive mindset. He was an attack-minded full back with an aggressive streak, which occasionally boiled over. He lacked pace, which meant he had to work that bit harder to survive in the professional game and his tendencies were naturally aligned to Dave Bassett's mantra. Wilder dug in and stuck resolutely to the challenge of winning an initially sceptical new manager over to his virtues.

Bassett built his reputation on assembling teams worth far more than the sum of their parts, turning lower league journeymen like Bob Booker into Premier League players in the process. He knew that his only way to compete, at higher levels with limited resources, was through strong organisation, superior physicality and by eking every last ounce of commitment and endeavour from his players.

Bassett was unrelenting in the demands he placed on his players and Wilder wasn't spared the occasional hellfire of his manager's tongue, all designed, in Bassett's words, "to toughen him up." Neither was Bassett averse to berating his players publicly, once referring to Simon Tracey as having "the brains of a rocking horse" following a sending off at Tottenham. Bassett was a masterful motivator and reverse psychology was one of a variety of methods he used to extract the most from his players. Meanwhile, a young Wilder, already cutting his management teeth in the Meadowhall Sunday League with Bradway, listened and learned.

Other similarities are apparent between mentor and protégé in their approach to camaraderie and team-building. As Booker recalls, there was "no hiding place" in that Bassett dressing room and "you either joined in or fell by the wayside." Not a million miles away from Wilder's "you're either in or you're out" perspective, emphasising the importance of 'the group.' So Wilder's public rebuke of his players following the Hull defeat was delivered, in contradiction to his claim, precisely because he does "care" – possibly more than any of his predecessors. A "reaction" was what he wanted and got, with normal service resumed away at Reading four days later as the Blades saw out the month of February with an unflattering 3-1 victory.

One of Wilder's many notable achievements, in his still relatively short Blades tenure, is his reunification of the various elements of the club – players, staff, owners and, most importantly, supporters. As a DNA Blade he understands profoundly the requirements and expectations emanating from the Lane terraces. Only foolhardy United supporters expect their team to be challenging for trophies on a regular basis or spending countless millions on players. What they demand is an honest day's endeavour; "leaving everything out there" in Wilder speak. They also want to be entertained with attacking, purposeful football. Wilder provides an unfiltered channel for these sentiments into the dressing room. He gets it, and ensures his players do likewise.

Consequently, the Blades' support base remained consistently positive, vocal and on side despite the team's post-Coutts injury form slump. Indeed, the main threat to the Blades' recovered sense of common purpose occurred in early February – not on the field of play but in the boardroom, in Riyadh and S2. The first clear indication that all was not well between Sheffield United's co-owners, Kevin McCabe and Prince Abdullah, came when McCabe made his "perhaps we need an ownership structure that works" comment, during an appearance at Sheffield University's Octagon Centre on February 5.

Not long afterwards, the club released a statement confirming "His Royal Highness Prince Abdullah … and Kevin McCabe are in discussions regarding the transfer of ownership and control of Sheffield United Football Club to the Prince." Nothing too surprising in that, taken at face value, given the full buy out option built into the initial deal agreed between McCabe and the Prince back in 2013. The reason for concern and intrigue among Blades fans emanated from seemingly connected positioning and manoeuvring by the Prince in respect of personnel changes at boardroom level.

The club's original press release confirming the commencement of discussions stated: "The Prince and Kevin McCabe want to reassure everyone connected to the club that the current negotiations and transfer of ownership will have no impact on the club's management and its staff." Had there been a speedy resolution to discussions that may have been the case. But, as weeks passed without further clarification, Wilder was questioned on the subject and made clear his concern. "I don't know the direction the club is going," he said. "It would be good to know from my point of view, of course."

It was proving an unhelpful distraction for Wilder, who was already a once in a generation manager. With reasonable backing, he could become a once in a lifetime one. Any tendency to take Wilder's devotion for granted, given his genetic affiliation to the Blades, should be strongly resisted. He is nobody's fool and will not hesitate from speaking out, as he memorably did at Northampton and later at United.

Wilder's Blades ended February in sixth place, one higher than they entered the month and with promotion to the Premier League still very much achievable and while their team's promotion prospects occupied the thought space of many supporters, the club's long-term future was still in the balance.

16

Brooks comes back with a bang
March 2018

Just over 100 days after their remarkable nine-goal thriller at Bramall Lane, Sheffield United and Fulham locked horns again on a Tuesday evening by the Thames. But much had changed since November, when Fulham's 5-4 win in South Yorkshire saw United tumble out of the Championship's automatic promotion places and moved Slavisa Jokanovic's men up to 14th in the table. Between the turn of the year and the return fixture against Chris Wilder's side, Fulham had taken 29 points from their 11 league games and signed Newcastle's £13m striker Aleksandar Mitrović on loan, as well as rejecting an £18m offer from West Ham for their captain Tom Cairney. Mitrović earned between £50,000 and £60,000 a week and although United travelled to Craven Cottage just seven points behind the Londoners in the table, in financial terms they were a world away.

Afterwards, with a predictable brace from Mitrović and Cairney's strike sealing Fulham's ninth home win on the bounce, Wilder was in defiant mood and the visiting Blades fans certainly got the upper hand in the battle of the supporters at least, a seemingly-endless repetition of one chant emanating into the West London night while their side chased shadows on the pitch. "Mitrović should be playing in the Premier League," Wilder insisted, "but sometimes you've just got to take your medicine and give credit to who you've come up against. Obviously we wish we'd have swallowed it slightly differently but the way they went about their work, the way they kept on going right until the end, meant the lads could come away with their heads held high."

Defeat at eventual play-off winners Fulham – regarded by many Blades supporters as, over the two legs, the best side they had faced all season – would not define United's promotion prospects, but Wilder knew that the story of the game could have been vastly different had skipper Billy Sharp and Clayton Donaldson, replacing injured top-scorer Leon Clarke, put away early chances when the score was goalless.

In what was to become a theme of Wilder's press conferences up until the end of the season, the message focused on being ruthless against top sides when chances were presented but – as the United manager said to his players in the dressing room at Craven Cottage, and with full respect to the teams involved – he would still rather be involved in occasions like this, after United's six years in the backwaters of League One.

By no means, though, was Wilder content to simply tread water in the Championship. And he was left frustrated when his side made the long trek to Ipswich Town's Portman Road and came back with only one point, despite again enjoying some golden opportunities to win the game. Ched Evans made a rare start upfront after recovering from ankle surgery and regaining fitness in the U23s, but midfielder John Lundstram spurned the best chance by far when he skipped through one-on-one with Bartosz Białkowski, but elected to try and square the ball to Evans instead of finishing himself.

Loanee James Wilson came off the bench and went even closer when his snapshot from outside the box hit the post, but on a cabbage-patch of a pitch Ipswich offered little threat of their own. Given the malaise at Portman Road, not in real relegation trouble but with no realistic, immediate chance of promotion, it was perhaps unsurprising when Ipswich parted company with Mick McCarthy. Under Wilder, it seems inconceivable that United will ever drift for as long.

The eventual goalless draw, though, placed extra importance on United's next outing, a rearranged home clash with Nigel Clough's Burton Albion after the original game fell foul to the 'Beast from the East' snowstorm that left the Bramall Lane concourses and surrounding areas unfit, and unsafe, for fans.

Despite an impressive record at United on paper – he led them to two major cup semi-finals and the play-offs in his two seasons in charge of Bramall Lane – Clough remains a polarising figure at his former club due to his defensive leanings, but his Burton side showed they could be a dangerous outfit by hammering Sheffield Wednesday 3-0 at Hillsborough earlier in the season.

The more pessimistic Blades amongst the fanbase saw the game as a textbook 'banana-skin' and the tense atmosphere was lifted a little by Enda Stevens' opener just before the half-hour mark, although Hope Akpan and Nathan Dyer both squandered good opportunities for the hosts. Then David Brooks replaced Wilson from the bench and put the game to bed with his first senior goal at Bramall Lane, a confident first-time finish after Sharp and Mark Duffy had combined superbly. The moment was especially sweet for Brooks, who had missed a large chunk of the season after contracting glandular fever and even had his own water bottle to avoid passing the illness on, but more importantly it helped United cut the gap to the play-offs to just two points.

"What strikes me about Brooksy is that he's just a real nice lad," Alan Knill, United's No.2, said. "There's nothing about him. He's a Wales international, but you wouldn't know. He's ridiculously talented. We watch him in training and go 'wow'. He does things with the ball that no-one else can do, and has an unpredictability about him. Some of the stuff he does, I just want to stop and applaud it. He's not fazed by who he's up against, he just wants to play football and if something doesn't come off for him, he just tries it again. He's going to be some player and although he doesn't yet have the football intelligence of, say, Duffy who's changed his role over the years, that'll come with experience. We're just gutted that we couldn't see more of him due to his illness."

The Blades were buoyed by the Burton win but failed to consolidate their position any further at home to Nottingham Forest, the former European champions turned lower-mid-table Championship side who travelled to South Yorkshire amidst another snow storm. For the first time in the club's history, the Bramall Lane pitch markings were turned red to aid visibility in the snow – and ensure the goal line technology worked – but the game was perhaps more memorable for an extraordinary miss from top-scorer Clarke, who somehow headed John Fleck's superb cross wide from around three yards with the goal at his mercy.

For once, United's 6ft 6in goalkeeper Jamal Blackman was not the most imposing player on the field – Forest's Costel Pantilimon stood two inches taller – but the on-loan Chelsea man was the busiest, denying Ben Brereton, Matty Cash and Daryl Murphy with impressive saves. Some of the growing frustration on the terraces showed when the ground staff called onto the pitch to clear snow in Blackman's goalmouth were bizarrely booed by fans, but Pantilimon had the final word when he parried away Fleck's late effort to once again blunt the Blades.

Wilder felt Blackman's subsequent man of the match award was more a product of United's profligacy in front of goal – he, rightly, suggested that a goalkeeper hadn't won the vote too many times during his time at Bramall Lane – but the mood in the media suite lifted a little when Wilder revealed the reason behind Chris Basham's absence from the teamsheet. "I got a call off Bash saying he had to shoot up to Newcastle because his wife was just about to give birth. That was a change we didn't expect because the baby was due in the international break. It was a frustrating day but if anything good has come of it, we've got another little baby Bash in the world."

Dad Basham was back in the team for Good Friday's trip to Brentford and, on a sodden pitch in west London, poetically opened the scoring with a deflected volley, prompting wild scenes in the Griffin Park away end. But the lead lasted just 13 minutes as Chris Mepham smashed home the equaliser, prompting a strange incident between Blackman and Brentford's Ryan Woods in the immediate aftermath. Both were sent off, replays later showing a petulant coming-together when diminutive Woods raised his hands at Blackman and the goalkeeper slapped him back right in front of the referee, but United had the better of the game with ten men and Donaldson and Clarke both forced excellent saves from home goalkeeper Dan Bentley as the search for that all-important winner proved elusive.

Wilder's recollection of the red-cards incident raised a laugh amongst journalists afterwards – "I don't know what Woods is thinking about, dealing with a 6ft 7in lad when he's 5ft 5in" – but his frustrations were again evident at his side's finishing. A local writer stood alongside former Blades striker Keith Edwards in the Griffin Park media room and when Wilder said "there's a bloke at the back who would have put a few of those chances away today," he wasn't talking about the journalist.

Away from the field, and sandwiched between the draws at home to Forest and away at Brentford, TalkSPORT aired an interview with striker Evans, talking to host Jim White about his return to the game after his rape conviction was quashed and he was found not-guilty in a re-trial. Evans, who insisted he holds no feelings of bitterness over the 30 months he spent in prison after being wrongly convicted, revealed he is abused at 70 percent of away grounds he visits with United, with "the favourite [insult of] 'you're a rapist', and this and that. Personally it doesn't affect me whatsoever, but when you go around the country and you've got people screaming and shouting those sort of words – that's not normal.

"But after five years of absolute abuse and scrutiny, I'm back where I belong and that's playing football, so people screaming and shouting at me is nothing compared to playing football again. I'd love to be selected for the Wales squad again and I'd love to play in the Premier League; promotion would be the ultimate prize for me and the club. I want to repay the club and the fans who have been absolutely amazing with me. I couldn't thank them enough."

Enter the dragon
By David Brooks, attacker

It was a great feeling to score my first goal at Bramall Lane, and in front of the Kop as well, because it had been a long road back after I picked up glandular fever. Hopefully there are many more like that to come. I was still having off days towards the end of the season but I feel good when I'm playing, and to get that goal against Burton Albion and the three points helped me feel back amongst it again.

The illness itself was a bit of a weird one. Obviously I didn't know it was glandular fever but I just felt really tired all the time, and when they finally diagnosed it as that it was a bit too late. I'd taken antibiotics before but they didn't really work, and it got to the day before the Preston game in December and I couldn't eat or sleep. The club ended up sending me home and the day before Christmas Eve, I couldn't move and kept throwing up, and had lost a lot of weight. I ended up on a drip on Christmas Eve, of all days, and was thankfully let out just before Christmas Day so I made it home to Warrington.

The drip helped me feel a lot better on Christmas Day but still, I was seeing the family for 25 minutes or so at a time and then I had to sleep for an hour. My emotions were all over the place and I had no energy to do anything. That was all out of the window completely. Anyone who's ever seen me play will know I don't rely on my strength, but when I started to come back I felt weaker in everything, even running. All my power seemed to have gone. People on *Twitter* were wondering why I wasn't playing with 'only a throat infection' but it was quite obvious that I was flagging towards the end of games. Getting back to full fitness has been a slow process but to get back on the pitch and score that goal against Burton was a great feeling after going through all that.

I grew up in Warrington supporting another United, just down the road in Manchester, but played for City as a youngster. I did well there until around U16 level when I became a scholar; all my teammates shot up physically and I just didn't. All of a sudden I couldn't get in the team because my physical frame just wasn't there at the time. My last year at City was the first year they moved into the Etihad and you could see the direction they were going in with the investment, even down to players they were signing at youth level. The coaches there made it clear to us that the chances of playing in the first team are very slim but it went in one ear and out of the other, to be honest; every footballer needs to think they will succeed otherwise the doubt takes over. But it doesn't really sink in until your time at a club comes to an end.

I remember them pulling me into the office unplanned, after a game I think, and said it might be best for me to move on and that they weren't going to stop me progressing my career elsewhere. I was devastated, and there were a few tears involved, but it worked out for the best in the end. I remember going to Bolton and they said they wouldn't invest the time in me as I was so small, so I came to United, played a couple of games and told my mum and dad that I loved it here. They offered me a contract and I signed it straightaway. Even then, I needed time. There was a picture going round early on of the United kit hanging off me, and I didn't realise at the time how small and underdeveloped I was, but the contract gave me time to develop physically and as a player. The main thing was just a bit of patience, really, and United had that with me.

I signed a professional contract in 2015 under Nigel Clough and trained with the first team once or twice under Nigel Adkins, but I moved up to the first-team building when Chris came in and it brought me on leaps and bounds. The tempo is quicker and playing with better, quicker and stronger players develops you, as well. The gaffer came in and made it very clear what he wanted to do, he's a massive Blade and a big figurehead for the club. The transformation since is credit to him and his staff. He drills the same principles into us every single day; work hard and the quality will follow. And it's worked.

I was a little frustrated not to make my debut in the promotion season but the gaffer was determined to win 100 points, and I understand it wasn't the right time. And we went on to do it too, so I can't complain really! The young lads were also very much a part of the celebrations. It was a mad couple of months, although there was no chance of me making a speech on the Town Hall steps when the gaffer tried to force me to. I'm shy and nervous enough without doing that as well! But to be involved in the celebrations was a nice touch.

Then for me, everything really changed that summer. I went

away with England and we did well in Toulon and within a couple of months, I'd been called up to the senior Wales squad. It felt like one moment I was on the outside looking in, and the next I was very much in the middle of it, all in the space of one or two months. It was crazy really, a bit surreal, but a great period. I'd always had the Wales kits growing up and always wanted to play for Wales, because my mum is Welsh, but I can't lie and say I never wanted to play for England. As a young kid, you want to represent your country and when the chance came to play for Wales, it was too good to turn down. At the time I wanted to play for Wales and thankfully they gave me the chance. It felt right at the time. I went away with the Wales U21s and I liked what they were doing, so when the first team came calling it was a no-brainer for me.

It could have all been different if I'd gone on loan to Chesterfield as planned, but football's about luck at times and it's worked out very well. My first senior call-up came just a few days after the Sheffield Derby win at Hillsborough, so that was another whirlwind few days – and my mum was in tears when I told her! Beating Wednesday was definitely the highlight of my United career; the day had everything, apart from a goal! I've got a nice picture of me nutmegging Jack Hunt which a few fans sent me, and there are pictures in the gaffer's office and in the tunnel at Bramall Lane. I can't remember much of the actual moment, as it's just spontaneous, but the clips have been everywhere and the picture is a bit of an iconic one really. It's probably not the best picture for him, but I don't ever tire of seeing it!

I also wasn't expecting to be man of the match at all. I got taken off and a few of the boys on the bench were winding me up, saying I should be practising my speech, but I thought Leon should have got it because he played so well as well as scoring twice. But it was a nice surprise. I was buzzing with that, it topped the day off nicely and it's safe to say that the gaffer loved every single minute of it too. Those are the types of games you want to be involved in, especially when you come out on the right side. It didn't feel any less important because I am not a Blades fan – we all knew how important it was, and we all wanted to win as badly as each other. They made it a bit edgy by equalising, but Duff's goal was an incredible moment. And produced another iconic image from the 'Bouncing Day Massacre'!

I didn't manage to make my Wales debut the first time I was called up but it eventually came at the Stade de France in November. My mum, dad, nan and grandad all came over on the ferry and I saw them in the crowd when I was warming up at half-time. It was a proud night for them all. In the players' lounge after the Panama game, my little brother was mesmerised by all these star players walking through. He was asking me why I was there alongside them! But there was a bit of that for me as well when we played France, if I'm honest. We went to do a training session and they were walking in as we walked out, and there were all these players I'd only ever seen on TV so I felt a bit starstruck. I play as some of them on FIFA 18, so it was a bit weird at the time! But I loved every second of it.

It did cost me a hoodie, though! I came back to United and didn't think the boys were in that day, so chanced a pink hoodie. I came back in after training and my shoes were hidden, my gear was everywhere and they'd signed my hoodie. I think it was their way of making sure I didn't get carried away! But I don't think I've changed much as a person from when I was 17 or 18. I'm more confident as a person but I don't think in my head I've changed too much. I like to think that my family – and my teammates – wouldn't let me.

March 2018 – One eye on the boardroom
By Neil Hoyle and Sam Tweed, Kop

United's start to March was delayed by the 'Beast from the East', which hit the Burton game, and it's always a strange weekend when a Blades game gets called off. You try to pretend you are interested in other results, but it's just not the same. Except of course, for when our near neighbours implode as they did down at Bristol City, losing 4-0.

Instead, we had to concern ourselves with the off-field goings on in the boardroom, with co-owners Prince Abdullah and

Kevin McCabe locked in negotiations to take sole control of the club. I feel that any "official" information so far had been very ambiguous, which only fans the flames of speculation and can quickly turn into a game of Chinese whispers. It didn't help that McCabe's planned meeting, on the day of the Burton game, was also hit by the snow, but I do wonder if any definitive answers would, or could, have been provided and my only fear was that the boardroom wrangling would distract Chris Wilder and the players from their play-off push. Did it? Who knows, but on the impasse went.

I also wondered at the time whether the games against Fulham and Ipswich, both away from home, would spell the beginning of the end of our play-off hopes. Losing at Fulham highlighted the difference in quality between a bona fide promotion contender, and a team that have punched above their weight. Just look at Aleksandar Mitrović, who scored twice. I see him as one of those players who is top quality at this level, but not quite a Premier League player (at least on a regular basis). All that being said, he was more than good enough to get the better of our defence.

With the money he is on, he should have been. It always seems to be the answer for fans when a team seems to be approaching its ceiling, to 'spend some money'. But seeing Mitrović playing against us got me wondering whether I'd like to see players of his ilk coming down from the Premier League and trousering such sums of money from United. I would say no. Too much of a compromise to our ethos. Without going too much into the finances of football, Fulham also averaged less than 20,000 in the season they had Mitrović, and they ended up winning promotion through the play-offs, so the gamble was obviously worth it. Aston Villa, who they beat at Wembley, threw the dice in a similar way with John Terry and lost. It's a fine tightrope that I, for one, am glad we're not balancing on.

At the start of this season, fresh out of League One and into the Championship, a point at Ipswich would have seemed reasonable enough and would have been accepted by the vast majority of right-thinking Blades fans. But ultimately it was part of a slow slide towards disappointment, an unavoidable feeling as the early bar was set very high. Come the end of the season, our board, whoever is sitting on it, need to give serious consideration to what sort of club they would like us to be. Honest triers who might hang on to the coat-tails of the big hitters, or a team that can afford to fund a seat at the top table?

It's an interesting conundrum, especially if Wilder is successful in leading United back into the Premier League. If or when that happens, we'd need to add quality or if we do go up, it could be an embarrassing situation – as others have found when they were there. It was back to business a little against Burton, when it was rearranged, and great to see David Brooks announce his comeback with a well-taken goal after good team build-up. Elsewhere on these pages he revealed he had received some stick from Blades fans while he was suffering with glandular fever, which is a shame, because from the outside he seems a great lad and can be an exceptional player. If only we had had him for the full season. Who knows what could have happened.

On the face of it, four points from two home games wasn't a bad return after drawing at home to Forest, but yet there is the feeling of missed opportunity prevailing. All in all, it brought a functional win against a Burton team who eventually lost their grip on the Championship that season, and a point against a Forest team who I think, under Aitor Karanka, are going to be one of the threats in 2018/19.

I thought our display away at Brentford was an improved performance that arguably deserved better than the point we had to settle for, especially given that other results amongst some of our rivals went our way. I personally thought the sendings off of Jamal Blackman and Ryan Woods were a bit much to be honest, a bit of handbags that could have been put to bed with a talking to with both players. But football in 2018 is very different to bygone years and if you raise your hand to the face of an opponent, you're asking for trouble.

Off the field, the Ched Evans interview with TalkSPORT dominated some of the headlines on the day it was released. There have been many things in our history that have divided our fanbase, but few as much as this saga. The question now has to be, has his resigning been worth it from a team point of view? To be fair, injury hasn't really helped Ched's cause and it'll be interesting to see whether he can recapture some of the old form that we remember from his first spell at United.

17

No fools here
April 2018

It was probably intended as a forgettable, throwaway remark but instead ended up helping to fuel Sheffield United's push for a second consecutive promotion. "Well, I don't think you'll go down" was the dismissive assessment of United's chances in the Championship in 2017/18, uttered by a member of Neil Warnock's coaching staff at Cardiff after the two sides met at the start of the campaign, and Wilder ensured the words were repeated on a motivational poster on the walls of their training ground at Shirecliffe.

It was that remark, rather than the return of Warnock to Bramall Lane, that dominated the talk ahead of the Easter Monday return clash between the sides in South Yorkshire, although the presence of the polarising, pantomime villain in the away dugout was always likely to turn heads. In the end, Warnock's return to 'his' club was relegated to nothing more than a sideshow – save for a trademark rant at the fourth official, which the South Stand crowd gleefully seized upon – as United cut their automatic promotion-chasing visitors to shreds, before and after Leon Clarke opened the scoring with his first goal since New Year's Day.

But Cardiff improved after throwing on £6m man Gary Madine, an unpopular figure at Bramall Lane not just for his Sheffield Wednesday connections, and Aron Gunnarsson and Kenneth Zohore both went close. At the other end, sub Clayton Donaldson hit the post from close range and Lee Evans should have had a penalty after being bundled over, but the hammer blow came in the 91st minute when United's defenders failed to properly deal with a long ball and sub Anthony Pilkington volleyed home the equaliser, sending Cardiff's fans – and bench – wild.

Warnock, who had a largely successful spell as manager of United after growing up supporting the club, left a sour taste in the mouth of some supporters with his typically over-the-top celebrations at the end of the game, and there was a healthy dose of social media schadenfreude days later when Warnock's Cardiff missed two injury-time penalties and lost to title rivals Wolves. Molineux boss Nuno sprinted to celebrate with his players, Warnock blatantly swore at every Wolves player and staff member he encountered and then, after refusing Nuno's apology and attempt to shake his hand with another four-letter outburst, accused his opposite number of lacking "manners and a bit of class".

"I thought we played really well at Brentford, who were on a run, battered Cardiff and the same with Boro a bit later," said Wilder. "Again, it's fine, dividing margins. We missed three or four great chances in the second half at Brentford and then we battered Cardiff all over the pitch, physically stood up to the challenge and outplayed them, and then made poor decisions. To only take two points from that weekend was a big blow to the players. They knew they'd played well and didn't need telling. We'd gone toe-to-toe with two decent sides in the division, but to only pick up two points was hugely disappointing."

With Warnock approaching his 70th birthday and still involved in football, controversy has a habit of following him around but under Wilder, and still very much involved in the promotion picture, United were now only looking forward rather than back. And their next encounter, a South Yorkshire derby away at struggling Barnsley, appeared a welcome opportunity for them to get over their Bluebirds blues. The short trip to Oakwell is always a highlight for a visiting journalist, too, despite the intermittent internet access and bizarre folding desks with a mind of their own, memorably sending a costly MacBook flying into the Barnsley air on one occasion. An old toilet block behind the West Stand was sadly recently demolished but the press room portakabin – named after Benny Hill, a respected local journalist rather than the comedian – stands firm. A reminder that this remains, in an era of soulless, identikit stadia, a proper football ground.

United, in contrast, were unidentifiable in the first half at least, and were perhaps fortunate to be only a goal down at half-time, to Gary Gardner's stunner from outside the box. Evans paid the price for the slow start and was dragged off before the break – although, in mitigation, either of his fellow midfielders John Fleck or John Lundstram could have suffered the same fate – but, as United made their way back to the Oakwell dressing rooms and jogged past their supporters, they were supported rather than scolded. "To know the supporters are behind us like that, I can't tell you what a lift it is," Chris Basham later reflected. "A few years ago, we'd have been getting slaughtered. People pay their money and are entitled to their opinion, but the supporters could see we were giving everything."

Second-half goals from Clarke and Fleck turned the game around, but the impressive Oli McBurnie dragged the Reds back on level terms and two minutes before the end, sub Tom Bradshaw headed in a cross from Kieffer Moore to send Oakwell wild. United, Wilder admitted, had proved themselves in the Championship but were perhaps missing something of a spark to take them to the next level and, either way, teams cannot play well for 20 minutes of a game and expect to win it. Wilder's mood at full-time was in stark contrast to that of Jose Morais, the Barnsley boss, whose beaming smile lit up Benny's press room. In midweek, his reserve goalkeeper Nick Townsend had broken a finger after an 'altercation' – described as a "duel" by Jose Mourinho's former No.2 Morais – with teammate Dimi Cavare but similar fighting spirit on the field was evidently lacking and they eventually suffered relegation to League One.

United, though, were looking to get out of the division through promotion, rather than fearing the trapdoor, but the Oakwell setback placed extra scrutiny on their midweek encounter with Middlesbrough, then placed sixth in the table and four points ahead of Wilder's men. Despite Boro's £50m outlay following chairman Steve Gibson's vow to "smash the league" United should have taken a point from the first game at the Riverside earlier in the season, and remained within touching distance of their big-spending opponents in the race for the play-offs.

Now under the guidance of former Stoke manager Tony Pulis, complete with trademark baseball cap, Boro named £15m striker Britt Assombalonga on the bench at Bramall Lane but it was United's Welshman Evans, a £750,000 January signing from Wolves, who lit up the game with a truly breathtaking opening goal, in just the second minute of the game.

After Enda Stevens' cross was cleared high into the Sheffield sky, Evans had work to do to actually reach the ball as it dropped but as he met it perfectly, the midfielder calmly side-footed his volley into Darren Randolph's top corner with searing pace. Bizarrely, Aston Villa's Jack Grealish scored a competent volley of his own on the same night against Cardiff City, which was later included in a Sky Sports 'goal of the season' poll on *Twitter*. The fact Grealish's strike was screened live on the network must have helped his cause; it was a decent enough strike but was not even the best Championship goal of that evening, never mind the season. Evans, for good measure, added a second volley before half-time that many Blades thought was better than his first, mainly because of the build-up; David Brooks sent Jonny Howson flying with a sublime Cruyff turn and his perfect cross was smashed home by his Wales teammate.

Two ahead at half-time, United's path to a momentous victory should only have been made more straightforward when Boro captain Grant Leadbitter was sent off for two first-half fouls but after a number of setbacks in big games over the years – in the last 20 seasons alone, they have lost five major cup semi-finals and failed in six play-off attempts – those on the Bramall Lane terraces knew better than to take anything for granted. Their nerves wouldn't have been helped when Daniel Ayala pulled one back for Boro just three minutes into the second half, after Pulis made a triple change at half-time, but United held firm and went to within three points of sixth-placed Millwall; who, by a quirk of the fixture list, visited Bramall Lane the following weekend.

The game was also Wilder's 100th in charge of United and the similarities between the Blades and Millwall – who had also dramatically exceeded all pre-season expectations after being promoted from League One – and Wilder and Neil Harris, who had two spells as a player with Millwall before taking over as manager, promised to make the game an absorbing contest. As predicted beforehand, both sides went toe to toe in front of 27,454 at Bramall Lane but Wilder's landmark occasion proved to be one of disappointment and frustration rather than celebration, with familiar failings to blame. United found Millwall's erratic goalkeeper Jordan Archer in fine form, denying Richard Stearman, George Baldock, Evans and Billy Sharp with spectacular saves, but eventually broke the deadlock when Jack O'Connell headed Evans' deep cross back across goal and Clarke made no mistake from close range for his 18th of the season. The noise inside Bramall Lane was deafening but many fans had barely taken their seats when, straight from kick-off, Millwall equalised, Steve Morison volleying home a long punt upfield after hesitant defending from the hosts.

"It's our player of the year do tonight," Wilder smiled afterwards, "and I think I'll probably be buying my own drinks because I've been critical of the lads in the dressing room. Once again, we're waiting and relying on other results but, with three games to go, our season is still alive." Goalkeeper Jamal Blackman, who faced the press after his manager, agreed – apart from one part. "I think we should all be queuing up to buy him a beer ... For the work he's done, for the work he's doing, every one of us should be getting him a drink." Wilder, in typically honest mood, also admitted that the visitors should have had a penalty when Basham barged over Jed Wallace and reserved some scathing words for referee David Coote, who Wilder remembered having a poor game when he was in charge of Halifax. "In short, I don't think he's a very good referee," was the takeaway summation.

With his side's game the early kick-off in the day, the division's other matches were well underway by the time Wilder made his way up to United's media suite and with *Sky Sports News* playing on a TV set to his left, the boss answered a question with a glance over at the half-time scores. "Go on Burton [who were playing Derby], I'll take Boro and Bristol City drawing ... go on Hull [against Wednesday], that's an obvious one isn't it? I fancy QPR against Preston, I'm not that bothered about Reading v Sunderland but the bottom one [United 1, Millwall 1] is the most frustrating." In the end, Burton held on for an unlikely win over Derby, Middlesbrough found a winner and Preston beat QPR. United remained ninth – still three points off sixth-placed Millwall, but with games rapidly running out.

The defining one proved to be away at Birmingham City as the big-spending strugglers put a huge dent in United's promotion hopes, while boosting their own survival chances, with a 2-1 win at St Andrew's. Ahead of the game Clarke was named in the PFA's Championship team of the year – the first United striker ever included at this level – and spoke of his pride at being honoured by his fellow professionals, but a back spasm made him a notable absentee from the Blades line-up when the teamsheets were handed in before kick-off. One name that was on it, though, was that of Mark Duffy, the former Birmingham man who admitted beforehand that he was desperate to play against his old club, and score, because of social media abuse he endured from Blues fans during his time in the Midlands. Poetically, United took the lead in the seventh minute of the game from the left foot of Duffy, who was subsequently booked by the referee for his subsequent celebration.

That goal lifted United up to seventh in the as-it-stood Championship table but they tumbled to tenth when Marc Roberts scored possibly the easiest goal of his career from a scuffed corner, and their misery was compounded when former Wednesday man Jacques Maghoma was sent free one-on-one to seal victory for the hosts and condemn United to a defeat which, with results elsewhere going against them, left their top-six task almost impossible. But it was the manner of the defeat, rather than the scoreline, which incensed Wilder, who felt this was up there with the poorer days of United's season so far – especially considering the potential prize that lay ahead of them.

The manager also scolded Duffy for his celebration, arguing that his goalscorer had done the hard bit by netting and didn't need to antagonise the home support any further, and when he finally emerged to face the media around an hour after the final whistle, only some of the emotion had subsided. The race was run, Wilder admitted, for some of the players that season and although he had to be careful to distinguish between those running on empty and any who he suspected were beginning to 'coast', changes were mooted for the final home game, against Preston.

"It's not an excuse, but I think tiredness did come into it for us," Alan Knill, Wilder's No.2, admitted. "At Birmingham, we were shouting for Jack O'Connell to get forward and he just couldn't move. He was trying to, but just couldn't do it. That's where the teams with bigger squads come into it. Throughout the season, none of the so-called big teams really fazed us but Fulham had some proper players and then added Mitrović to it and against Villa, the only difference between us and them was Robert Snodgrass. There was a proper belief that we could have done something, but it's a really intense league and a very tiring one. We'll learn the lessons and come back stronger."

Derby's midweek victory over Warnock's Cardiff, plus their superior goal difference, all-but ended United's top-six hopes for the season but by Thursday morning, spirits amongst the group at the training ground seemed high. Jake Wright and Fleck seized their opportunity on the pool table at Shirecliffe while Paul Coutts conducted an interview on a nearby sofa and Duffy, his mood visibly lifted after his beloved Liverpool beat Roma 5-2 in their Champions League semi-final first leg, waited to take on Ched Evans. Wilder, not for the first time, then praised his players in the interview room next door, admitting that they had picked him up in the week rather than the other way around, and conceded he may have been a touch harsh with some of his criticism in the visiting dressing room at St Andrew's.

In the end, the wholesale changes that many anticipated didn't materialise but United's faint play-off chances were officially ended when Alan Browne scored the only goal of a largely-forgettable game against Preston at Bramall Lane. The real fireworks were saved for afterwards, upstairs in the media suite, as an emotional Wilder opened up about what he perceived to be a lack of "direction, clarity and dialogue" from co-owners Kevin McCabe and Prince Abdullah, whose bitter legal battle to gain full control of the club still showed no signs of a resolution. "It's 100 percent critical it gets resolved," Wilder said. "I can't do my job properly unless there is a direction and decision from them. Any club that wants to be successful has to have harmony, direction and a plan. There isn't a plan, there isn't direction, and there isn't harmony either. That, unfortunately, is fact."

Pressed further on whether he had questioned his own future at his club, Wilder – who had had cut an unusually subdued figure throughout the game and wiped away tears as the Kop sang his name during the end-of-season 'lap of appreciation' – pulled no punches. "If it stays the same, I don't think anybody would be surprised if I questioned where my career is going," he admitted. "I want to progress my career, the careers of the staff and the players and, most importantly, give the supporters hope we can have a genuine club with a strategy and plan to move forward. I want to lead it, but I need a bit of help. I am the only voice that comes out of the club. There are a lot of things which need to happen, and they need to happen soon. This is a brilliant club which is close to my heart and I want it to move forward in our own way."

The following evening, as Fleck was crowned United's official player of the year at a glittering awards ceremony at Bramall Lane, McCabe addressed the room and agreed that harmony and direction was vital. Representatives of Prince Abdullah were also present at the awards – as was Wilder – but by the following Friday, when the Blades boss faced the press for the final pre-match briefing of the season, there had still been no communication. Wilder's mood had improved somewhat from the Monday evening – at an awards ceremony when he took exception to a comment from host Mark Clemmit describing United as a 'mid-table side' – but the line of questioning ahead of the weekend's trip to Ashton Gate was still focused on matters in the boardroom, not Bristol City.

"I have obviously had calls from family, concerned about what's happening, but they know through experience with me what football is all about," Wilder admitted. "But I don't think anybody thought we would have this season, and be in this situation at the end, where a year on, we have an issue at boardroom level." To further muddy the waters, Wilder was by now the overwhelming favourite to take the Sunderland job after the Black Cats, relegated to League One, sacked former Wales boss Chris Coleman. The Stadium of Light job which appeared to be a poisoned chalice did, underneath the surface, have its advantages; Ellis Short, the American billionaire, agreed to write off around £140m of debt as part of the sale of the club to a consortium headed by businessman Stewart Donald – who enjoyed a good relationship with Wilder when the two worked together at Oxford some years before.

Some Blades, remembering Wilder's decision to swap the promotion-chasing U's for relegation-threatened Northampton earlier in his career, resigned themselves to losing their manager while others resolutely remained convinced he would stay. In truth, the only men who had the power to decide either way were battling in the Bramall Lane boardroom and, at this point, were barely on speaking terms. Both will have heard the message loud and clear, though, when almost 2,000 Blades made the seven-hour round trip to Ashton Gate and, within a minute of kick-off, were united in one voice. *"Chrissy Wilder ... we want you to stay."*

As ever, each chant of his name was met by a thumbs-up from the manager and a scintillating first-half display, which saw them go into the break 3-0 ahead, improved the mood in the away end a little and it was noticeable that Wilder celebrated Billy Sharp's goal, which was sandwiched between similarly stunning efforts from Clarke and Kieron Freeman, as if it had sealed United's play-off place. It was, in the end, perhaps a fitting microcosm of United's season that they were below-par in the second half and conceded two goals from set-pieces to cling on for a 3-2 victory.

But there were bigger concerns at hand. A rousing rendition of "Chrissy Wilder and Alan Knill" to the Tom Hark theme was the soundtrack to another standing ovation after the game, and some supporters wondered if this was really goodbye. After an emotional moment in the dressing room, where Wilder expressed his pride in his players, some of them thought it was too and the manager was again pressed on his future when he appeared for his post-match briefing.

But instead he preferred to focus on the achievements of the past 46 games rather than look forwards – with a pointed grin when he remembered "a few decent results away from home". One in particular, no doubt, was still vivid in his mind.

Reflecting on his first season at Championship level, Wilder said: "On days when the likes of Fulham turn up and say 'yes' and Wolves do likewise, they're very good and we struggled to live with them. There were some brilliant individual performances against us, like Sam Johnstone and Robert Snodgrass for Villa, and powerful teams like Cardiff. A lot of players are capable of producing that bit of magic from nothing but there were other times when our players more than stood up to the challenge. We enjoyed it and more than played our part in the division, played comfortably well and held our own. We need to keep that going, but we attacked the division in a way I really enjoyed watching.

"We thought we might have to take results on the chin every so often, but we only really took a 'doing' at Wolves when they were head and shoulders above us on the night. But even at Fulham away, we had two of the best opportunities of the game and then Aleksandar Mitrović goes up the other end, scores and the game is gone in a heartbeat. They are the differences we need to try and bridge.

"The league table doesn't lie, but I feel our season was more than a tenth-placed finish, the way we attacked the division. It was a great effort. We did feel for the majority of the season that we had a great opportunity to get amongst it, and finishing tenth doesn't quite tell the true story of what we've done. We felt we should have been a little bit closer but when you look at the pivotal moments like the Easter weekend, games against Millwall and Preston when we conceded sloppy equalisers, games against Bristol and Villa where we dominated and lost in the last minute … it could easily have been a different story.

"But to go to Bristol on the final day and play like that … I thought they were outstanding. The players once again gave everything, and that epitomised what this group is all about. A lot of clubs, with nothing to play for, would have gone out the back door and been on the beach a little bit, but they gave everything. Afterwards, like I had the season before, I thanked the players for their efforts and told them that I thought they'd been outstanding. There were a lot more highs than lows and we put a mark on the division in which many people thought we'd struggle. We never struggled. And I told them that the way they'd acted and behaved, and gone about attacking the division, was a credit to themselves."

After victory in the south west saw United achieve Sharp and Wilder's agreed top-ten finish – a target set at the start of the season after a meeting between skipper and manager – the latter jetted off on holiday but, perhaps then more than ever, struggled to switch off from football – even taking in a game as former United manager Adrian Heath's Minnesota United lost 2-0 at Los Angeles FC. With the link to Sunderland refusing to go away, McCabe and Prince Abdullah agreed to meet in a neutral hotel in Mayfair and iron out Wilder's budget for the coming season, while also continuing their battle for control of Bramall Lane.

Wilder, who had been as short as 1/4 with one leading bookmaker to leave United for the Stadium of Light, met with both co-owners after returning from his break in California and ended weeks of speculation by signing a new contract tying him to United until the end of the 2020/21 season. The sighs of relief from the red half of the Steel City were almost palpable. There was work still to be done – the depth of disagreement between the club's co-owners was laid bare in the High Court, and Brooks was sold to Bournemouth – but at least immediate fears that this could be the end of the Wilder era at Bramall Lane were allayed. Instead, the manager's message was clear. This was only the start.

'Don't write me off just yet'
By Leon Clarke, striker

I got told about being in the PFA's Championship team of the year by a text message and then the manager mentioned the award before training one day. He knows I'm not someone who likes to be the centre of attention and probably thought I'd get a bit of stick! But the lads were brilliant. It's probably the best group I've ever worked with. We enjoy ourselves and we play with a freedom. Credit has got to go to the manager and his staff for that, because of the way they set things up. Everyone gets along and there are no cliques in the dressing room. People here help each other out and that goes a long, long way in any walk of life ... not just sport. There's experience in the squad and if results don't go our way, we rally around as a group. We speak about it, take positives out of the game if we haven't got a good result and take it into the next one.

It doesn't feel like a chore here at all, like it can at some places. You can't help but enjoy yourself here; especially in my position because everyone has seen the amount of chances that we create. We've just got to keep trying to drive things on. That's what I did before coming here and, after I'd arrived, when I was injured for long periods too. I've always had the manager's backing though and knew, as long as I worked hard, that I'd get a chance. Even in the Championship, when things haven't gone so well, he's kept faith in me. That means a lot.

The season has been all about proving a point for me. A lot of people were saying at the beginning that I couldn't score goals in the Championship anymore. They thought it was above my level. I didn't really listen but I knew that if I had a chance, if I played games, that I could do it. I never stopped believing, I knew that if I had a chance to play consecutively, week in, week out, then I'd be fine. There have been times when I've played in the Championship but never as much as I have this season. The coaching staff still trusted me and put me in the team and I'd like to think I've repaid them with what I've done. Scoring 19 goals has proved a few people wrong. I might not say it or show it with my emotions, but to do that is really nice for me.

Then there was the month with nine goals; that's something I'll probably never achieve again in my career and it was a special month for myself personally, although the results didn't go the way we wanted them to. But to score nine goals in one month is a great achievement and it was a great season. It would have been nice to get a few more goals but it's been quite easy in this team, to be honest, with the way we play, the amount of chances we create and how we get their fans on their feet. As a striker, you just have to put yourself in the right place and you know you'll get chances all the time.

If you ask me what my game is about; I run, I chase, I harry, I make it difficult for centre-halves. If the ball's there to be won, I'll go and win it. If the ball's going over the top, I'll chase it down. And I've scored goals this season. But I'd like to think some of the centre-halves I've come up against, it's not been an easy afternoon for them, it's been a tough one – and that's maybe why I got voted in the team of the year. To be recognised by your fellow professionals is obviously really nice; it's a good accomplishment for me and a reward as well for the team, and what we've achieved this season.

As a person, I'm very laid back, calm and chilled. Some people take it the wrong way but I don't mean it to come across as rude or ignorant. That's just how I am, calm and relaxed. But on the pitch, I just go into games wanting to work as physically hard as I can; run, challenge and head the ball. I try to do all of the right things and the fans appreciate that. Obviously I can hear when the crowd chant my name and that's really nice. I remember coming here with other clubs, and in derbies with Wednesday, so I knew all about the roar of the fans. This club was in League One for far too long and when we won promotion, you could see how much it meant to everyone; from the fans to the people who work at the stadium.

When I knew there was an opportunity to come here, I couldn't turn it down. I think there was a chance to come to United when I was at Coventry. There was more interest in Callum Wilson than myself, but there was an interest there. I didn't get involved. I left the two clubs to sort it out and nothing happened in the end. But I'm here now, which is the most important thing. And I was delighted when the club wanted to extend my contract during the season; it was an easy decision to make. There was talk about other clubs being interested in me but it never crossed my mind; I just try to focus on helping the team as much as I can, with or without the captain's armband on.

To captain a great and historic club such as this isn't something

I'm used to, but it's a real honour. I really didn't expect it. I had the captaincy at Coventry for maybe 20 games but I try to play my normal game regardless of being the captain or not. If I work really hard, hopefully other people will follow. But I'm a different captain from, say, Chris Morgan! He was scary when you played against him. You knew he was a leader because he had that real presence about him. I'm more of a leader in terms of how I try to play. I'm a much quieter captain than Morgs but probably a lot more hard working. Don't tell him I said that!

The manager has put his faith in me since signing me, and I've tried to repay him for that. He's driven us on for the last two seasons and is different to a lot of managers that I have worked with. He drummed a philosophy into us and let us know what promotion would mean to everyone at Sheffield United. Really, it starts with him and, as players, we follow. Big things are possible; the manager wants to take the team to the Premier League and hopefully, in the future, we can do that.

April/May 2018 – In two minds about the months
By Sam Parry, Kop

April was the disappointing bookend on the end of a shelf holding more colourful titles.

Come off it. We'd have taken all this before the start of the season, wouldn't we?

It's not pre-season though, is it? Don't get me wrong, it's not been a bad season whatsoever. Nonetheless, for me, it's petered out into something disappointing, mildly so.

We'd have taken tenth. I'd have taken top half, but tenth is some achievement. Think of the rubbish we've put up with. All those years of third-tier self-flagellation; play-off finals, Wembley, play-off semi-finals, Nigel Adkins, Dean Hammond. Then, bang; promotion and now tenth place in the Championship – come on.

Spade's a spade. We've missed a shovel-load of chances over the last few games – tons. Slipped from our grip. Look at it: five points from six games in April. Five! In three of those games – Cardiff, Millwall, Birmingham – we took the lead and threw it away. Win those instead of taking the grand total of two points and we'd have made the play-offs. Simple. We didn't and we haven't. End. Of. Story.

They were always going to be tough games. Look, Cardiff won promotion; a point against them is a good point, a really good point in fact. Birmingham were fighting to stay in the division and we didn't show up, but these things level out over the course of the season. It's the Championship, not League One. Granted, we gave a sloppy goal away to Millwall. We shouldn't have let that one through, but again, you can't legislate for individual mistakes and still, even if you add those mistakes up, the sum total is not a bad season. We won games that we never expected. Wolves. Derby. Nobody thought we'd thrash Wednesday …

… I did. And I don't mean to say it's a bad season. But hope builds up, you know? And to see it simmer away into nothing like that – argh. It rattles your bones. There was a play-off place on a plate for anyone who could dig deep, to anyone who could muster that ounce more of toil. Even after dropping the ball against Cardiff, we still go and beat 'Boro and give ourselves a shadow of a chance – what do we do after that, eh?

Point taken. Against Middlesbrough, I thought we'd found that bit of steel, maybe even a bit of luck. Not that we were lucky, those goals were screamers. Evans' volley was the equal of Browny's. And Brooks' Cruyff-turn-look-and-cross, within the boundary of his own singular stopping distance, was magic. You must slow it down to see it at all.

But then Birmingham happened: 1-0 up and we threw it away. Donaldson on his lonesome up top didn't seem to be a smart move by the gaffer, but the players looked more dead on their feet than I do first thing on a Monday morning.

I know, I know. It was poor. Not arguing otherwise. Still … Bristol away on the last day. Blades in the sunshine. That first half with those goals and that sonorous din of "He's one of our own." I almost had to ask the bloke next door to keep it down.

It was brilliant, no doubt about it. Still too little, too late. The thing that winds me up, is that we've shown that we are plenty good enough. We've gone toe-to-toe with the lot of them. Don't forget that *they* told us that we were entering the cut-throat arena that is La Liga. Well, if *they* were correct in their analysis of England's second tier, then La Liga is well and truly our level. And, do you know what I think? I think that April, more than any month of this campaign, typified our ability to be every opposition's equal without the rewards that should follow: the points. That's the season in a nutshell.

And despite that we were only a few points off. Look at this last stretch of season, it tells us that what Chris Wilder is lacking is that tiny bit more quality. Just a bit. If that comes in during the summer, we'll be more consistent, more adroit, more likely to mount a real hammer-and-tongs run at the play-offs. And who knows, automatics?

The pessimist in me says 'I'll reserve judgement'. Perpetual exasperation no matter what. Win. Lose. Draw. Okay, so we improve the squad. It doesn't mean we're going to wind up any nearer the top. Teams around us will improve and look at those coming down. There were even worries if Wilder would be here to oversee it.

"Nobody's patsy," he said. Damn right. Wouldn't want it otherwise. But just look at the performance in the Bristol game; the players gave him (and us!) everything. I don't know an intelligent soul that didn't desperately want him to stay. And, if the board want to measure up our success I can give them the dimensions right here, right now: a five-foot-odd silhouette of a 50-year-old bloke, Peroni bottle in hand. I mean, it's taken us the best part of ten managers to find Mr Right – we couldn't go losing him now.

Still work to do in the boardroom. I'm not interested in picking a side; I chose mine a long time ago. Red and white.

Can't agree on that much, can we?

18

He's one of our own
By Dan Atkin, Kop

Let me start by saying, I wanted Nigel Adkins. I had grown tired of Nigel Clough's prosaic, don't-lose footballing mentality and his negative and often confrontational interviews and press conferences. I hoped that Adkins' approach and positivity would be a refreshing change of pace and a real antidote to the previous 18 months. Unfortunately, between the two of them, they contrived to do what I had always thought would be impossible. They made my interest in United wane.

As far back as I can remember, the United result has always dictated what sort of weekend or even week I have. A good win has usually meant everything is right with the world but a bad result or performance and I've been known to be poor company. Brian Deane's sale to Leeds United in 1993 pretty much ruined a fortnight in Portugal and my ex-missus was adamant that I loved United more than I loved her. In fairness, she was 100 percent correct.

But what started during the Clough era, and continued throughout Adkins' tenure, was a growing feeling of apathy within towards the team. And it wasn't just specific to me; several of my closest mates, all diehard Blades, were starting to feel the same. Anyone who has had the misfortune to be sat near me on the Kop during the 27 years it has been seated will attest to the fact that I'm known to be somewhat vociferous, or words to that effect. During Adkins' time at the club I was asked several times if I was okay, as I was so quiet and unmoved by events on the pitch. In fairness to Clough he did give us two fantastic cup runs but memorable matches against Nottingham Forest, Charlton, Hull and Spurs were very much papering over the cracks.

When Clough was relieved of his position, the firm favourite with the bookies was Adkins and I for one was delighted with this. In reality, what was a full rebuild job at Bramall Lane was beyond him and as we finished 11th that season, the divide – not only between the club and the fans, but within the fans themselves – was palpable. We were crying out for someone to not only address the issues on the pitch, but to reunite the club as a whole. And in Chris Wilder, we got that.

If there is a manager in the whole of English football who is more of the antithesis to his predecessor than Wilder, then I would be amazed and although it took a little longer on the pitch, from the minute he walked through the door he just got things right. Pretty much his first act as manager was to appoint local lad, Blade and top goalscorer Billy Sharp as captain – it seemed to be a message to the fans that Wilder had got our back and with himself, Sharp and co-owner Kevin McCabe, supporters were now represented in the boardroom, in the dressing room and on the pitch. Job one, get the fans onside: tick!

Wilder's overall approach to transfer policy was refreshingly different, to what we had experienced over previous years. Long, fruitless and at times embarrassing pursuits of players were no more, and United were no longer to be squeezed for more money by current players or transfer targets. Targets were given Wilder's vision of the team and the club, told what was on the table and that was that. Players, both existing and new, were made aware of what was expected of them in no uncertain terms, what the prerequisites were and given a clear vision of how Wilder wanted the team to play. Anyone who didn't buy in, or was unable to meet the physical demands, was quickly and ruthlessly jettisoned. You were either in or you were out.

After everything Wilder and his coaching staff have achieved at United, this may sound like a strange thing to say but taking us from the depths of ignominy to the League One title within the space of 12 months was not, for me, his most significant accomplishment. It probably isn't too dramatic to say that Wilder healed this football club. When he took over, we were experiencing mediocrity on the pitch and the club had lost its identity. More worryingly, the rifts within the club and the fans had turned the Lane into a pretty toxic place to be on a Saturday afternoon.

For as long as I have been a Blade, the club has always functioned better when we have a team that the fans can identify with, be it Dave Bassett's mix of waifs and strays and genuine talent that punched above their weight for so long on an absolute shoestring, or Howard Kendall's ultra-stylish collection who were a broken arm and a wonder goal away from promotion. The last side that the fans had a genuine affinity with was the one that Neil Warnock put together, which went up into the Premiership and were one goal away from staying there a year later. In fact, from that moment on we went from one short-term fix to another, with decisions on appointments taken with all the coordination and forethought of a punchdrunk boxer. Every single manager appointed appeared to have a different philosophy on how the game should be played and, as such, we lost everything that makes us what we are: an identity. A vision. A togetherness.

When this club gets on a roll and the fans are united it becomes a genuinely special place to be, and this is what Wilder did when he came back. The record books will say 'Sheffield United, 2016-17 League One champions' and also that we accumulated 100 points that season. But what they won't say, what only people whose hearts beat to the tune of the Greasy Chip Butty will know, is that Wilder gave us our club back.

The fractured fan base was pulled together again. No longer were fans bickering about whether Clough was hard done to or whether Adkins should have been given more time. No longer did we have to put up with the Dean Hammonds and Conor Sammons of this world. No longer did away teams simply have to turn up and frustrate for the first 15 minutes of a game, secure in the knowledge that the first time they got a throw in the natives would revolt and turn on their own. Suddenly the Lane was a place where visiting teams had to be prepared to fight and scrap for every single inch of turf if they wanted to come away with anything. The Greasy Chip Butty was now being belted out like a battle cry before games, unlike in previous seasons when it had an almost Pavlovian feel to it. A sense of going through the motions.

The term 'kissing the badge' has become a modern day parlance to describe mercenary footballers who profess undying love for a particular club, only to jump ship for their new employers five minutes later when presented with a large amount of Middle Eastern petrodollars. But to see Wilder roaring at the crowd and thumping his chest after an important victory is a thing of beauty, and has the hairs on the back of my neck standing up as I write this. The poignancy being that this is a bloke who, had he not been blessed with the talent to be a professional footballer for many years and then honed his talents as a football manager, would be with us; the bloke in the Golden Lion or the Sheaf before the game, discussing who the best centre half we have ever had is. Reminiscing about John Francis' last-minute diving header to beat Brighton 5-4, or laughing about getting chased coming out of Maine Road in the 1990s. He is one of us, he is living all our dreams for us and he's given us our club back.

Thank you, Chris. You really are one of our own.

Epilogue: The last word
By Chris Wilder, manager

The author of this book asked me to sum up how it feels to be the manager of Sheffield United, and I have to say that I have loved every single moment of it. The sun hasn't always shone since I took the job, but I get a real buzz from driving into work, towards either the training ground or Bramall Lane, or getting on the coach for an away game and seeing the support for us at the ground. There is no getting away from it – as manager of my club, there are times when it's like New Year's Eve after a win and other times when I just want to curl up and go to bed, or retreat to my house, shut the door and the curtains and hide away.

It's been tough for my family, as well, and they've supported me brilliantly. My wife, Francesca, has been a fantastic support for me too. She knows how much it means to me and how I feel, and is there in bad times as well as good; which is the most important thing, really. It's quite easy for people to jump on the bandwagon when the sun is shining and things are going well, but I have good people around me – friends and family – which I really appreciate.

Ever since I started out in management all those years ago it has never left me, but it consumes you and takes hold of you even more when it's your club. There's a lot of expectation to do well from my pals! We still sit in the pub on Sunday and have those conversations about United … the only difference being I'm now the one making the decisions when it was someone else before! It's changed my life and we turned it around a lot quicker than anyone thought we would.

I have to say, I've also loved watching my team play; the way they go about their business, and the attitude of the group throughout. As I say, the sun hasn't always shone but Rory McIlroy will sometimes smack an 82. Most of the time, though, he's at it and most of the time, my group is at it too. It hit home again on the last day of the season, at Bristol City – I'm a supporter of the club as well as an experienced manager, and watching my team who had nothing to play for take apart a team who had been up there all season was brilliant.

Then, there was the reaction of the fans towards me, during the game and afterwards. After my comments to the press about the direction of this club from the owners, the support was brilliant from the fans. I was in a difficult position because I am emotionally connected to this football club, but professionally I had to make the right decision for my career as well as the future of the club.

I look back at it and stand by what I said, 100 percent. I was genuinely concerned and want the club to go in the right direction. I was the voice of the club in a difficult period, and something needed to happen sooner rather than later. Thankfully, it did.

It was a tough time, a lot of reflection and thought and things had to be sorted out upstairs. I'm glad they have been. After the last game of the season I thanked the players and the staff for their efforts and it was a bit emotional. I did wonder if this was the last time. It was the same after the Preston game, when we did the lap. I thought 'will I get another chance to walk around this pitch?' I did get a bit emotional because I didn't know what would happen in the summer. The reaction then, and at Bristol City, was incredibly humbling.

We're not powerhouses of the Championship in certain aspects, but we add a lot to it in other areas. I've enjoyed being a part of it over our first season back, and there are hopefully many more to come. I'm often asked what it feels like to hear the fans sing my name, and it's quite a strange one. I want to acknowledge them every time, and I think it's important that I do that, but I obviously want to concentrate on the game too.

I don't want to stick my thumb up and the next second, the ball's in the back of our net! But seriously, they know I speak their language and know where the fans are coming from. The biggest thing when I came into the club was that they needed a style and an identity bringing back, because I felt they'd lost that a little bit. We've done that – myself, the players and the staff – and it's something the fans appreciate.

The big thing for me, when I first came in, was giving our fans value for money; having a go, working hard and always giving everything, no matter what. I think people buy into that. They'll get behind anyone who they see is ready to leave it all out there. There's nothing worse, even more so than a defeat, if you're sat in the stands and the people out there playing give you the impression they're taking it easy or swinging the lead. You have a connection to a club and it's not always because you want or expect to see a really good game. Once you connect yourself, you go out of loyalty, through thick and thin, because it's a part of your life. That's what you do.

I should imagine, over the years, folk have come out of our place and said 'I'm not going again, that was crap, I've had it and I'm never going back.' Then, when the next weekend comes, you end up ringing your mates up, arranging to go down to Farm Road Club, have a couple of pints and walk to the game. That's the loyalty, and our fans are amongst the most loyal in the business. But we want them not to just come out of loyalty. We want them to come because they're enjoying themselves and are being entertained. We can't always guarantee we'll win and we get pushed back at times. But the one thing I'll always highlight about my lads is that they'll really try and take it to opponents.

I'm sure they'll not always be singing my name when we go through difficult periods, but they know what they'll get from me … honesty, and no rubbish or spin. I manage and coach, and I played, in a way I think represents the football club and what it's about … not boastful or arrogant or spending money left, right and centre. We want to build, of course, but there are clubs in the summer who had to release or sell players because they'd overspent, and I've seen the other side of staff in the canteen or the office not being paid, or being let go, because the club has spent so much money. We can't take that gamble.

I think the way we go about things suits us. But I also think it gives the people who come to watch us something back, because they spend their hard earned money to be there. Times are hard out there at the moment and, although I think we get our pricing structure right, coming to the football can still be an expensive day out. So surely it's in everyone's interests to give them something to get behind. Yes, I know we can all get frustrated at times but we all want the same thing. If I was in there with the fans, I would enjoy watching this team because from the touchline, I enjoy watching them. We're not perfect but they're honest, they give everything and they always put it in. The backing has been the same and, although we might get caught at times, I'm proud of the attitude out there on the pitch and, just as importantly, on the terraces too.

I've said a few times since taking over that I never craved the job at Bramall Lane, but once it was offered to me I wasn't ever going to turn it down. I'd have been absolutely kicking myself if I'd said no, and wasn't ever offered it again in the future! I don't want to smash the previous manager because at the time, everyone thought it was the right appointment. But the supporters vented their frustrations at what followed, the decision was made and my appointment was met in a decent light. I had a big job on my hands. As managers, we all work in different ways but I felt it really needed a shake up and the power needed to come back to the club.

Obviously I've supported the club all my life but it had been a while since I had been in the inner sanctum, and the size of the club really impressed me. It was a huge organisation, but had just finished 11th in League One. I remember going for a pint with John Garrett, and he was saying he'd never been so low as a Blade.

Then, it's safe to say we didn't have the start we perhaps wanted but we saw that the players were running around, and I think we would have turned the corner sooner rather than later. After promotion – which came, incidentally, at our previous club Northampton, almost a year later to the day since we took them up on the same ground – we managed to drag the celebrations out for about four or five weeks! But the standard of what the players were producing, in training and in games, was as high as ever. After we finished on 99 points at Northampton, I was desperate for us to get to 100 that season because I wanted us to leave our mark on the division, and wanted this team to leave their mark on the history of this great club. I understand it wasn't in the Premier League and these things are relative, but I wanted this team to go down as one of the great ones in United's history. I certainly believe they deserve to be up there with the others.

We'd heard all the stuff from the other side of the city about the big scary Championship, and what a powerful division it was. We'd watched it and there were some unbelievably talented teams and players, but we'd also seen a lot of average teams and average displays by top teams as well. We were a bit of an unknown quality with a lot of our players experiencing the Championship for the first time, but all we kept hearing was how the league was going to 'do us' and we'd take shoeings every four or five games. But after the first three or four games went pretty well, we decided to stick to our approach, do it our way and give it a right go.

I'm proud of how we went about it. We competed very, very well in the Championship, with some memorable days and some frustrating ones, and we'll be looking to build on that in the future. A lot was made about my background in Sunday League playing and management when I took the United job, but that's not something I am, or ever will be, embarrassed about.

Someone showed me a comment from a Wednesday fan when I took over, about their manager being Champions League and United's being from the Meadowhall Sunday League. I remembered that and managed to ram it down their throats when we beat them 4-2 at Hillsborough, on that day in September! There shouldn't be a stigma about Sunday League. I learned a lot with Bradway and it helped me to where I am today. I don't think my career's been a Sunday League one, either. I started off at a decent club, Southampton, in the old first division and if I could take a club there, it'd be a huge achievement for me and a very proud moment.

There's a lot of good things that have to be done until that's a possibility, of course, because it's an incredibly tough league to break into. But there's always a dream at the end of everything we do, and sometimes they do come true. That's what we're looking to do, with this great club. I obviously signed a new contract back in May and I think it sent a message out to all of our supporters, who have backed us tremendously. It settled everybody down and it was important to get it sorted, 100 percent, after a very important period which allowed me to reflect and get my thoughts together with my staff.

We have had two fantastic seasons and I was delighted that both owners put their trust in me. I had to make the right decision, and I believe I have. Did I think after the season we had in our first year, coming out of League One in the manner we did, that I would be contemplating my future a year on? No I didn't. But these things happen in football. Things get lost and go in a different direction, and it was important things were brought back together. That's all I have ever wanted, the best for the football club. To lead from the front and bring it together, and have a clear positive message for the supporters.

I think there's more to come from this group, and the profile of the club has undoubtedly gone up. Last season, we were one of the most-covered teams on Sky Sports. All I have ever wanted to do is move forward. I have worked hard in my career to get in this position and I am hugely ambitious, as are the players. We want to drive the club forward and be involved in the top part of the division. I think I can fulfil all my ambitions at this club.

Being the manager has changed my life. I've had to quieten down a little bit, which I have done even though people might not think so, but I've seen the effect the club has on everyone's day-to-day life, both individually and collectively as supporters. What's the secret to management? I don't think there is one. It's like asking a top golfer what the secret to success is. A lot of things have to be brought to the table and done well. You have to have a talent and an in-depth knowledge of every part of the game, and surround yourself with good people.

I think there is a bit in me to lead, yeah. I'm opinionated and

I'm driven. All the staff I have here are. I don't think we'd have had the careers we have, on and off the pitch, if we weren't. Over the years you change through experience, knowing what works and what doesn't, but I still manage on gut and have the same principles that I won't change. They underpin everything. I've always tried to surround myself with good people, and the staff are brilliant. The players need to be good characters; they've got to want to work, enjoy coming to work and want to be successful.

I have always given 100 percent for every club I've been involved in but I can't get away from it; the highs at United are a lot higher but the lows are a lot lower, too. Being surrounded by people that have followed the club for years, you feel the highs and lows with them. Something I've heard a lot, though – and if I had a pound for every time, I'd be living somewhere else for sure – was that we'd given the fans their club back.

Every time I hear it, it brings a lump to my throat because it's the most humbling thing anyone can say to me, my staff and the players. All I can say, as a supporter, former ball-boy, ex-player and now manager, is that it's been an absolute pleasure. I have loved every minute.

Statistics

Chris Wilder, as a manager

Alfreton (2001–02) P42, W35, D4, L3. Win: 83%
Halifax Town (2002–08) P312, W120, D77, L115. Win: 38%
Oxford United (2008–14) P269, W121, D70, L78. Win: 45%
Northampton Town (2014–16) P126, W61, D28, L37. Win: 48%
Sheffield United (2016–) P103, W55, D20, L28. Win: 53%
Total (2001–) P852, W392, D199, L261. Win: 46%

Statistics: Soccerbase (correct as of July 1, 2018)

Honours

Alfreton
NCEL Premier Division: 2001–02
NCEL League Cup: 2001–02
NCEL Presidents Cup: 2001–02
Derbyshire Senior Cup: 2001–02
Halifax
Conference play-off final runners-up, 2005–06
Oxford United
Conference play-off final winners, 2009–10
Northampton Town
League Two title, 2015–16
Sheffield United
League One title, 2016–17

About the author

Danny Hall is a sports journalist at *The Star* newspaper in Sheffield. He's a previous winner of the 'weekly sports journalist of the year' gong at the Regional Press Awards and 'sports journalist of the year' at the O2 Media Awards. Danny was shortlisted for the regional sportswriter of the year award at the Sports Journalists' Association awards in London this year and helped to cover Sheffield United in FA Cup and League Cup semi-finals and a play-off final at Wembley, as well as the 2016/17 League One promotion season.